"Christopher Gehrz's tough-minded yet open curiosity about Charles Lindbergh's perturbing spirituality—an amorphous Jesus and nebulous Christianity melded with pantheistic religiosities, eugenics, antisemitism, White supremacy, and American nationalism—brings forth a religious biography as compelling as it is fascinating. An absorbing, necessary American read."

— **Jon Butler**
author of *God in Gotham: The Miracle of Religion in Modern Manhattan*

"Charles Lindbergh was a celebrated aviator, the father of the baby abducted in the 'crime of the century,' a Nazi sympathizer, and a believer in eugenics. He also carried a small New Testament with him as he entered the South Pacific theatre of World War II. In this fascinating, informative, and accessible biography, historian Chris Gehrz helps us make sense of the religious life of this 'infamous pilot.'"

— **John Fea**
American historian and executive editor of *Current*

"This short and crisply written biography tracks Lindbergh's life and 'spiritual but not religious' leanings. Lindbergh followed his own spiritual compass, yet towards a path that led him to sympathy with some of the worst political and social ideas of the twentieth century. The mixed brew he concocted, as Gehrz makes clear, reinforced rather than challenged his sympathies for anti-Semitism, eugenics, and white supremacy. Gehrz clearly and powerfully captures the sad ironies of this tale of a man who flew solo into heroism and into dark places."

— **Paul Harvey**
author of *Howard Thurman and the Disinherited: A Religious Biography*

"In a portrait of Charles Lindbergh that is both soaring and sober, Christopher Gehrz pilots us from the transcendence of flight into the darkness of bigotry and infidelity. Yet Gehrz is our guide, not Lindbergh's judge. Gehrz reveals Lindbergh's long search for a spirituality that affirmed his own sense of purpose but did not shackle him to a church or require him to repent. He sees in Lindbergh a nation bewitched by its technological accomplishments, confident in its innocence, and callous toward inequality."

— **John G. Turner**
author of *They Knew They Were Pilgrims:*
Plymouth Colony and the Contest for American Liberty

LIBRARY OF RELIGIOUS BIOGRAPHY

Mark A. Noll, Kathryn Gin Lum, and Heath W. Carter, series editors

Long overlooked by historians, religion has emerged in recent years as a key factor in understanding the past. From politics to popular culture, from social struggles to the rhythms of family life, religion shapes every story. Religious biographies open a window to the sometimes surprising influence of religion on the lives of influential people and the worlds they inhabited.

The Library of Religious Biography is a series that brings to life important figures in United States history and beyond. Grounded in careful research, these volumes link the lives of their subjects to the broader cultural contexts and religious issues that surrounded them. The authors are respected historians and recognized authorities in the historical period in which their subject lived and worked.

Marked by careful scholarship yet free of academic jargon, the books in this series are well-written narratives meant to be read and enjoyed as well as studied.

Titles include:

Abraham Lincoln: Redeemer President
by Allen C. Guelzo

Sworn on the Altar of God: A Religious Biography of Thomas Jefferson
by Edwin S. Gaustad

Duty and Destiny: The Life and Faith of Winston Churchill
by Gary Scott Smith

A Christian and a Democrat: A Religious Biography of Franklin D. Roosevelt
by John F. Woolverton and James D. Bratt

Harriet Beecher Stowe: A Spiritual Life
by Nancy Koester

For a complete list of published volumes, see the back of this volume.

CHARLES LINDBERGH

A Religious Biography of America's Most Infamous Pilot

Christopher Gehrz

WILLIAM B. EERDMANS PUBLISHING COMPANY
GRAND RAPIDS, MICHIGAN

Wm. B. Eerdmans Publishing Co.
4035 Park East Court SE, Grand Rapids, Michigan 49546
www.eerdmans.com

27 26 25 24 23 22 21   1 2 3 4 5 6 7

ISBN 978-0-8028-7621-8

Library of Congress Cataloging-in-Publication Data

Names: Gehrz, Christopher, 1975– author.
Title: Charles Lindbergh : a religious biography of America's most infamous
    pilot / Christopher Gehrz.
Description: Grand Rapids, Michigan : Wm. B. Eerdmans Publishing Co.,
    2021. | Series: Library of religious biography series | Includes bibliograph-
    ical references and index. | Summary: "A short biography of Charles
    Lindbergh that traces his varying interests in faith and spirituality and
    explores how this aspect of his life influenced both his famous achieve-
    ments and his infamous sympathies for white supremacy and eugenics"—
    Provided by publisher.
Identifiers: LCCN 2021000659 | ISBN 9780802876218 (hardcover)
Subjects: LCSH: Lindbergh, Charles A. (Charles Augustus), 1902–1974. |
    Lindbergh, Charles A. (Charles Augustus), 1902-1974—Religion. |
    Air pilots—United States—Biography.
Classification: LCC TL540.L5 G46 2021 | DDC 629.13092 [B]—dc23
LC record available at https://lccn.loc.gov/2021000659

Unless otherwise indicated, Scripture quotations are from the American
Standard Version.

In honor of another descendant of Swedish immigrants: Dick Peterson—for whom physics is an act of worship, whose career confirms Anne Lindbergh's instinct that "the true scientist [is] akin to the artist and the saint," whose life demonstrates that "The heavens declare the glory of God; and the firmament showeth his handiwork" (Psalm 19:1)

Contents

Acknowledgments

I usually end this part of any book with my family, but this time I'm going to start the acknowledgments with my wife, children, and parents. If it weren't for them, I'd never have given a second thought to Charles Lindbergh—and I'd never have been able to study his life.

One weekend in August 2016, the kids and I drove Katie to a workshop in St. Cloud, Minnesota, which left Lena, Isaiah, and me free to pay our first visit to the Lindbergh House, just up the road in Little Falls. That autumn, as we spent a sabbatical together on the East Coast, my son researched the *Spirit of St. Louis* for our visit to the National Air and Space Museum. After that trip to Washington, I started thinking seriously about the notion of a "spiritual but not religious" biography of Lindbergh. That project never would have happened if my parents, Dick and Elaine Gehrz, hadn't hosted us for that 2016 sabbatical, and if Katie, Isaiah, and Lena hadn't spared me for a long summer research trip in 2018 and then put up with endless Lindbergh conversations and trivia ("Did you know that . . . ?") over the following two years.

The next most indispensable figure in this project was Heath Carter, who had an inkling that a tall, introverted Minnesotan of Swedish ancestry might be the ideal person to study Charles Lindbergh—then helped fill in the gaps of this Europeanist's knowledge of US history. With Kathryn Gin Lum, Heath continues the excellent work started by Mark Noll in editing the Library of Religious Biography, several of whose prior entries I used to research my own contribution. Among many other people at Eerdmans who labored on this particular biography, let me thank Laurel Draper, Tom Raabe, Laura Bardolph Hubers, and David Bratt, who helped me realize that a biographer doesn't have to like his subject to tell an important story.

While a spiritual biography of Lindbergh is unusual, I built on the work of many predecessors, particularly A. Scott Berg, Susan Hertog, Bruce L.

Larson, and Grace Lee Nute. Their research and writing helped Charles, Anne, and the rest of the Lindbergh family come to life for me.

Nute worked for the Minnesota Historical Society, which remains one of the finest organizations of its type. I'm grateful for the staff and volunteers who make the Gale Family Library such a comfortable place to do research, and for the friendship of Kent Whitworth. Just before Brian Horrigan started his well-earned retirement from that organization, he shared some invaluable advice about doing Lindbergh research in Minnesota and beyond it. Melissa Peterson was a generous host at the Charles Lindbergh House and Museum in Little Falls.

Just down the road, Ann Marie Johnson of the Morrison County Historical Society kindly met my spur-of-the-moment request for some oral histories and newspaper clippings. The COVID-19 pandemic kept me from spending time in St. Louis, but Bryan Morey pointed me to some of the Lindbergh artifacts digitized by the Missouri Historical Society. The rangers and other National Park Service employees who operate the Wright Brothers sites in Dayton, Ohio, and Kitty Hawk, North Carolina, helped me better understand the earliest days of American aviation history.

The archivists and other staff of Yale University's Sterling Memorial Library and the Library of Congress's Manuscripts Division made my 2018 research trip more fruitful than I could have hoped. It was a particular honor to chat with Judith Schiff, who spent years helping Charles Lindbergh build his collection of private papers at Yale and then coedited his posthumously published autobiography.

That those collections are open to researchers is thanks to the Lindbergh children, who have had to put up with far too much public scrutiny over the years—yet still make it possible for people like me to offer critical assessments of their father. I'm especially grateful to Reeve Lindbergh, a lovely person and gifted writer who had already shared much insight through her own books, yet still took time to answer my occasional questions about her parents.

Thanks also to Bethel University, which awarded me the sabbatical that started this project, the grant that enabled my research trip out east, and the course release that made it possible to jump-start my writing. For eighteen years now, Bethel has been an ideal academic home, populated by committed teachers and scholars who are not just good colleagues but dear friends. With this book, I've been particularly influenced by Marion Larson, Amy Poppinga, and Sara Shady, whose commitment to love their non-Christian neighbors via interfaith dialogue and service helped inspire my engagement with someone who both admired Jesus and rejected Christianity. My teaching assistant Collin Barrett assisted me early in my research, especially with Lindbergh's opposition to US involvement in World War II. Among our wonderful librarians, I owe special thanks to Ann Gannon for hosting a presentation where I took a first shot at narrating this story for potential readers, and to Sandy Oslund and Kaylin Creason for filling dozens of requests for books and articles. (When the COVID quarantine shut down libraries like ours, the Internet Archive became an invaluable substitute for more traditional interlibrary loan services.)

Bits and pieces of this book first took shape as I "thought in public" about Charles Lindbergh at my personal blog, *The Pietist Schoolman*, and at the Patheos group blog *The Anxious Bench*. From the latter's distinguished group of contributors, I'm particularly grateful to Philip Jenkins (who was a regular source of suggestions, particularly when it came time to write about the America First movement), David Swartz (who pointed me in the direction of Kendrick Oliver's religious history of the space race), John Turner (whose own book on Brigham Young remains the best religious biography I've read), and Kristin Kobes Du Mez and Beth Allison Barr (who were never too busy with their own, more significant books to take time to encourage my writing).

Phil Anderson taught me more about the Swedish immigrant heritage the two of us share with Charles Lindbergh. Peggy Bendroth and John Lawyer helped me speak the language of Congregationalism and Episcopalianism, respectively. Many others shared ideas, resources, and encouragement via social media, email, and informal conversations, including Amy Artman, Jon Butler, Mark Healey, Tim Johnson, Craig Miller, Nick Pruitt, and Paul Putz. Whatever mistakes that follow are my responsibility.

Chris Gehrz
Roseville, Minnesota

Introduction

At first, the clerk at Brentano's might not have recognized Charles Lindbergh. Even in wartime, Manhattan's most popular bookstore had customers walking in from Rockefeller Center. And by 1944, Charles Lindbergh no longer looked like his most iconic images. Forty-two years old that April, his blond hair was starting to thin, his lanky frame starting to soften. But before too long, the clerk must have realized that the next customer was none other than the quiet Minnesotan whose solo flight across the Atlantic Ocean in May 1927 had made him the most famous man in the world.

Then the next chapters in Lindbergh's biography may have come to mind: the marriage to an ambassador's daughter . . . the tragic kidnapping and murder of their young son . . . the family fleeing to Europe to escape the press . . . then returning to oppose US intervention in World War II. Perhaps the clerk had even been at Madison Square Garden three years before, where Lindbergh was the featured speaker at multiple America First rallies in the months preceding the Japanese attack on Pearl Harbor.

But if the Brentano's employee noticed the bundle under Lindbergh's arm and wondered why the country's most infamous isolationist had just bought a military uniform, he was soon distracted by the book Lindbergh handed over for purchase: the New Testament.

"Since I can only carry one book—and a very small one," Lindbergh reported to his diary, along with other preparations for his secret deployment to the South Pacific, "that is my choice. It would not have been a decade ago; but the more I learn and the more I read, the less competition it has."[1]

"The Famous Unknown"

At this point, most of you are probably feeling like that bookstore employee. It's nearly a century after his historic flight to Paris, so it may take you a moment to recall the Lindbergh story. But at least some of it remains familiar: the *Spirit of St. Louis*, of course, and his son's kidnapping; perhaps the Midwestern origins.

Or if you've seen Lindbergh's name in the news recently, it's likely because of ongoing debates over the memory of a man who explained his opposition to World War II in terms that were anti-Semitic, racist, and even pro-Nazi. "Whatever his merits in the field of aviation," concluded a 2017 op-ed in the largest newspaper in Lindbergh's home state, "that the main airport terminal [for Minneapolis–St. Paul] continues to be named after a prominent anti-Semite and Nazi sympathizer is at once an insult and a disgrace."[2] As I wrote this book, HBO aired *The Plot against America*, a miniseries based on Philip Roth's alternate history novel, in which Lindbergh defeats his nemesis Franklin D. Roosevelt in the 1940 presidential election and sets the United States on the path to fascism.

But in our actual timeline, did you know that a middle-aged Lindbergh flew fifty combat missions in the spring and summer of 1944, bombing Japanese positions and shooting down an enemy plane? Or that his experience of history's bloodiest war tempered his earlier enthusiasm for science, technology, and even aviation itself?

Do you have any idea why a self-educated reader of voracious appetite would have selected the New Testament alone, among all the other options crowding Brentano's shelves? Or why he would then spend so much of the last thirty years of his life writing about metaphysics, theology, and spirituality?

Six years after his daring flight to Paris made Lindbergh a global celebrity, aviation promoter Harry Bruno concluded that even Lindbergh's closest friends "never saw into the inner heart and mind of this famous unknown."[3] All these decades and biographies later, nothing remains less known about this most famous American than the story of his spiritual quest.

Spiritual but Not Religious

Charles Lindbergh did read and reread the New Testament, but his is not a story of Christian conversion. The Gospels taught him to admire Jesus but not to accept him as the Savior who redeems us, nor as the Lord who reigns over us. Lindbergh had little interest in most other Jewish and Christian Scriptures. His tombstone does bear the words of a psalm, but stripped of any mention of God. Never more than a curious visitor to churches, Lindbergh was spiritual but not religious.

Nowadays, that phrase is often used to describe the nearly 30 percent of Americans who don't affiliate with any particular religion or denomination but who are not atheists or even agnostics.[4] Also called "religious nones," for its pattern of nonaffiliation, this group has never before been so prominent a segment of the population.

But it has never been absent from US history. In fact, some of this nation's best-known citizens have been spiritual but not traditionally religious. In the first great American autobiography, Ben Franklin explained why he "early absented [himself] from the public assemblies" of Christian churches, yet he "never was without some religious principles," including beliefs in God, the immortality of the soul, and the afterlife.[5] Earlier in this same series of religious biographies, Allen Guelzo probed the theological struggles of Abraham Lincoln, who "could not come the whole way to belief" in the deity whose judgments and providence are so central to that president's Second Inaugural Address.[6]

But Charles Lindbergh is a particularly good subject for a "spiritual but not religious" biography at this point in the twenty-first century. Unlike Franklin, who chose to stop attending the Presbyterian meetings of his Massachusetts childhood, or Lincoln, raised by sectarian Baptists in Kentucky and Indiana, Lindbergh rarely attended church even during his early days in Minnesota. The child of a mother who questioned the veracity of the Bible and a father who found God in nature, he has much in common with the increasing share of "nones" who grew up with no church background: people who had no particular childhood religion to renounce but followed their own path to an adult spirituality.

"A Lapsed Presbyterian"

By contrast, his wife is more like those who remain deeply spiritual but no longer affiliate with the churches that raised them. Anne Morrow Lindbergh adopted a more eclectic set of beliefs and practices as she aged, to the point that she called herself a "lapsed Presbyterian."[7] But the adjective shouldn't obscure the importance of the noun; she never entirely shed the religious language and imagination of her upbringing. For example, while reading the Bible was a midlife choice for Charles, it was a lifelong habit for Anne, whose books, journals, and letters quote the American Standard Version almost as often as her favorite poets.

While this book is not a dual biography, she is a secondary protagonist. Anne Lindbergh was both a key influence on Charles, encouraging and shaping his fledgling interests in literature, art, philosophy, and religion, and a particularly close and perceptive observer of her husband, sympathetic but also critical. (As is their youngest child, Reeve, through whose eyes we'll often see a different perspective on her parents.)

Anne was the foremost of the many conversation partners who spoke into Charles Lindbergh's spiritual development. That list starts with his parents, grandparents, and a preacher great-grandfather and grew in adulthood to include the pilot-poet Antoine de Saint-Exupéry and his fellow French Catholic Alexis Carrel, a Nobel-winning surgeon who balanced interests in anatomy, eugenics, and mysticism. In turn, Carrel encouraged Lindbergh to explore Eastern religions and introduced him to Jim Newton, a Christian businessman who became a lifelong friend. Newton could never convince Lindbergh to join Protestant minister Frank Buchman's Moral Re-Armament (MRA) movement, but at an MRA congress in Switzerland, Lindbergh did meet a Maasai tribesman. That encounter helped spark the aviator's latter-day fascination with African and Pacific Island people groups that tended to find God within the wildernesses and waterways that Lindbergh worked to conserve.

A SOLITARY SPIRITUALITY

As extensive as this network was, it shouldn't cause us to miss the most distinctive feature of Charles Lindbergh's "spiritual but not religious" journey: how lonely it was. As Jim Newton grudgingly accepted, his friend was "no joiner."[8] "You have caught the Divine flash of spirituality and recognized its reality," acknowledged Paluel Flagg, the Catholic physician who introduced Lindbergh to Alexis Carrel, "but you refuse to accept any briefing [sic] as to your course, your deployment and your eternal objective."[9] Others could ask questions and suggest answers, but the man who flew solo across the Atlantic had to chart his own spiritual path.

So we need to be careful with our terms. While "spiritual" is a word often used in Christianity to describe intense personal experiences, Paul Heelas and Linda Woodhead emphasize that the approach to spirituality of most religions is still "focused on something which is and remains external to and higher than the self." By contrast, the goal of what they call a "subjective-life" spirituality is "living one's life in full awareness of one's states of being; in enriching one's experiences; in finding ways of handling negative emotions; in becoming sensitive enough to find out where and how the quality of one's life—alone or in relation—may be improved. The goal is not to defer to higher authority, but to have the courage to become one's own authority. Not to follow established paths, but to forge one's own inner-directed, as subjective, life."[10]

They don't point to Charles Lindbergh as an example of such a spirituality, but they might have. Unwilling to submit to any authority beyond himself—whether an inspired text, venerable tradition, or ecclesial hierarchy—Lindbergh struggled to fit together the religious bits and philosophical pieces he collected into a coherent understanding of humanity and divinity, morality and mortality. Thirty years after his visit to Brentano's, he spent the last week of his life designing his own funeral, which sampled everything from Christian hymns and Jewish Scriptures to readings from Native American poetry and the Mahatma Gandhi.

Lindbergh drew on Christian beliefs and practices as they suited him, but in a piecemeal fashion that left unchallenged some of his cruelest convictions. He had no concept of sin to help him make sense of the brutality he witnessed in World War II, and he didn't share his wife's interest in the power of grace and forgiveness. Most strikingly, Charles Lindbergh spilled much ink on the purpose and dimensions of human existence but never seems to have taken seriously the biblical claim that *all* humans are made in the image of God (Gen. 1:26–27). On the contrary, he concluded that equality was a false idol, "a concept of man, and not of God," and persisted for years in defining the "quality of life" in terms that borrowed heavily from eugenics.[11]

So Lindbergh's story is a warning that "nones," like the more traditionally religious, can fuse spirituality with white supremacy. It's no coincidence that he began to advocate for eugenics at the same time that he began to look for truth beyond natural phenomena. Under Carrel's influence, Lindbergh spoke of "racial decline" and "spiritual decline" in the same breath. The free-thinking aviator may have seen himself as one of those "who believe in God and who search honestly for His way,"[12] but he discovered a deity whose laws happened to coincide with his own belief in the necessity of racial competition. Furthermore, Lindbergh's insistence on flying solo meant that no external authority would contest or complicate his inner convictions.

TELLING THE LINDBERGH STORY

Nearly half a century after his death in 1974, Charles Lindbergh continues to inspire admiration, revulsion, and curiosity. I can only hope that the portrait I sketch will be as complicated—and neither too familiar nor too different.

I have worried that even a critical appraisal of Lindbergh's life might needlessly burnish his celebrity. But at a time when "America First" is back in our discourse and Nazis are back on our streets, when Americans are again turning away asylum seekers and demonizing religious minorities, I'm convinced that the failings of Charles Lindbergh make his story more relevant, not less.

For if it's his extraordinary accomplishments that sustain a perpetual market for Lindbergh biographies, it's in part the ordinariness of his prejudices that makes it worthwhile to examine Charles Lindbergh yet again. To be sure, not everyone who shared his views reached his conclusions. In the debate over US intervention in World War II, few America First-ers actually wanted to join Nazi Germany in building a "Western wall of race and arms,"[13] or blamed Jewish propaganda for preventing such an alliance. But in Lindbergh's time or ours, there's nothing all that unusual about a white American wanting to disenfranchise fellow citizens, to keep refugees out of this country, or to control the "reproduction of our less able groups."[14] For all the trails he blazed in aviation, scientific research, environmental protection, and spirituality, Charles Lindbergh followed a well-worn path in coming to assume the superiority of those who looked like him and in perceiving threats from those who didn't.

Yet even so critical a biography of Charles Lindbergh must live up to the innovative standard of his own autobiographical writing, especially the much-admired *Spirit of St. Louis* (1953). In a small homage to the most distinctive feature of that book, our otherwise linear narrative will sometimes jump back and forth in time.

Because of its focus, this Lindbergh biography may seem to skip too quickly through the details of the 1927 flight and 1932 kidnapping, both of which have inspired hundreds of articles and books of widely varying quality. As Lindbergh himself understood, any "biographer can only preserve a portion of [a life's] richness."[15] Those seeking a more comprehensive account will want to supplement this biography with Scott Berg's, the first written with full access to Lindbergh's private papers and still the best. But I'll try to say enough about the flight to Paris's Le Bourget Field and Lindbergh's response to his eldest son's death to keep those who already know that version of the story attentive to the less familiar tale of the flier's spiritual quest.

It is the years least familiar to most students of Lindbergh that are most central to my version of his story: the partnership with Alexis Carrel, the postkidnapping exile in Europe, the experience of World War II and its aftermath, and Lindbergh's latter-day exploration of environmentalism and what he called "primitive" cultures. Along the way, I'll occasionally pause to consider how religious individuals and institutions responded to a pilot whom one eyewitness at Le Bourget called "the new Christ," and how Lindbergh's achievements in aviation helped make flight—on Earth, then beyond it—into its own kind of secular religion.

Our story starts long before May 1927, even earlier than Charles Lindbergh's childhood in the Upper Midwest and his first encounter with the airplane. First, we must understand the spiritual biographies of his parents and grandparents. For Lindbergh was convinced that "life's values originate in circumstances over which the individual has no control."[16] A man who made much of heredity would insist that we account for his spiritual ancestry.

CHAPTER ONE

Ancestors

> I am not well grounded in family history, although I have
> become more interested in it as I learned more about the
> principles of heredity. When I was a child, people disdained
> ancestors and recognized little value in good birth.
>
> —*Charles A. Lindbergh (1938)*[1]

S IX WEEKS BEFORE he bought a New Testament in New York,
Charles Lindbergh was not far from his birthplace in Detroit. Since
1942, the aviator had helped his friend Henry Ford test warplanes at Willow Run, the famous Michigan factory that churned out a B-24 bomber
every hour. On Sunday, February 20, 1944, Charles Lindbergh took the
morning off to do something he rarely did: go to church.

Not at the factory chapel that Henry and Clara Ford dedicated to their
mothers, but in an older sanctuary thirty miles to the north, on the shore
of Orchard Lake. As the Lindberghs drove up, Anne took mental notes
about a church that reminded her of the farmhouse in Grant Wood's *American Gothic*. "In the middle of the white snow, facing the frozen lake, oak
trees around it. It must have looked much the same" as it did a century
earlier, when Charles's great-grandfather preached there. Initially disinterested in his family history, the pilot's growing commitment to eugenics
in the 1930s had made him more eager to trace his own bloodlines.

The Lindberghs joined about thirty other congregants that morning:
"Middle-class, healthy, rather dull, respectable, and good people," judged
Anne. Though the young minister was "shy, stiff" as he read his sermon,
Charles perked up at the topic: baptism. "After the service," Anne reported
to her diary, "C., never out of place, went and talked to the preacher—

blushing and shy—about his great-grandfather and said the sermon was interesting to him since his great-grandfather, he had been told, baptized by total immersion in the lake!"[2]

THE LODGES AND THE LANDS

Lindbergh's great-grandfather, Edwin Albert Lodge, was "tall, spare, and dark, with a scraggly beard and piercing brown eyes" that Lindbergh's mother, Evangeline, remembered decades later. Born in England in 1822, Lodge immigrated to North America as a teenager and eventually settled in Detroit. He was much in demand as a doctor and pharmacist, but at least as committed to his work as a pastor. (He lacked traditional credentials for any of these jobs: his medical training came from homeopathic schools, and he never attended seminary or underwent ordination.) Evangeline Lindbergh recalled watching her grandfather consult his Bible as he prepared sermons, underlining Jesus's words with red ink and the disciples' in blue. He honed his penmanship by writing out the Lord's Prayer on a piece of paper the size of a dime. Lodge preached "earnestly and sincerely" in the church on Orchard Lake, where he "donned his hip boots & waded into" the water to perform baptisms. "No sprinkling on the head for him," explained Charles. "He believed in ducking them right under."[3]

What his great-grandson only dimly understood was that Edwin Lodge was not a Baptist, but belonged to a group founded by the Scottish Presbyterian minister Thomas Campbell and his son Alexander.[4] (Coincidentally, the Orchard Lake church had joined a Presbyterian denomination by the time Charles and Anne visited it.)[5] Preaching on the American frontier during the Second Great Awakening, the Campbells and Barton W. Stone sought to restore Christianity to the pure simplicity of the first communities of Jesus followers. Like Baptists, these Restorationists baptized believers by immersion ("ducking them right under"), held the Bible as their sole authority, and sought to keep the church separate from the state. But they also took seriously the New Testament's many admonitions to maintain Christian unity and hoped to overcome the religious divisions that had only deepened since the Protestant Reformation. Stone's followers accepted no label more particular than Christians; the Campbells' adherents called themselves the Disciples of Christ.

Lodge's commitment to Restorationism is clearest in a church history lecture he delivered in 1859. "For three hundred years after the death of the Saviour," he began, "the glorious Gospel, which he gave to Man, was promulgated by his faithful disciples in all simplicity." But in the fourth century the conversion of the Roman emperor Constantine replaced "the pure primitive love of the lowly Jesus" with "the cold formality and the heartless pomp of a State religion." As his version of the story reached the sixteenth century, Lodge praised Martin Luther for "denouncing with fiery zeal the informalities of a perverted Church." (His great-grandfather, Charles Lindbergh admitted, "reviled the Catholics and the pope with theological fanaticism.")[6] But three centuries after Luther, Lodge decided that the "present condition of the Religious world calls for another Reformation" to bring about "a truer faith and a truer life. . . . Luther aimed high[;] we need the aid of one who shall aim higher. Instead of a Reformer with the spirit of a St. Paul we need a Regenerator in the spirit of a St. John, teaching of the Doctrine of Love which will save the world."[7]

Lodge's "truer life" included a particular emphasis on observing the Sabbath, as a day to welcome Jesus into the household. "The whole day will be none too long," he lectured, "if you love the Lord sufficiently. If this His Day is a weariness, in any one of its hours, then you are growing tired of your guest. You wish his absence rather than his company."[8] To help his family maintain its religious focus on Sundays, he banned newspapers and discouraged his wife from spending time cooking hot meals.

While Lodge's restrictions on pastimes like dancing and card playing didn't survive his children's generation, much of that branch of Lindbergh's family tree remained devoutly religious.[9] When she and Charles paid a visit to the Lodges in 1935, Anne Lindbergh felt "very uncomfortable" meeting a great-aunt named Harriet: "She is intense, ascetic, and Isaiah-looking. But there is an integrity about her that I like. The disconcerting large framed picture of Christ on the wall. C. and Aunt Harriet underneath it talking about the modern generation smoking and drinking, C. in a loud voice. (She is deaf.)"

As they left, Aunt Harriet gave Anne an "ascetic kiss in the back of the neck (C. gets kissed too!)," then told her and Charles "with glowing simplicity and conviction, 'People forget that God still rules the world. It can't be so bad.'" Anne went on, "We burst outside, and yet her integrity is compelling."[10]

When he first started to write an autobiography, three years after the encounter with Aunt Harriet, Charles Lindbergh described Edwin Lodge as "fanatically religious," albeit "interested in many fields." By the time that memoir came out, in 1953, "Great-grandfather Edwin" was still "extremely religious" but saw no necessary conflict "between science and God. His studies of biology didn't convince him that all existence ends with the flesh. He had faith in some quality that is independent of the body."[11]

If he came to admire a certain version of his great-grandfather, Lindbergh identified far more closely with his grandfather. He recalled Charles Henry Land as a self-taught dentist who "used to carry on long philosophical discussions with his patients, who liked to talk to him because of his free, original ideas. . . . He was not a church goer. His practise embraced patients of various faiths," including a Christian Scientist whom he asked about "the relation of the spiritual to the mental" as he operated on her.[12] A later biographer concluded that "Charles Land's interests were catholic, his horizons without limit. He listened to a bird call, looked at a wild flower, took care of his patients, experimented with his porcelain, worked on his air conditioner, played with the children and speculated about evolution—all with the same interest and relaxed intensity."[13]

That originality and open-mindedness got Land in trouble with the Michigan Dental Association, whose more conservative members didn't appreciate the new devices and techniques he introduced. But we'll see that Land's laboratory occupied a prominent place in the memory of his similarly curious, trailblazing grandson.

Land had joined the Lodge family in 1875, when he married Edwin's daughter Evangeline in a Disciples of Christ ceremony. ("The blessing given, the ring is on," their wedding record is inscribed. "And at god's altar radiant run / The currents of two lives in one.")[14] Named for the Greek word for the Christian gospel, Evangeline Lodge was "a kindly, quiet woman, wonderful with children," like her grandson Charles.[15] Edwin Lodge kept all his daughters from attending even Restorationist colleges, which had long been open to women. Instead, Evangeline's education consisted mostly of preparation for motherhood and study of the Scriptures. At age nineteen, she received a Bible as a Christmas present. "Study it daily," her father directed, "and prayerfully."[16] After marrying Charles

Land, Evangeline Lodge passed down both her name and that Bible to her first child, born in 1876.

Her husband preferred to spend Sundays taking a break from the city, but the Land family did worship at Detroit's Central Christian Church, where Edwin Lodge occasionally served as guest preacher.[17] Young Evangeline's Sunday school teacher—the daughter of her mother's Sunday school teacher—once offered a prize for reading the entire New Testament. She said she and a friend took turns reading "aloud as fast as we could, alternating when one grew tired," finishing "without an idea of what we read. But we received prizes." It wasn't the only hint that the future Evangeline Lindbergh would hold her faith more loosely than her grandfather or mother. On summer visits to Grandpa Lodge's lakeside church, she amused herself during the family's evening prayers by "counting feet."[18] Her son Charles came away "deeply impressed by the fact that [his] preacher great-grandfather had failed to convert his own granddaughter to his faith."[19]

As strict as her grandfather was, Evangeline's inquisitive father was equally committed to preserving "a large amount of freedom for his children—constantly saying they must learn sometime."[20] Not only did the upwardly mobile Dr. Land pay to send his daughter to a private girls' school, but she continued her studies at the University of Michigan, at a time when one medical student recalled how it was "impressed upon the women of our department that the U of M was a men's school & often we had the feeling that we were trying to rob men of a livelihood."[21] An heir to her father's fascination with science, Evangeline graduated in 1899 with a degree in chemistry.

Eager for adventure, she looked for teaching jobs on what remained of the frontier. Evangeline dreamed of teaching "chemistry to the children of miners" but had to settle for the offspring of mill workers and farmers.[22] In September 1900 she relocated to Little Falls, Minnesota, where she would be paid $55 a month to teach not just chemistry but also biology, physics, and geography. Anne Morrow Lindbergh concluded that her mother-in-law had been "lured by unrealistic ideas about the romance of the frontier." Evangeline Land was prepared neither "for small-town life in Minnesota" nor for marriage to the fellow University of Michigan graduate she met the night of her arrival in Little Falls: a lawyer named C. A. Lindbergh.[23]

THE LINDBERGHS

As he and Anne flew over the Swedish province of Skåne in 1933, Charles Lindbergh looked down at the dark green forests, deep blue lakes, and golden yellow fields and wondered why his folks "ever left that place"![24] His paternal grandparents were among the first of the 1.25 million Swedes who emigrated to North America between 1850 and 1930. Like nearly a quarter of that total, they settled in the state of Minnesota, whose landscape does look uncannily like that of southern Sweden.

Later Swedish immigrants to Minnesota tended to find work in the Twin Cities of Minneapolis and St. Paul, but the early wave either farmed land richer than the rocky soil of their home country or took small-town jobs related to industries like logging or the railroad. Not all came to the Upper Midwest in search of better economic opportunities. Some were avoiding mandatory military service, like one of my great-grandfathers; others were religious minorities fleeing persecution, like the pietistic Baptists who founded Bethel University in St. Paul.[25]

Then there was Ola Månsson, who left Sweden for none of those reasons.

In fact, before migrating, he had been a prosperous farmer who won election to Sweden's parliament, the Riksdag. Part of the progressive wing of that body, Månsson (b. 1808) backed citizenship for Jews and called for the state church to loosen its hold on the kingdom's increasingly diverse religious life. (While Månsson, like most Swedes, remained Lutheran, everyone from the Methodists to the Mormons made gains in the mid-nineteenth century.) But in the summer of 1859, the farmer-legislator suddenly undertook a ten-week journey from Stockholm to the tiny village of Melrose, Minnesota, one hundred miles northwest of Minneapolis. Already in his early fifties, Ola Månsson was starting over, trading the work of a European politician for that of an American settler. His new life came complete with a new wife (nearly thirty years his junior), a new son (not yet two years old), and a new name, August Lindbergh.

For over a century, the reasons for this set of abrupt, profound changes were unclear, even to many of August Lindbergh's children and grandchildren. "Probably no one but Ola Månson [sic] himself knew the real motive for his migration to America," his son Perry told Grace Lee Nute of the Minnesota Historical Society in 1936.[26] When historian Bruce L. Larson published his biography of Charles August Lindbergh thirty-five years later, he repeated Nute's judgment that Ola left Sweden because his political enemies had had him charged with embezzling funds from the Bank of Sweden.[27]

Nute had discovered that there was more to the story, but it wasn't until Scott Berg released his biography of Månsson's aviator grandson in 1998 that the full truth came out. Ola had fled Sweden and reinvented himself as August Lindbergh not just because of political battles and legal problems, but because he had had an affair with a young waitress, Louisa Callén, that produced a son, Charles August (C. A.). Leaving behind his first wife and their children, August started a new family with Louisa and C. A. in a new land.[28] Notably, he chose to live in a place that was home to few Scandinavian immigrants.

And to few churches as well, as central Minnesota was very much part of the American frontier in 1859. Fretting over the souls of indigenous persons and white settlers alike, some East Coast Protestants who advocated westward expansion had founded the American Home Missionary Society (AHMS). "While we sympathize in whatever tends to increase the physical resources and prosperity of our country," wrote an AHMS agent in 1850, "we can not forget that with all these dispersions into remote and still remoter corners of the land the supply of the means of grace is becoming relatively less and less."[29] In 1860, that society dispatched a Congregational pastor named Charles S. Harrison to Sauk Centre, Minnesota, ten miles from August Lindbergh's homestead in Melrose. The two men met in August 1861.

In Sauk Centre to mill wood for an expansion of his growing family's new farmhouse, August Lindbergh suffered a gruesome accident. He fell into the saw, whose blade cut so deeply into August's left side that an eyewitness claimed to see his heart beating. Rev. Harrison arrived on the scene to help tend Lindbergh's injuries, then raised $25 to pay the doctor who finally arrived to treat the farmer.[30] (C. A. later told Charles that "a man of ordinary endurance would not have been able to survive the time which passed before the surgeon arrived.")[31] The following year Harrison recounted the story for readers of the *Home Missionary*, explaining that Lindbergh was in "voluntary exile here, on account of hatred raised against him for energetic measures against the established, and in favor of free religion, as the state Church was too exacting." As he continued, Harrison turned the horrific account of the sawmill accident into a conversion story:

> We feared he would die before the surgeon came, and I was anxious to do something for his soul. I could not talk fluently with him myself, so I rode in haste, eight miles, for a good Scandinavian brother who labored with him faithfully all night, and in the morning the stern fortitude of this strong man softened into the calm serenity of the Christian's hope. It was a sublime spectacle—a great man lying on his lowly couch. He had no tears for his own bitter anguish; he wept not at the agony of his loved companion; but when the love of God flooded his soul, with streaming eyes and touching eloquence he spoke, in broken language, of his new found joys. It was the most eloquent sermon I ever heard. His neighbors were assembled, and there was hardly one who did not weep with him. At length, after over thirty hours' waiting, the surgeon came; his arm was amputated, and he lives, praising God's mercy in afflicting him, and quoting that passage which speaks of "entering into life *maimed*" [Matt. 18:8]. It was indeed a wonderful providence, sent on purpose for his soul's salvation.[32]

Not long before that accident, Harrison had apologized in the same publication for not raising more funds ($1.50 for the year ending March 1861), explaining that the people in that part of Minnesota "are poor, and there are but few of them professors of religion."[33] So he may have been tempted to embellish the spiritual elements of August Lindbergh's accident, for the sake of AHMS supporters eager to see more "professors of religion" on the frontier. Neither August's children nor his most famous grandson mentioned anything like a dramatic conversion when they told the sawmill story.[34]

That's not to say that the Lindberghs professed no religion. (And it's worth noting that Harrison briefly reentered the Lindbergh story years later, to officiate the wedding of Charles's half sister Eva.)[35] C. A.'s younger brother Frank remembered their father reading the Bible "a great deal"— perhaps the Swedish Scriptures that he passed down to C. A., along with a treatise by the Lutheran theologian Johann Friedrich Fresenius and a church history textbook.[36] C. A.'s sister June recalled their father enjoying a history of the Reformation, whose "terrible pictures of tortures" still scared her decades later.[37] Though August continued to read in his native language, he "insisted that his children speak only English in the home"—and at worship.[38]

In September 1878, Melrose became the home of Trinity Mission Church, a new Episcopal congregation. Though Trinity didn't last long, its surviving parish record book includes the names of its founding families. Only one entry bears a Scandinavian name: August and Louisa "Lindburg" and their children.[39] Having chosen to live in a town with no other Swedish immigrants, August had little choice but to opt for a mainline American denomination, not one of the Midwest's many Scandinavian Lutheran synods. (We'll see that C. A. made a similar decision, despite having Swedish options readily available.)

"Prayers were not a regular part of the household routine," recalled Perry Lindbergh, who left his mother—August's first wife—in Sweden to help his father after the sawmill incident. But C. A. and his younger brother Frank attended Sunday school.[40] Their father helped start a one-room schoolhouse a mile from the farm, then found C. A. a spot in Grove Lake Academy, a private preparatory school near Sauk Centre.[41] Run by an Irish Catholic priest named Daniel J. Cogan, the school was open to children of all denominations. In its short life span, Grove Lake Academy educated two future congressmen: C. A. Lindbergh and Minneapolis lawyer and judge George R. Smith, who served alongside Lindbergh in the US House of Representatives for four years.[42]

Father Cogan's school boasted a rigorous curriculum, but it's easy to imagine a young C. A. tuning out his teacher as he gazed wistfully out the classroom window.[43] "I had become so imbued with the grandeur of God's Creation," he admitted to prospective voters in 1914, "that, when a school was started, I could not divert my attention from Nature to books."[44] Nevertheless, his graduation from Cogan's academy qualified him to attend law school at the University of Michigan. (Minnesota's land-grant university didn't establish its own law school until 1888.) After graduating in 1883, C. A. Lindbergh returned to his home state and set up a law practice in Little Falls, some forty miles northeast of Melrose.

Now a town so unassuming that it bills itself as the place "where the Mississippi pauses," Little Falls in the late nineteenth century was a bustling village on the verge of explosive growth. From an 1890 census count of 2,354 residents, Little Falls nearly doubled in size within two years, after a new company headed by Charles A. Weyerhaeuser built a mill that kept hundreds of employees busy cutting upwards of 60 million feet of timber per year.[45] In the years to come, C. A. Weyerhaeuser and C. A. Lindbergh would work often—and worship occasionally—together, and their sons became playmates.[46]

In 1889, an ailing August Lindbergh moved to Little Falls to live with his son. He died four years later. In its obituary, the local newspaper celebrated August's "integrity and uprightness of character . . . his excellent moral worth. . . . As a Christian he was unobtrusive, speaking more by acts and an unblemished life than by words, yet during his [last] sickness he expressed many times his firm hope in Christ as his Saviour." For the memorial service, the pastor preached on an Old Testament passage that must have seemed appropriate for a farmer who had endured his share of trials over eighty-five eventful years: "Thou shalt come to thy grave in a full age, like as a shock of corn cometh in his season" (Job 5:26).[47]

That funeral was held at the Congregational church in Little Falls where C. A. attended services with his first wife. Like his sisters June and Linda, C. A. had married a Roman Catholic,[48] but Mary LaFond Lindbergh broke with the church of her French Canadian and Irish ancestors and became "quite a worker" among the Congregationalists in town.[49] Tragically, the Lindbergh family returned to that church for another funeral in April 1898, after Mary died of surgical complications at age thirty.

Throwing himself into his work, C. A. enrolled his daughters, Lillian and Eva, at a boarding school in Minneapolis and took a room on the second floor of the nicest hotel in Little Falls. In September 1900, the local school superintendent introduced him to the newly arrived science teacher, Evangeline Lodge Land, who rented a room just upstairs from the widowed attorney. Just twenty-four years old, Evangeline was closer in age to Lillian Lindbergh than to C. A., but the courtship proceeded quickly. "Signals were easily arranged," Evangeline wrote later, in a notebook intended for their son. "And usually he walked with me or I walked with him on the way to school. There was nothing so very unusual about it all. Father was simply outstanding in appearance and personality."[50] Frustrated with its rules and facilities, Evangeline soon quit Little Falls's school, but not Little Falls. She had decided to accept C. A.'s marriage proposal. On March 27, 1901, the pastor of Detroit's First Congregational Church married the couple in the Land home.[51]

C. A. built his bride a well-appointed three-story house on a plot of land along the Mississippi River, just south of Little Falls. The following winter Evangeline returned to her home city, where on February 4, 1902, her physician uncle delivered her first, and only, child: Charles Augustus Lindbergh.

CHAPTER TWO

A Boyhood on (and beyond) the Upper Mississippi

I have never gotten over my original feeling that in Minnesota, all the elements of my father are finally brought
together, and that here, if I can only pay close enough attention, he will be fully restored to me, time and time again.

–Reeve Lindbergh (1998)[1]

FORMALLY WELCOMING Charles Lindbergh back to his homeland
two weeks after his historic flight to Paris, President Calvin Coolidge
described the young flier as "representing the best traditions of this country," a new pioneer who descended from "a stock known for its deeds of
adventure and exploration."[2] But Lindbergh himself was conscious that
the frontier was already gone by the time he was born: "Indians had been
assigned to reservations. Horses replaced oxen. Forests were disappear-
ing."[3] His youngest child, Reeve, attributed such "wistfulness" to her father
"wondering if perhaps he had been born too late" to share the experience
of European settlers like his Swedish grandfather.[4] Instead, Charles would
find his own opportunities for adventure and reinvention as he explored
the frontiers of human achievement and understanding with what his
widow called "pioneering energy."[5]

Lindbergh recognized that he "grew up in a generation torn by the impact of new scientific knowledge on old religious dogma."[6] He was raised,
writes historian Thomas Kessner, when a "new spirit of speculative thought
and imaginative experimentation" was "replacing an inscrutable cosmos
filled with biblical miracles with one anchored in empirical knowledge."[7]

Young Lindbergh's first guides on the contested boundary between
past and future certainties were adults willing to abandon traditional

beliefs and institutions to pursue the scientific and political progress of modern civilization. His father, mother, and other mentors, the _New Yorker_ noted in 1953, were "men and women with strong opinions and still stronger wills . . . who had got somewhere in the world, but not at the expense of their own precious singularities."[8] As Charles's best biographer perceptively observed, his freethinking family taught him "the principles of self-reliance—nonconformity and the innate understanding that greatness came at the inevitable price of being misunderstood." The Lindberghs and Lands "were prideful to the point of arrogance," Scott Berg concluded, and "so evangelical as to appear fanatical"—just not about religion.[9]

LITTLE FALLS: "TWO SALOONS FOR EVERY CHURCH"

Born in Michigan four years before his father ran for the United States Congress, Charles Lindbergh would do some of his growing up in Detroit and Washington. But most of his memories of childhood and adolescence center on Little Falls, Minnesota. Not far from Sauk Centre, where August Lindbergh nearly died in a sawmill and Sinclair Lewis later learned to doubt that "every Sunday, sweet-tempered, silvery pastors poured forth comfort and healing," Little Falls was reputed (in Evangeline Lindbergh's telling of things) to have "two saloons for every church and a church for every creed."[10]

So, which church did the Lindberghs attend, and how often were they there? Lindbergh biographer Joyce Milton mentions Evangeline taking her young son "to services at the Lutheran church" in Little Falls.[11] It's an understandable but mistaken assumption.

From its founding in 1892, Bethel Evangelical Lutheran Church had been a center of community for the town's Swedish American residents. "Being newly arrived immigrants," a later pastor wrote, the congregation's first members "were not rich in earthly possessions, but it is quite evident that many were deeply and sincerely concerned about spiritual things, and earnestly desired to have a Lutheran Church in their community and a Lutheran pastor to serve them." Little Falls's burgeoning lumber industry and surrounding farmland drew more Swedish immigrants up the Mississippi, about fifteen hundred of them by the turn of the century.[12] In 1903, a year after Charles Lindbergh's birth, the Bethel congregation was large enough to pay for the construction of a new brick church, less than two miles upriver from the Lindbergh farm.[13]

C. A. Lindbergh certainly knew parishioners at Bethel Lutheran Church. In 1895 he sold some of his property to Bethel's new sister church in Darling Township. Years later he employed Bethel's former pastor as his legal secretary.[14] But like his father, C. A. chose not to take his family to a Swedish church.

Of the many possible reasons for that choice, the most practical is the most likely. While C. A. knew enough of his father's native tongue for occasional use in his legal practice, neither Evangeline nor their son ever learned Swedish—which remained the language of worship at Bethel Lutheran throughout Charles's childhood and youth.[15] It wasn't until after World War I—when the use of Swedish, like German, seemed suspicious to a certain kind of patriotic Minnesotan—that the church finally added English services two evenings each month. Bethel Lutheran didn't complete the transition to English until the beginning of the Second World War, when the church called its first American-born pastor.[16] It wasn't just the Swedes; even First English Lutheran Church of Little Falls didn't stop using Norwegian until 1926.[17]

Instead of either Scandinavian Lutheran congregation, or the Swedish-speaking Mission Covenant church, the Lindbergh family attended First Congregational Church, where C. A. had buried his father and first wife in the 1890s. That congregation had formed in 1857 as an outgrowth of the work of missionaries Frederick and Elizabeth Ayer. By the time C. A. came to town, First Congregational had settled into a new wood-frame structure, just a few blocks from his law office. In 1893 the church completed the brick building that the young Charles Lindbergh came to know.[18]

In choosing such a church, in marrying a woman of British ancestry, and in raising their son to speak only English, C. A. Lindbergh was shaping his child's sense of identity. Charles would grow up to think of himself less as a Swedish American than as a member of "the white race." It was a transition that many European immigrant groups made in the early twentieth century, but the racial anthropology of the time gave people like the Lindberghs particular advantages.[19] "The concept of Nordic whiteness," explains historian Erika Jackson, "granted social privilege to those who could claim Scandinavian heritage." Having "become white" by the decade of

Charles Lindbergh's famous flight, many Swedish Americans would support efforts to restrict immigration from places other than northern and western Europe. Some would even join fellow "Anglo-Saxons" in the revived Ku Klux Klan.[20] Charles Lindbergh himself would eventually speculate about disenfranchising African Americans and allying the United States with Nazi Germany as a "western wall" against "Asiatic" threats.

But at the turn of the century, why did the Lindbergh family join the Congregationalists, out of all the Protestant English-speaking options in Little Falls? (There were also two Catholic parishes in town, plus a community of Franciscan sisters that ran a hospital and orphanage.) Why did C. A. not do like his father and attend the local Episcopal church, founded in 1885? Or the Methodist congregation, which merged with the Congregationalists in 1969? There was no Disciples of Christ presence in Little Falls, but one wonders if Evangeline ever walked past First Baptist Church and thought of her grandfather immersing the faithful in the waters of Orchard Lake.

It's possible that two people as fiercely independent as Evangeline and C. A. Lindbergh simply felt a spiritual kinship with the traditional autonomy of Congregationalism. But here, too, more pragmatic answers suggest themselves.

By 1915, the two hundred members of First Congregational included citizens as prominent as Charles A. Weyerhaeuser and Drew Musser, who ran the Pine Tree Lumber Company.[21] "Mrs. Weyerhaeuser, whose contralto voice was most pleasing, sang in the choir," Evangeline Lindbergh recalled. "Many of our friends attended this church, as well as the Lindbergh relatives."[22] Indeed, her son assumed that his family's involvement in any Christian church had less to do with religious commitment than with social and political ambition. Not only did First Congregational give them a place to hobnob with local elites like the Weyerhaeusers and Mussers, but after C. A. was elected to the US House of Representatives in 1906, public worship let him reassure God-fearing voters of the Lindberghs' devotion to a higher power—and to each other, at a time when his marriage to Evangeline was starting to fall apart.

When Charles Lindbergh first attempted to write about going to church, in 1949, he stretched his memory back over forty years, to a stifling summer day during his father's first congressional campaign:

It's to be my first day in church. Mother has dressed me in a gray woolen suit, long black stockings, felt hat, and brown kid gloves. It's all terribly uncomfortable. . . . Church! How I dislike that word, although I'm not quite sure what it means. It's keeping me away from the farm where we usually drive on Sunday mornings. . . .

Why do I have to go to church? Well, my father is going to be a Congressman in Washington. He's going to represent all the people of the town and of the country around it for miles and miles. It's a very important position, and the family of a man who holds such an important position is expected to go to church. Besides, I'm 5 years old, and it's time for me to learn something about a mysterious and disturbing being called God. Church is the place where one learns about him.

But as young Charles fidgeted in the hard pew, sweating in his heavy clothes and dreaming of cool river waters, he found it hard to think theologically: "The words of the Preacher drone in my ears, one merging into another until all are meaningless. Now and then he mentions God; but he says nothing I can understand about Him." And when "one doesn't understand" religion, he realized, "it's awfully uninteresting."[23]

He kept revisiting that episode as he finished *The Spirit of St. Louis* (1953) and turned to the long-gestating memoir published posthumously as *Autobiography of Values* (1978), but the small details and larger themes remained consistent.[24] Incommodious, incomprehensible, and inauthentic, "church was an ordeal to be cautiously avoided" throughout Charles Lindbergh's childhood. It's not clear how often he succeeded in staying home on Sunday mornings. Lindbergh insisted that "he revolted so effectively" that he was never taken to church again, but his mother claimed that there was "considerable regularity" to the Lindberghs' churchgoing.[25] Even if we trust Evangeline's sometimes unreliable memory, it's unlikely that her son found answers to his earliest theological and metaphysical questions in the sermons, Scriptures, hymns, and prayers he heard at First Congregational. He claimed that one childhood encounter with church was enough to leave him "a skeptic toward religion, questioning the beneficence of God."[26]

What image of God did young Lindbergh glimpse in church, or glean from mentions "in story books, in the cursing of lumberjacks, in the blessing of an old aunt"? The leading Congregational hymnal of the early twentieth century opened with a hymn encouraging congregants to "gratefully sing [God's] power and his love," but Charles had little sense of a God whose "bountiful care . . . breathes in the air . . . shines in the light."[27] Instead, he imagined God "as a stern old man living in Heaven, somewhere off in the sky like clouds, knowing about and judging every act you made. When you died, He might make you pay for all the things you did wrong, like staying home on Sunday or scratching the bottom of a pew's seat." This was a deity to match the punitive unpleasantness of church, a Lord best loved with "long, serious faces."[28]

Yet even as he worried that an "all powerful God . . . might take some of [his] possessions out of the boxes [he] locked them in," young Charles remained curious about the divine.[29] "If God made everything, who made God?" Lindbergh remembered wondering. "An eight-year old child's questions confound church and university alike, portraying vividly the rational boundaries of both science and religion."[30] When Charles would ask churchgoing Congregationalists such theological questions, they might respond with "one of those authoritatively evasive answers so baffling to a child's mind: 'We must speak of God only with the greatest respect.'" He added, "As though I'd been wrong in even thinking of the question."[31]

From its start, Charles Lindbergh's spiritual journey led him away from religion, whose certainties squelched curiosity, whose community stifled individualism. So if not from the dull rituals and dour strangers of church, where better to seek answers than at home, from parents whose growing distance from each other never stopped them from being close to their son?

Little Falls: The Lindbergh Library

In the summer of 1938, Charles Lindbergh invited historian Grace Lee Nute to visit him and Anne at their new home on the remote French island of Illiec. Working on a biography of C. A. Lindbergh, Nute jumped at the chance to pepper his son with questions. For example, she asked if he could recall his father's views on religion and parenting:

I know from his letters that he thought a good deal about such matters and his own views were very liberal. I should like to know the practical expression of his views. It is one thing, for instance, to have arrived at a broad and unconventional creed one's self,—by the route of long years and much experience,—and quite another to teach that same creed to an inexperienced child. But in lieu of doing that, must one make the child start where the father did, just as if no generation could learn these things from others, but must go through all the turmoil and doubts itself? I should like to know your father's answer to this age-long problem. The same question arises, of course, in the realms of morals and philosophy.[32]

Alas, we have no record of his answer, and Nute never completed the biography. (When Bruce Larson revived the project years later, he covered C. A.'s religious beliefs in a single paragraph.)[33] Nor did Charles say much on this subject in his own autobiographical writing, or in the pages and pages of critical notes he took on the work of his invariably inadequate biographers.

But one way or another, he came to hold a creed at least as "broad and unconventional" as that of his parents. Exploring Evangeline and C. A.'s philosophical and theological interests at least foreshadows some later themes in Charles's spiritual biography.

Our best source for the Lindberghs' spiritual and intellectual life is intriguing but problematic: the books shelved in the drawing room of the Lindbergh House historic site in Little Falls. Charles Lindbergh warned Grace Nute that the family library was "broken up on several occasions." Not only did the Lindberghs' first home burn to the ground when Charles was three years old, but the smaller replacement (built in 1906) was ransacked by souvenir-seekers after his 1927 flight.[34] But as part of the Minnesota Historical Society's decades-long restoration of that home, a number of books belonging to Lindbergh's parents were collected and catalogued.[35] Ranging far beyond the chemistry and law textbooks that you'd expect a high school science teacher and small-town attorney to own, the Lindbergh library suggests an intellectually curious couple who were eager to consider divergent points of view on the most fundamental, controversial questions of their age.

Perhaps least expected are all the religious publications. The Lindbergh House library includes at least five Bibles, ranging from Lodge and Lindbergh family heirlooms to a 1917 copy of the _Scofield Reference Bible_, the standard text of dispensationalism. "My mother read the Bible to me," Charles recalled, "but explained that no one knew how much of it was true."[36] Nonetheless, Evangeline's share of her family's collection also includes Alexander Cruden's biblical concordance, Puritan minister John Flavel's _Christ Knocking at the Door of Sinners' Hearts_, and John Ruskin's _Sesame and Lilies_, perhaps from a family member who worried that a college education would make Evangeline neglect what Victorian Christians like Ruskin saw as the God-appointed duties of women in the domestic sphere. It's not clear which of the Lindberghs owned _The Great Controversy between Christ and Satan_ (1911), by the Seventh-day Adventist prophet Ellen G. White, or _The Church and Modern Society_ (1903), a two-volume set of addresses by John Ireland, the Catholic archbishop of St. Paul.

But aside from what they inherited from their families, none of C. A. and Evangeline's religious books seem to have been read all that intently, judging by their lack of notations, dog-ears, tears, smudges, or other hints of even casual use. By contrast, it's evident that both of Charles's parents devoured the works of modern skeptics. For example, Evangeline marked David Hume's paragraph wrestling with the question of whether God must "be the ultimate author of guilt and moral turpitude in all his creatures," in a 1904 paperback of _Enquiry concerning Human Understanding_ that was issued by the same Chicago company that published her copy of Immanuel Kant's _Prolegomena_.[37] Charles's half sister Eva remembered their father reading works by Thomas Huxley (whose biography of Hume is in the collection) and Charles Darwin (whose _Origin of Species_ is lightly annotated). In addition, C. A. owned several books by philosopher John Fiske, who did much to popularize Darwinism in Gilded Age America.

But Eva added that her father respected William Jennings Bryan, the evangelical populist with whom he shared views on political progress, if not evolution.[38] And the one author we know to have been read by both Lindbergh parents was most famous for trying to bridge the religious and skeptical sections of their library: Henry Drummond.

If he lives on at all in modern memory, it's as the name of the Clarence Darrow character who debates a Bryan surrogate in _Inherit the Wind_. But the actual Henry Drummond was a Scottish evangelist who both worked with Dwight L. Moody and made a Christian case for Darwinian biology. The American publisher of Evangeline's copy of Drummond's *Evolution of Man* praised him as "the foremost living member of that group of writers which may be generally called the reconcilers of science and religion." Though "Evangelicals did not at once know how to take" his method of reconciling Scripture and science, "a large proportion of thoughtful, conscientious and earnest Christians, wavering in their faith because of the new light which science had thrown upon religion, have given an eager welcome to his teachings and have found in them the solution of their doubts."[39]

Though it's not clear if he read Charles Darwin's *Descent of Man*, C. A. Lindbergh made extensive notes in Henry Drummond's *Ascent of Man*. "If the theological mind be called upon to make this expansion [to embrace evolution]," began Drummond, "the scientific man must be asked to enlarge his view in another direction.... The social and religious forces must no more be left outside than the forces of gravitation or of life." Or, as Charles Lindbergh put it in 1966, "We reach a point in observation and analysis where the human intellect stares past frontiers of its evolutionary achievement, toward unreached areas infinitely vast—the mystical realm of God."[40]

At a time when Darwinists like Herbert Spencer (represented twice in C. A.'s collection) advocated for the "survival of the fittest," Drummond insisted that "it is only when both the Struggle for Life and the Struggle for the Life of Others are kept in view, that any scientific theory of Evolution is possible."[41] Charles Lindbergh would later see strife as something like a divine imperative driving human progress, but Drummond denied that evolutionary theory required its adherents to view the world as "one great battlefield heaped with the slain, an Inferno of infinite suffering, a slaughter-house resounding with the cries of a ceaseless agony." Instead, through evolution God had granted humanity a beneficent kind of "sovereignty" that would have appealed to a Progressive Republican like C. A. Lindbergh:

> The moulding of his life and of his children's children in measure lie with him. Through institutions of his creation, through Parliaments, Churches, Societies, Schools, he shapes the path of progress for his country and his time. The evils of the world are combated by his reme-

dies; its passions are stayed, its wrongs redressed, its energies for good or evil directed by his hand. For unnumbered millions he opens or shuts the gates of happiness, and paves the way for misery or social health. Never before was it known and felt with the same solemn certainty that Man, within bounds which none can pass, must be his own maker and the maker of the world.[42]

Not only did Drummond anticipate Charles Lindbergh's adult obsession with improving humanity's "quality of life," but Drummond's earlier attempts to identify connections between the spiritual and physical worlds—in *Natural Law in the Spiritual World* (1884)—anticipate Lindbergh's later notion of being connected to a pantheistic "life stream" that preceded birth and survived death.

Given his dismal early experience of organized religion, it's easiest to imagine a young Charles joining his father in highlighting Drummond's closing critique of "the parasitic habit [of] *Going to Church.*" Not that Drummond opposed religious practice in its own right, but as a member of Scotland's Free Church, he disdained the clergy-dominated formalism that can discourage individual piety and inquiry. In the end, Drummond predicted that a "formal religion can never hold its own in the nineteenth century. . . . We must either give up Parasitism or our sons." All three Lindberghs—mother, father, and son—could have quoted Drummond's defiant conclusion to describe their own philosophy:

> Better far be burned at the stake of Public Opinion than die the living death of Parasitism. Better an aberrant theology than a suppressed organization. Better a little faith dearly won, better launched alone on the infinite bewilderment of Truth, than perish on the splendid plenty of the richest creeds. Such Doubt is no self-willed presumption. Nor, truly exercised, will it prove itself, as much doubt does, the synonym for sorrow. It aims at a life-long learning, prepared for any sacrifice of will yet for none of independence; at that high progressive education which yields rest in work and work in rest, and the development of immortal faculties in both; at that deeper faith which believes in the vastness and variety of the revelations of God, and their accessibility to all obedient hearts.[43]

LITTLE FALLS: "NATURE-WORSHIP"

Charles Lindbergh recalled being "surprised by the amount of reading [C. A.] apparently did at one time or another," and it's possible that his parents talked to him about the philosophical, religious, scientific, political, and other materials they read. But young Charles's own limited library consisted primarily of adventure tales, and he claimed to know comparatively little about his father's taste in reading. "The times we were together were usually spent in out-door activities."[44] Likewise, Lindbergh's "reminiscent letter," *Boyhood on the Upper Mississippi* (written in 1969–1970 and still a key source for the Lindbergh House tour), says little about books amid its detailed descriptions of hunting, fishing, and farming.

Lindbergh wouldn't want us to make too much of his outdoor conversations with his father. "As a matter of fact," he told Grace Lee Nute, "our discussion on these occasions was much more likely to be about the scarcity [*sic*] or abundance of partridges and prairie chickens, about campaign trips, the farm at Little Falls, or my father's hunting trips near Sauk Center [*sic*] when he was a boy."[45]

But from early on, the land around Little Falls must have provided as much intellectual and spiritual formation for Lindbergh as any school or church. "It was here," Reeve Lindbergh believed, that her father "grew to value the wilderness that seemed so close in time, and the natural world that still spread, relatively undisturbed, all around him." She went on, "His years in Minnesota certainly nourished in my father a concern for the natural environment that remained one of the central themes in his life."[46] Looking back at his time in Minnesota, Lindbergh wrote, "God had been manifest to me through nature; never through a church. In churches, I had always longed to get outdoors to wash off what seemed a shallow, dogmatised religion."[47] Likewise, when he and his mother went to Panama in 1913 to see the canal being built, Charles recorded seeing "a few old cathedrals" but was far more excited to spot monkeys, alligators, flying fish, and other fauna and flora.[48]

Even when he was a child, some saw a spiritual dimension to the time Charles spent outside with his father. As Nute conducted interviews for her project, a Lindbergh family friend named Mrs. A. M. Opsahl recalled how C. A. and his son "would spend quiet hours of contentment, strolling through the wood-lands, gleaning bits of nature-lore through their own observations, exchanging perhaps a half-dozen remarks in as many hours. Or, it may be, they would enter into long discussions of philosophy, scientific research, religion, and sociology. . . . So keen was the delight these two took in the great world of out-of-doors that it fairly amounted to nature-worship."[49]

We don't have a record of Charles's more philosophical or religious conversations with his father, who had been so "imbued with the grandeur of God's Creation" in his own youth that he could not divert Lindbergh's attention from nature to books. But perhaps C. A. repeated something like the speech that stuck in the memory of his business partner, Carl Bolander:

> I was with him once on a trip through the lake country to the north of us. We halted for the view at the top of a hill overlooking a lake, and the long, yellow road through the pines, and suddenly my companion broke a long silence with an outburst of such eloquence and impassioned feeling as I'd never heard from him before. "Some men tell us there is no God!" he said, "or that God is a puny creature shut up in Churches and creeds. I need no scientific analysis or theological arguments to show me the reality or the bigness of *my* God when I look at this!" and his long arm swept the horizon.[50]

DETROIT: "THE DEVIL'S WORKSHOP"

"Instinctively I was drawn to the farm," recalled Charles Lindbergh, "intellectually to the laboratory." For while the former acquainted him with the miracles of nature, the latter enchanted him with its "magic: the intangible power found in electrified wires, the liquids that could dissolve either metal or stone, the lenses through which one could see the unseeable."[51]

The laboratory he had in mind was not his mother's classroom in Little Falls; she didn't return to teaching until after her son went to college. Instead, Charles thought back on his many visits to the Land family in Detroit. Evangeline fondly recalled for him how her mother became his friend and confidante and her father made a "pal" of him and thoroughly enjoyed him.[52] More than that, Dr. Charles H. Land helped Charles Lindbergh understand "the fascination of science itself—the opening of a new, adventurous, and amazing era for mankind."[53]

One of the most evocative flashbacks in Lindbergh's book *The Spirit of St. Louis* comes about a third of the way into his flight to Paris. As he gazes at the night sky from nine thousand feet above the Atlantic Ocean, his mind wanders back to a gray house in downtown Detroit, where Dr. Land invited his grandson to join him at work in his dental laboratories. "Grandfather is a scientist who invents all sorts of things," Charles remembers. "Here, I live amid turning wheels, the intense heat of muffle furnaces, the precise fashioning of gold and platinum, and talk about the latest discoveries of science." When grandfather and grandson finally emerge from the basement for dinner, Charles gets "to listen to discussions of philosophy and the latest scientific theories." Sermons and speeches could only "hum" in his ears, but the language of science was "clear-cut."

> People have been preaching about God and arguing about government for hundreds of years, and still they don't agree about who's right and who's wrong. Science isn't like that. It confronts opinion with facts. In science men are measured by what they really do. There's no unfairness about it. It doesn't matter whether you believe in God, or whether you are a Republican or a Democrat. Your experiment works, or it doesn't. A machine will run, or it won't. You can't prove that the atheists are wrong, and you can't prove that the Democrats are wrong, but the arguments of science can't be denied when an airplane actually flies or a human voice is carried from one city to another without wires.[54]

Of course, things weren't quite so "clear-cut" as that. Lindbergh later denied biographer Walter Ross's claim that the Lands were "scientific determinists."[55] As the flashback continues, Grandfather Land finds problems with the application of science, as he worries how technological innovations in transportation and communication will affect humanity. Even the laboratory, for all its wonders, carried some sinister connotations in Lindbergh's memory. He ended up cutting from his manuscript a paragraph that attributed to his grandfather's dental chair "the attributes of Satan." He went on, "It's as intriguing and as representative of hell. I can hardly bear to work in the nearby laboratory when my grandfather bores into a living tooth. . . . There's no sign of God around that chair. In fact God just doesn't fit very well into a scientific, laboratory life. You're so occupied with your physical surroundings, and your mind is so busy thinking—creating things for itself—that you don't have much time left for Him."[56]

Charles may have associated his grandfather's lab with Satan, but, in Joyce Milton's words, "it was the devil's workshop that he found more fascinating."[57] While churchgoers in Little Falls had little patience with a child's confusion, Dr. Land was always ready to answer his questions. While Christianity struggled to make its God known or relevant, science offered clarity—and hope for progress. "Science is a key to all mystery," Lindbergh remembered deciding as a child in Detroit. "With this key, man can become like a god himself. Science is truth; science is knowledge; science is power. . . . By its growing proofs of evolution, it's confounding preachers with their fables of Adam and Eve." While Henry Drummond tried to help readers like Evangeline and C. A. Lindbergh reconcile Christian belief with Darwinian biology, their son came to suspect that evolution "may prove there isn't any God." For if Grandfather Land was right that scientists could discover "the missing link" between humanity and its evolutionary ancestors (one of whom was depicted in a drawing on the wall of his operating room), then "the Bible would be proved wrong. And if it lies about Adam and the Garden of Eden, how can one trust what it says about Heaven and hell, and God?"[58]

Washington: "Cheese"

His visits to Detroit made such an impression on Lindbergh that he considered going into the Land family business, studying biology and medicine so he could "explore the mysteries of life and death." As an adult he would achieve some surprising success as a biological researcher, but young Charles decided that "these sciences belonged to well-grounded, brilliant minds; their study was intricate, and [his] school marks were poor in the subjects they demanded as a background."[59]

"He was not hard to teach," Charles's educator mother told reporters after his 1927 flight, "but, I must confess, did not study hard on things which did not interest him." It certainly didn't help Lindbergh's educational struggles that he rarely spent more than a few months in one place. "He was very unfortunate in not being able to get his schooling in a regular manner," Evangeline admitted.[60] "My school career was always in a chaotic condition," Charles Lindbergh told Grace Nute, "due somewhat to our constant moving back and forth between Little Falls and Washington."[61]

C. A.'s political career also helped deepen his estrangement from his second wife, which was permanent by the time he was sworn in for a second term in 1909 (though they agreed to avoid the public scandal that would have come with divorce). Nevertheless, his father continued to be an important presence in Charles's life. For most of C. A.'s ten years in the House of Representatives, Evangeline and Charles relocated to the nation's capital for the winter, stopping in Detroit on the way to and from Minnesota.

In Washington Lindbergh "started school, most unwillingly."[62] Several schools, actually—all unwillingly. (It didn't help that classmates took to calling him "Cheese.")[63] For parts of 1913–1916, for example, Lindbergh was enrolled at Friends School, an elite academy near the White House. Founded in 1883 by Quaker educator Thomas Sidwell, Friends advertised itself as "nonsectarian." Even as it "[strove] constantly in a quiet way to apply to daily school life the principles of Christianity," the school's curriculum included no coursework in Bible, theology, religion, or church history.[64] While Sidwell's teachers were better than those of the public schools he had attended, Charles still had great difficulty with his studies and "did not find much friendship" among the politicians' and diplomats' children enrolled there.[65] "How is it possible?" a former Sidwell classmate asked a reporter after Lindbergh burst on the global scene in May 1927. "'Cheese' was always of the most quiet, retiring nature."[66]

Meanwhile, he received a political education, accompanying his father on the floor of Congress and even attending the inauguration of President Woodrow Wilson in 1913. When C. A. introduced his son to Joe Cannon, the powerful Speaker of the House struck Charles as "an old man with a white beard, rather like a God on his throne." He went on, "[He] looked at me as though I should not have been there, which was probably true."[67] At the Capitol, Charles learned that "Government, with its tremendous powers, was quite a bit like God." He added, "Only instead of being Christians, people who believe in good government were called Republicans, like my father; the others were called Democrats. . . . Unlike God, Government was a tangible thing, but it didn't seem to have much more effect on life."[68]

But Lindbergh disliked that kind of schooling as much as the others, since the House of Representatives reminded him "of church. It was always too hot, and rather stuffy, and its speeches went on and on like sermons from a pulpit; only instead of talking about heaven and hell, like ministers, Congressmen were more interested in things like tariffs and trusts." He went on, "Sometimes you got a headache as you listened." As a politician's child, he "lived with famous figures, saw history in the making. But one forgot about the sunsets and lost the feel of branch to muscle."[69]

WASHINGTON: "A KIND OF MARTYRDOM"

Perhaps C. A. wished that Charles would show more aptitude for school or more interest in law or politics, but he seemed content to let his son find his own path. Indeed, Representative Lindbergh's campaign platform in 1914 emphasized the importance of freeing the potential in children, quoting poet Ella Wheeler Wilcox's dictum: "Trust in thine own untried capacity as thou wouldst trust in God Himself." (Wilcox was a member of the spiritualist New Thought movement, and her understanding of God was as unconventional as C. A. Lindbergh's.)

Returned to Congress with a ten-point victory, C. A. continued to champion the rights of the people against the power of the "Money Trust." But it wasn't just powerful financial institutions that concerned him. In 1916 he asked the House to investigate charges that the Roman Catholic Church was trying to erode public education, the free press, and other American institutions. He had been educated by a Catholic priest; his first wife was raised Catholic; and, according to his son, he "never held any antagonism for that faith."[70] But the populist in C. A. Lindbergh did resent the contrast between well-funded church properties and the poor houses surrounding them, and he now echoed the old charge of Protestant nativists that American Catholics rejected the separation of church and state.[71]

Yet C. A. wasn't averse to using religious language to advance his own political agenda. "If we adopt an honest system and make use of what

God has given us to make use of," he proclaimed in 1914, "everyone could enjoy what now only the few enjoy. The natural laws are simple and just. Man's laws, as now administered, create a Hell on Earth for the most of us, because they violate Nature's laws."[72] In 1916 C. A. decided not to seek reelection and instead set his sights on the Minnesota governor's mansion. His preliminary platform for that office supported woman suffrage and condemned "the unfavorable economic and bad moral effect" of "the liquor traffic." Above all else, he sought "to emancipate The 98 Per Cent from the shackles of industrial slavery." For "when God's Creative Forces respond as they do," he concluded, "we are at fault if we let the Subsidized Wealthy fix the times to suit themselves."[73]

After the Democratic incumbent died and was succeeded by the Republican lieutenant governor, C. A. shifted to the race for the US Senate. With fourteen-year-old Charles as his driver, Representative Lindbergh campaigned across Minnesota but finished fourth in the Republican primary, well behind Frank Kellogg (who would be US secretary of state at the time of Charles Lindbergh's flight to Paris).[74]

As his political career stalled, C. A. Lindbergh faced another family tragedy: his youngest daughter, Lillian, was dying of tuberculosis. (Charles drove his mother all the way to California to attempt a reconciliation with her ailing stepdaughter.) On one of his last visits, C. A. said he was struck that his daughter's "eyes—always clear and beautiful—this time were different." He went on, "not less beautiful or clear, but death seemed to be pictured in them for the body, and the light of the soul—spirit eternal for the little girl whom I adored as my daughter." Lillian died on November 4, 1916. "However much we miss our loved ones under ordinary conditions," her grieving father wrote, "we do not get a full realization of their worth to us, till a loved one is about to be transfered [sic] from this world to the eternal state."[75]

Three days later, Woodrow Wilson narrowly won reelection, in part because he took credit for having kept the United States out of World War I. But in January 1917, German submarines resumed their attacks on American shipping, and the Wilson administration began to prepare seriously for war. In one of his last acts as a lame-duck congressman, C. A. Lindbergh joined thirteen other representatives that March in voting against arming merchant ships. A month later, Wilson asked a joint session of Congress to declare war on Germany. "It is a fearful thing to lead this great peaceful people into war," the president acknowledged. "But the right is more precious than peace, and we shall fight for the things which we have always carried nearest our hearts." A pastor's son who became a Presbyterian elder himself, Wilson finished his address by casting America's duty in terms of Martin Luther's famous statement of Protestant principle: "God helping her, she can do no other."[76]

Wilson received his declaration of war, but six senators and fifty congressmen voted against him—including C. A. Lindbergh's successor and three other representatives from Minnesota. It wasn't just their German American constituents who opposed the war. Given their cultural and religious ties to Germany and their homeland's historic tensions with Russia, Swedish Americans like Lindbergh had generally resisted efforts to commit the United States to the Allied cause. A day after Wilson's war address, twenty Swedish Mission Covenant pastors composed a joint antiwar statement: "Humanity can not be helped nor our rights and honor vindicated by dragging our country into the war in order to help one violator of international law and American rights punish the other."[77]

But once war was unavoidable, most Swedish Americans took part, their "response to the call of duty . . . as whole-souled and hearty as it was from those whose ancestors came from England," according to one University of Minnesota professor.[78] Eager to prove their patriotism, observes Erika Jackson, they "began to refer to themselves as part of the Nordic race for the first time in an effort to link racial fitness to American loyalty." In the process, they adopted the language of eugenicists like Madison Grant, who had just declared that the "Nordic race in its purity has an absolutely fair skin and is consequently the white man par excellence."[79]

But C. A. Lindbergh stubbornly refused to cease his critique. Though fond of Mark Twain's warning that "the whole nation—pulpit and all—will take up the war-cry," the now-former congressman wasn't averse to using the language of the pulpit as he continued his fight against the war.[80] In his 1917 book, _Why Is Your Country at War?_, C. A. quoted an antiwar poem that ended at the foot of the cross:

I see HIM there;
I see HIS blood stained cross;
I see HIS saddened soul's despair.

I see—and yet
Betrayed and crucified,
In agony of soul HE weeps;
While all about
The shouts of frenzied men
Ring out their hideous cry for war.
WHAT FOR? WHAT FOR?[81]

C. A.'s critics turned such imagery against him during the 1918 guberna-torial election when he opposed his party's incumbent, a staunchly prowar Swede named J. A. A. Burnquist. One anti-Lindbergh poster asked which "cross" Minnesotans should take up: "The Loyal, Red-blooded American One, or The Yellow One of Chas. A. Lindbergh." Losing the war, Lind-bergh's opponents warned, would leave "civilization . . . crucified upon the iron cross" of German militarism.[82] While Lindbergh received the support of the radical Non-Partisan League, he lost to Burnquist and be-came persona non grata in the Republican Party.

His friends back in Little Falls fell back on religious language to pay trib-ute to C. A. Lindbergh's political career. "For want of a better expression, I shall call him a Seer," wrote Thomas Pederson, who wished years later that Minnesota would erect a shrine "to the memory of this apostle of economic equality and freedom."[83] Mrs. Opsahl told Grace Lee Nute that Lindbergh had had "to suffer a kind of martyrdom for the clear reasoning and sanity that established such views in his mind, and the unfaltering courage it required to proclaim them. A prophet without honor among his own,—how truly he illustrated this age-long truth."[84] Over twenty years later, Lindbergh's son would fight his own crusade against American involvement in a world war—and suffer his own "kind of martyrdom" in the process.

LITTLE FALLS: "STANDING AT A WATER-SHED"

World War I ended before Charles Lindbergh was eligible for military service, but that cataclysmic conflict did impact his life in other ways.

Settled back in Little Falls but continuing to struggle with academics, Charles took advantage of a wartime policy that gave him an alternative to flunking high school. The local principal decided to let students receive credit for working on farms, where the military draft threatened the labor supply. So Charles ended his high school career raising cattle, sheep, and chickens and tilling fields alongside farmhands like Daniel Thompson, a devout Norwegian who read the entire Bible every year.[85]

Charles intended to stay on the farm until he "enlisted in the Army or until the war was over—whichever came first."[86] He never fought on the western front, but the First World War did speed up the technological revolution that would carry Lindbergh far from rural Minnesota. Still a fragile novelty in 1914, limited to reconnaissance work, the airplane developed quickly over the course of the war. Had the fighting in western Europe not stopped on November 11, 1918, British bombers might have reached deep into Germany itself. A second world war would demonstrate the terrible power of aerial bombardment—and convince Charles to rethink his youthful faith in the clear-cut benefits of science—but in 1918 flight still retained its romantic allure for a teenaged boy pulled between the wildness of nature and the wonders of science.

In St. Cloud, Minnesota, for a talk in 1981, Reeve Lindbergh imagined her father as a boy, "standing at a water-shed in American history. On the one hand, there was the farm, and behind it the whole outdoor world that was such a profound part of this country's frontier experience. On the other hand there was the laboratory, and the machine, and the airplane. Which course would he follow, with his imagination so equally captured?"[87]

CHAPTER THREE

"The Winged Gospel"

The cockpit is the cradle of the future
and who rocks there now
will inherit the horizons of tomorrow.

—*Gill Robb Wilson* (1957)[1]

C HARLES LINDBERGH saw his first airplane in 1911.[2] Hearing the approaching sound of an unfamiliar engine, he climbed onto the roof of his home in Little Falls to spot "a biplane . . . less than two hundred yards away." For a dollar a minute, an early pilot was taking locals up for the ride of their lives. While the plane was "a frail, complicated structure," it captivated nine-year-old Charles. School was frustrating and church was stifling, but the mere thought of flight was liberating. He started to imagine himself with wings on which to swoop down off the roof into the valley, "soaring through air from one river bank to the other over stones of the rapids, above log jams, above the tops of trees and fences."[3]

The new contraption held just as much power over adult imaginations. A few years after Lindbergh first glimpsed an airplane, a Pennsylvanian named Gill Robb Wilson went to war in France, where he learned to fly in dogfights over the western front. He recalled that "the crudity of the aircraft of those days went unnoted in the all engrossing conviction that the airplane held the key to the future for better or worse. Time would take care of its perfection for whatever utilities might be desired. The pertinent fact was that the sky was a new medium of destiny, a frontier where hitherto only the mythologist and poet dared set foot."

Forty years later, Wilson couldn't even remember his first solo flight, for the "miracle of flight was so engrossing that indoctrination was a step to be hurried over as a matter of scant consequence except as a stepping stone."[4]

It's almost impossible to read the early history of airplanes without seeing words like "myth" and "miracle." The Greek story of Icarus leapt to many minds in the first years of powered flight, as daring pioneers soared toward the sun—and, all too often, came crashing back to the earth. But it was the language and aspirations of Christianity that transferred most easily to a machine-assisted ascent that narrowed the gap between earth and heaven and heralded good news of great joy for war-weary humanity.

Flight and faith seemed inseparable—and not just for Gill Wilson, who followed his father into ordained ministry but was better known for founding America's Civil Air Patrol and publishing *Flying* magazine. Almost from the moment two other preacher's kids invented it, the airplane inspired widespread devotion to a kind of technological religion: the "winged gospel," complete with its own evangelists and martyrs. "Sacrifices must be made," insisted Otto Lilienthal before he died of injuries sustained in an 1896 crash.[5] Gone were the days, wrote Wilson, "when men cajoled a moody God / and fawned on the inanimate forces / and fled because they dared not draw near." Pilots like Charles Lindbergh would instead "shed the fearfulness of ignorance / accrued from the foreshortened vision of yesteryear."[6]

"God Did Not Intend Man Should Ever Fly"

In the autumn of 1900, two sons of a United Brethren bishop left Dayton, Ohio, to test their design for an airplane on the windswept Outer Banks of North Carolina.[7] Their host in the isolated fishing village of Kitty Hawk described the attitude of the few hundred inhabitants of the town: "[We] were set in our ways. We believe in a good God, a bad Devil, and a hot Hell, and more than anything else we believed that the same good God did not intend man should ever fly." Otherwise, reckoned William Tate, God would have made man with "wing feathers . . . growing on his shoulders."[8]

Yet when Wilbur and Orville Wright took their *Flyer* on its first powered flights on December 17, 1903, one awed witness couldn't help but feel "kind o' meek and prayerful."[9] The brothers returned to Ohio the following year to conduct increasingly ambitious tests on a field outside of Dayton. The first person to publish a report on their gravity-defying activities was a local beekeeper who taught Sunday school, advocated for the prohibition of alcohol, and headed his January 1905 dispatch with a biblical exclamation: "What hath God wrought!" (Num. 23:23).[10] Turned down by the editor of *Scientific American*, Amos Ives Root could only share the miraculous story with the readers of his company's trade journal, *Gleanings in Bee Culture*:

> God in his great mercy has permitted me to be, at least somewhat instrumental in ushering in and introducing to the great wide world an invention that may outrank electric cars, the automobile ... and ... may fairly take a place beside the telephone and wireless telegraphy.... God's free air, that extends all over the earth, and perhaps miles above us, is our training field.... When you see one of these graceful crafts sailing over your head, and possibly over your home, as I expect you will in the near future, see if you don't agree with me that the flying machine is one of God's most gracious and precious gifts.[11]

Or, as a previously skeptical eyewitness stammered, again and again, as he watched Orville Wright soar overhead in 1908: "My God!"[12]

They had grown up in a devoutly pietistic church, and Wilbur strongly considered attending Yale Divinity School. But by 1903, both Wright brothers had ceased regular church attendance, influenced by the skeptical works of agnostic writer Robert Ingersoll.[13] Now a new kind of religion, fit for an age of technological progress, grew up around them. "Like the Christian gospels," Joseph Corn explains, "the gospel of aviation held out a glorious promise, that of a great new day in human affairs once airplanes brought about a true air age."[14]

Even more successfully than Henry Drummond's attempts to reconcile Christianity and Darwinism, the "winged gospel" fused two powerful forces in modern American life: evangelicalism and industrialization. "Preachers had extolled the prospects of replicating heavenly perfection right on earth, if only people had faith," writes Corn. "The combination of an optimistic, this-worldly religion with an industrial revolution encouraged many to view secular developments as evidence of religious progress.

Machinery became a 'gospel worker,' and devices of iron and steel seemed pregnant with great moral and spiritual implications."[15]

Like revivalists preaching the old-time religion, the evangelists for the new faith drew crowds to worship. When a plane first flew over Chicago in 1910, a million people turned out to watch it, including a pastor whose recollection sounds more than a little envious: "Never have I seen such a look of wonder in the faces of a multitude."[16] Corn suggests that the "first act of airplane worship" was performed by the Wright brothers themselves. In preserving their first airplane for posterity, they made the *Flyer* "the primary relic of that miracle, not simply a piece of the true cross but the cross itself." Soon the anniversary of their landmark flights became the high holy day of what adherents called "airmindedness." Every December, eight days before "Christians honored the birth of Christ, believers in the winged gospel solemnly paid homage to the original 'miracle' that took place at Kitty Hawk in 1903." On the twenty-fifth anniversary of the first flight, politicians, diplomats, and leading pilots made a government-sponsored "pilgrimage" to the North Carolina site that one speaker called a "national shrine." In 1932 a sixty-foot monument was installed atop Kill Devil Hill. Bearing an image of Icarus, the granite column pays tribute to the "dauntless resolution and unconquerable faith" of the Wrights.[17]

Americans weren't the only people enraptured by flight. After watching Wilbur Wright's hugely popular demonstrations at Le Mans in 1908, French writers resorted to religious analogies to make sense of the American. For example, one made much of the flecks of gold in his gray-blue eyes, claiming that they "ignite a passionate flame because Wilbur Wright is a zealot. He and his brother made the conquest of the sky their existence. They needed this ambition and profound, almost religious, faith in order to deliberately accept their exile to the country of the dunes, far away from it all."[18]

A young aviation journalist named François Peyrey noticed how those gold-flecked eyes grew distant; they reminded him "of those monks of Asia Minor who lived perched on the tops of inaccessible mountain peaks. The soul of Wilbur Wright is just as high and faraway." (It wasn't the last time someone would associate flight with the solitary, ascetic life of monasticism; the pilot of the *Spirit of St. Louis* felt like a "hermit," surrounded by "no unnecessary extras, only the barest essentials of life and flight.") The sight of Wright circling high above filled Peyrey with a sense of "religious grandeur."[19]

Such descriptions led cultural historian Robert Wohl to conclude that the dawn of the twentieth century left humanity "yearning for a new type of hero: someone able to master the cold, inhuman machines that the nineteenth century had bequeathed and at the same time capable of transforming them into resplendent art and myth." The Wright brothers crafted the first "epic poetry of technology deeds," but it was Charles Lindbergh who would best exemplify the archetypal attributes—what Wohl calls "the ascetic and spiritual qualities"—that François Peyrey first saw in Wilbur Wright: "the unusual eyes; self-reliance; determination; attention to detail; extraordinary patience; an artisan-like dedication to work; loneliness; genius; indifference to the superficial emotions of the masses; trustworthiness; imperturbability; purity; aesthetic sensitivity; spirituality; loyalty; simplicity; and above all, height and distance from the ordinary run of human beings."[20]

Learning to Fly

But most of that lay far in the future. Fifteen years after Kitty Hawk, few people who knew Charles Lindbergh would have ascribed determination or genius to a peripatetic student who barely graduated high school. The personal and professional travails of his parents forced Charles to cultivate self-reliance earlier than most teenagers, but toiling on the sandy soil of the family farm didn't lift him far above the ordinary run of life in central Minnesota. And it would take years for him to articulate any vision of the spiritual or the aesthetic.

In any event, the young Lindbergh's favorite pilot wasn't Wilbur Wright (who died of typhoid fever in 1912), his French rival Louis Blériot, or even the American fighter ace Eddie Rickenbacker. It was a fictional Scottish flier named Tam MacTavish.

The hero of *Tam O' the Scoots*, a World War I novel written by Edgar Wallace (more famous for later creating King Kong), MacTavish tried "every subterfuge, every trick, every evasion and excuse he could invent to avoid service in the army." But he turned out to be a natural fighter pilot: a fearless scout ("scoot") who shot down Germany's greatest aces and survived three bullets to the chest before retiring to marry an American nurse.[21] (Coincidentally, Tam was a "Wee Kirker"—like Henry Drummond, a member of Scotland's Free Church.) An early apostle of the "winged gospel," Wallace dedicated the novel to Quentin Roosevelt (d. 1918), the youngest son of Teddy Roosevelt, and all other "airmen, friend and foe alike, who have fallen in clean fighting":

> Nearer was he to the knowledge and splendour of God,
> Mysteries sealed from the ken of the ancient and the wise—
> Beauties forbidden to those who are one with the clod—
> All that there was of the Truth was revealed to his eyes.

As he rested from farm work, Charles thrilled to read Tam's exploits serialized in the pages of *Everybody's Magazine*. "In mortal combats with enemy pursuit planes, bombers, and balloons," he recalled, Tam "represented chivalry and daring in my times as did one of King Arthur's knights of old."[22]

Lindbergh determined that he would enlist in the army when old enough and "become a fighter pilot himself."[23] But the unexpectedly early end of fighting in November 1918 "raised major questions in regard to" his future, as his "dreams of being a scout pilot were replaced by the less romantic choice between another year of farming or college." Ultimately, Charles preferred the toil of the farm to the tedium of the classroom and so spent 1919 at home. Finally, in September 1920, eighteen-year-old Charles Lindbergh rode his motorcycle to Wisconsin, whose land-grant university he had selected "probably more because of its nearby lakes than because of its high engineering standards."[24]

Even when his mother joined him in Madison, Lindbergh found it hard to concentrate on his classes. "The long hours of study at college were very trying for me," he had to confess to his admiring public in 1927. "I had spent most of my life outdoors and had never before found it necessary to spend more than a part of my time in study." Having "been raised with a gun" in rural Minnesota prepared him to star on the rifle team of the university's ROTC chapter, but he made little progress toward a degree in mechanical engineering.[25] Lindbergh's brief college career ended, he said, "before the end of the first half of my sophmore [*sic*] year, a few weeks before I would have been dropped anyway because of poor marks and attendance."

By then he had resolved to enter aviation and learn to fly. "I had become fascinated by airplanes."[26] One of his friends on the rifle team tried to talk him out of taking up such a dangerous profession, but aviation, he said, proved "an irresistible force in my mind. Was a life of flying to be renounced because it shouldered danger?"[27] On April 9, 1922, he made his first flight, as the sole student of Ray Page's aircraft factory in Lincoln, Nebraska. He claimed that until that moment, he "had never been near enough a plane to touch it."[28]

"The Most Riveting Foolishness"

As a twenty-year-old dreamer, Lindbergh dismissed concerns for his safety. But as a fifty-year-old veteran writing *The Spirit of St. Louis*, Lindbergh recognized what had been at stake as he first took to the skies in what was still a "frail, complicated structure": "Behind every movement, word, and detail, one felt the strength of life, the presence of death. There was pride in man's conquest of the air. There was the realization that he took life in hand to fly, that in each bolt and wire and wooden strut death lay imprisoned like the bottled genie—waiting for an angled grain or loosened nut to let it out."

The Fokkers that chased Tam MacTavish weren't there to spit bullets at Lindbergh, but every flight risked death. Less than twenty years after Kitty Hawk, flying still pushed fliers against the limits of their maturing abilities to control an emerging technology. Not just pilot error but the mistake of a mechanic "meant a ship might crash; a man might die."[29] From the beginning, a young man who had always been more thoughtful than his schoolwork suggested had to have asked himself questions of mortality.

But also of immortality, as Lindbergh instantly felt flight caused him to "live only in the moment in this strange, unmortal space, crowded with beauty, pierced with danger."[30] As he grew more confident in his skills, Charles said, "[I] began to feel that I lived on a higher plane than the skeptics of the ground." Flying let him taste "a wine of the gods of which they could know nothing. Who valued life more highly, the aviators who spent it on the art they loved, or these misers who doled it out like pennies through their antlike days?"[31]

Lindbergh was also quick to risk another new invention that defied gravity and granted divinity. The parachute held, "with invisible threads, a human life, a man who by stitches, cloth, and cord, had made himself a god of the sky for those immortal moments." Two months after starting his flying lessons in Nebraska, Lindbergh crawled out on the wing of a plane flying two thousand feet above the earth and executed a *double* jump: cutting the first parachute in middrop, then releasing a second. "Afterwards," he admitted, "I learned that the vent of the second chute had been tied to the first with grocery string which had broken in packing the parachute." He fell several hundred feet, headfirst, before the second canopy finally slowed his descent.[32]

"Like other young men," comments Bill Bryson, "Lindbergh was capable of the most riveting foolishness."[33] Mastering the airplane combined his yearning for "freedom, beauty, adventure" with his love of science and interest in engineering. But there was no "scientific objective to be gained" in parachuting. Plummeting toward the ground, he felt a "deeper reason . . . beyond the descriptive words of men—where immortality is touched through danger, where life meets death on equal plane; where man is more than man, and existence both supreme and valueless at the same instant."[34]

Lindbergh would eventually wonder if such activities were "too arrogant," as "flying feels too godlike to be attained by man." Perhaps its inherent danger was a kind of divine judgment on mortals daring to enter that "strange, unmortal space": "When one obtains too great a vision is there some power that draws one from mortal life forever? Will this power smite down pilot after pilot until man loses his will to fly?"[35]

If such questions did occur to a younger Lindbergh, they didn't stop him from continuing his education in aviation. But the pilot he admired most in those days had been raised with the same religious objections that made the denizens of Kitty Hawk suspicious of the Wright brothers. "When I was a child," Harlan "Bud" Gurney recalled, "people were for the most part, very certain that God never intended men should fly. I know that my Irish, but very gentle Mother, felt that there was something almost sacrilegious about men's efforts to do so. She used to tell me, 'if God in His great wisdom had intended men to fly, He would have given them feathers and made all of their bones as hollow as their heads'!"[36]

Bud Gurney arrived at the Nebraska Aircraft Factory a year before Lindbergh arrived. Despite being three years younger than the Minnesotan, Gurney had already logged over two thousand hours before Lindbergh's first flight. Though he had defied his mother's advice, Gurney maintained a sober, pragmatic view of his work in aviation. While "most people thought of aviators as strange and daring men, hardly a human breed—men . . . who placed no value on their lives," Lindbergh learned to fly alongside a man who valued his life, he said, "as highly as anyone I knew." Gurney loved flying but also "flew to make enough money to marry his fiancée."[37]

Reckless enough to walk wings with Charles on barnstorming tours in 1923, Gurney knew that "it couldn't all be fun. There was work to be done."[38] For example, he jumped out of Lindbergh's Curtiss Jenny at an air show in October 1923, but only because he was paid $50. (Alas, Gurney was seriously injured and had to spend the money on his hospital bill, not to pay the tuition required to continue his schooling.)[39] If God did intend men to fly, they still had to find ways to remain grounded.

Lindbergh never abandoned his youthful conviction that flight necessitated danger. ("What civilization was not founded on adventure," he asked in *The Spirit of St. Louis*, "and how long could one exist without it?")[40] But however godlike flying felt, it was ultimately a matter of science and engineering. Writing just months after crossing the Atlantic, Lindbergh remembered thinking that "it would not only be possible to reach Paris, but, under normal conditions, to land with a large reserve of fuel and have a high factor of safety throughout the entire trip as well."[41] The same matter-of-fact tone runs through all of Lindbergh's first memoir, and in his last memoir, he recalled always knowing "that flying was dangerous." He went on, "But I was not foolhardy. I was prepared to plan. I was also prepared to take risks. To complicate the situation, experience had already taught me that neither intellect nor instinct could subjugate the other."[42]

"How ironic," mused Robert Wohl, that a young boy who grew up admiring the derring-do of "Tam O' the Scoots" would "be responsible for replacing the image of the hot-blooded and reckless ace with that of the cool, sober, and dependable aerial technician, the taciturn and unflappable captain who flies your commercial jet today."[43]

THE LAST FLIGHT OF C. A. LINDBERGH

One of Charles's first jobs as a solo pilot gave him his last intensive time with his father. In 1914 and 1916, he had served as C. A.'s driver during his father's political campaigns. In mid-1923, the two Lindberghs reprised the experience with an airplane.

Defeated handily in a halfhearted attempt to return to Congress in 1920, C. A. Lindbergh tried once more to revive his political career. He campaigned to complete the term of Senator Knute Nelson, who died in office five years after calling the antiwar Lindbergh "as disloyal as can be."[44] Having just bought his own plane in Georgia, Charles suggested that he could fly his father between campaign stops—perhaps hoping to take in some barnstorming income in his free time. (C. A. encouraged this thinking, telling his son to "make some spondulix" along the way.) His trip from the Southeast to Minnesota was Lindbergh's first solo flight across country.

At the many stops on the long journey, he continued to take up "any one who is sufficiently 'airminded' for a short flight over the country," charging five dollars for a ride no longer than ten minutes.[45] Some of the "airminded" were drawn to the "winged gospel" by more traditionally religious preoccupations. Stuck in rural Mississippi after a fast-approaching storm forced him to make a crash landing ("My first 'crack-up'!"), Lindbergh took up dozens of paying customers on short flights. One elderly African American woman asked how much he'd charge to fly her up to heaven—and leave her there.[46]

When he finally reached Minnesota, the aerial campaign got off to a rough start. Charles crashed outside Minneapolis and had to wait for a new propeller before joining his father at a rally in the southwest of the state.[47] At that point C. A. was supposed to scatter campaign literature from the open cockpit of Charles's Jenny, but instead he tossed the entire bundle of five hundred leaflets into the plane's stabilizer. Then in early June, they veered into a ditch during an abortive takeoff; neither Lindbergh was hurt, but the propeller and landing gear broke.[48] The flying tour was cut short, and C. A. finished last in the three-man primary for Minnesota's Farmer-Labor Party.

Still, Charles enjoyed the time with his father and marveled at the experience of flying over fields he had walked as a child. From the skies above the Lindbergh farm, he could "embrace its entire body in sight and consciousness at once—in a realization which previous generations assigned to birds and God." Landing for a visit, Charles reminisced with the Lindberghs' devout farmhand Daniel Thompson, who never thought he'd "live to see such a contraption" as an airplane. For his part, Charles realized that technological progress had closed a chapter in his life: "I knew that day," he recalled later, "that childhood was gone."[49]

The following spring he returned to flight training, becoming a cadet in the Army Air Service. But not even a month into a yearlong course at Brooks Field in Texas, he received a telegram from his sister that "exploded" through his life. C. A. had a brain tumor. Doctors at the Mayo Clinic operated without success and gave the former congressman just weeks to live. Lindbergh received a short leave and returned to Minnesota, where he found that his father—who had been considering a run in the 1924 gubernatorial election—"could not even speak." Lindbergh added, "But he recognized me at his bedside, and took my hand; that was all."[50] It was the last time father and son saw each other. Charles headed back to Texas, and C. A. died in Minnesota on May 24, 1924.

His funeral took place at First Unitarian Society in Minneapolis, where he had been attending services. According to his daughter Eva, C. A. "liked the lectures" from Rev. John Dietrich, a former Reformed pastor who had been defrocked in 1911 as he began to embrace what he called "religious humanism."[51] It's easy to see why a freethinker like C. A. Lindbergh would be drawn to a Unitarian minister whose addresses were advertised as not pretending "to offer any final conclusion on the matters discussed, but seek merely to promote clear thinking, to quicken individual conviction, and to inspire earnest action. In all these addresses it is understood that the speaker speaks for himself only, and commits nobody. Freedom of speech for the speaker, and freedom of judgment for the hearer,—that is the arrangement."[52]

For example, the same month that Charles saw his father for the last time, Dietrich spoke on "The God of Evolution . . . a conception of God so radically different from that of Christian theology that it is not recognized as God at all by those who have been trained in tradition and assumption, with the result that evolution is considered by the Christian church as a godless philosophy."[53] (Dietrich also deplored the First World War, to the point of hoping that Armistice Day would be set "aside as a day of mourning and penance"—a proposal that surely appealed to C. A. Lindbergh.)[54]

"Death did not bother him," Charles told C. A.'s biographer.[55] On one of their earlier nature walks, the elder Lindbergh had told his son that he wanted to be cremated. Having just visited his own parents' graves, C. A. had decided not to impose the obligation for their upkeep on his own children. "He wanted to disappear completely after he died," his son recalled. "His ashes should be 'thrown to the winds.'" So, several years later, Charles flew over the old Lindbergh family homestead in Melrose and scattered his father's ashes: "puffs of white in the slipstream."[56]

But one of C. A.'s friends insisted that being cremated and having his ashes scattered was not simply about saving money and bother. That "rite had to him a deep vital, underlying meaning."[57] It certainly did to Charles Lindbergh, at least in retrospect. "Time inverted while I flew," he remembered, as "past and present fused" and memories flooded into his mind:

> When I took off, I sensed my father next [to] me, not his ashes—as he had flown next [to] me campaigning, not many years before. Then, the country roads and villages I looked down on rose to surround us as I chauffeured him in early days of motor cars. We stopped to talk to farmers, to address political meetings, to eat lunch at country hotels. We hunted ducks in marshes, partridge in forests, prairie-chicken in open fields. The old homestead took us back to childhood, to brothers and sisters, and farm chores. Here, my father had arrived as a baby from Sweden, when my grandparents settled on the frontier, determined to make of it their home.

"It was," Lindbergh concluded, "as though I had drifted down with his ashes, as though I were in the wind that had taken his shape from the flames and carried it away."

Or so he remembered while writing and rewriting his autobiography in 1968, as part of a meandering meditation on what happened to humanity at the conclusion of "the momentary form of life." Scattering his father's remains made Lindbergh feel like he had "entered a spiritual framework as infinite, complex, and subtle as the magnitudes composing it."[58] But is that how he perceived that experience in the moment, or in retrospect?

It's a minor episode, but the story of his father's last flight points to one of the challenges inherent in understanding Charles Lindbergh. He eventually told and interpreted his own story—at greater length than any reporter or biographer—but most of that narration and analysis came in the second half of Lindbergh's life, much further along his spiritual journey. During the first half, including the years just before and just after the adventure that made him the object of so much interest, Lindbergh recorded almost nothing about what he thought, felt, and believed.

"To Know God's Earth and Air"

Lindbergh returned to Texas and completed his army training, graduating first in his class just nine days after nearly perishing in a midair collision. But even gifted fliers found few opportunities in the peacetime military, so Charles took a job with the Robertson Aircraft Corporation, flying bags of mail from St. Louis to Chicago. While the work may sound mundane compared to the flight Lindbergh was about to plan, he remembered it with the language of the sacred:

> We pilots of the mail have a tradition to establish. The commerce of the air depends on it. Men have already died for that tradition. Every division of the mail routes has its hallowed points of crash where some pilot on a stormy night, or lost and blinded by fog, laid down his life on the altar of his occupation. Every man who flies the mail senses that altar and, consciously or unconsciously, in his way worships before it, knowing that his own next flight may end in the sacrifice demanded.[59]

Laid down his life. Whether he adapted Jesus's phrase from the Gospel of John consciously or unconsciously, Lindbergh illustrates well Joseph Corn's observation that air-minded Americans often borrowed from

Christianity as they "searched for language appropriate to the excitement they felt for the airplane."[60]

On off days, Lindbergh supplemented his income by offering flying lessons. One of his oldest pupils in St. Louis—"close to sixty years age, and we look with doubt on any prospective student over thirty"—was a priest. Pastor of St. Henry's Catholic Church for twenty years, Father Henry Hussmann befriended his flying instructor, who later wrote this about the priest:

> [His] handling of the controls was just as bad as I'd expected. But how he loved to fly! I learned that he didn't care much about whether he soloed or not. He wanted to climb up above the earth and look down on its farms and villages, over its horizons, to see the great winding lengths of its rivers, and handle the controls of the plane he was in—wallow, slip, or skid as it might. He couldn't afford to fly often; but every week or two he came out to the field for another hour in the [OX-5] Standard. And he wasn't a fair-weather flyer. If it was windy or raining, he'd still go up with you if you'd take him, as though he wished to know God's earth and air in all their phases.[61]

By that point, Father Hussmann's young teacher was starting to prepare for a far longer flight, one that would show him more of God's air and earth than any pilot had encountered in a single stretch. In *The Spirit of St. Louis*, Lindbergh spends his hour aloft with the priest trying to figure out how to finance a flight from New York to Paris.

CHAPTER FOUR

"The New Christ"

Lindbergh saved souls. . . . Much has been said about materialism, about men losing their faith, about their doing nothing except for gain. Then comes along a simple man who
somehow has ideals in his soul and who restores humanity's
belief in human nature in the ability to do big things. Within
each one of us is that wellspring, the water of life. The realization of this is the vision each of us should have.

–*Rev. Randolph Ray (May 29, 1927)*[1]

O N MAY 20, 1927, everyone in Yankee Stadium talked to God. It was
a Friday night fight, not a religious revival. But before Jack Sharkey
and Jim Maloney threw a punch, the ring announcer asked forty thousand
boxing fans to pray for someone they'd never met. They weren't alone, according to humorist Will Rogers. "A . . . slim, tall bashful smiling American
boy is somewhere over the middle of the Atlantic ocean," he wrote in his
syndicated newspaper column. "He is being prayed for to every kind of
Supreme Being that had a following."[2]

Perhaps the prayers were answered. Or perhaps the Saint Christopher's
medal Father Hussmann had slipped into his flight instructor's jacket had,
as Lindbergh put it, "taken me where I wished to go."[3] For the next night,
wrote Frederick Lewis Allen, "something very like a miracle took place."[4]

On May 21, 1927, just over thirty-three hours after he took off from
New York's Roosevelt Field—and fifty-six hours since he had last slept—
Charles Lindbergh landed north of Paris, at an aerodrome called Le Bourget. As many as 150,000 people were waiting for him, desperate to catch a
glimpse of the first person to fly solo across the Atlantic Ocean. "It was like

drowning in a human sea," he remembered.[5] Fortunately, no one actually knew what the American mail pilot looked like, and two French fliers were able to remove him to the safety of a nearby hangar. It would be one of the last times for many years that Charles Lindbergh went unrecognized.

How? Why? Who?

"Young and old, rich and poor . . . Fundamentalist and skeptic," wrote Allen, in his "informal history" of the Roaring Twenties, "all with one accord fastened their hopes upon the young man in the *Spirit of St. Louis.*"[6] Almost from the moment he landed, Lindbergh was bombarded with questions from awestruck admirers as famous as kings and presidents and as anonymous as the tens of thousands who sent him fan mail.

As he sat down that July to dash off *"We,"* the memoir he had promised George Putnam, the publisher who would soon marry Amelia Earhart, Lindbergh was most willing to answer one question: *How?* Writing over two hundred pages in just three weeks, Lindbergh explained how he had made possible the impossible: how he had trained as a pilot through years of barnstorming and delivering the mail; how his monoplane was specially designed and constructed for its singular purpose; how he had painstakingly plotted his journey on nautical maps and eliminated every needless ounce of weight to maximize his fuel. Lindbergh even detailed how much water he drank—but left out his answer to the question King George V asked during a personal audience in London: "How did you pee?"[7]

But Lindbergh also refrained from answering the deeper questions everyone was asking, such as those that began *Why?*

Why fly solo across the Atlantic? Was he simply trying to win the $25,000 prize that hotelier Louis Orteig had been offering since 1919? No, money didn't interest him. *Did he seek glory and celebrity?* No, he never expected such adulation and mostly wanted to be left alone. *Was he a daredevil, risking certain death to experience life more intense than the comfortable banality of modern existence?* Several pilots had already perished on the same quest, including two French war heroes who had taken off from Le Bourget just days earlier and disappeared over the Atlantic. But Lindbergh insisted that he had weighed the risks and, on balance, deemed the journey a safe one.

In a book that revealed more about his plane than its pilot, Charles Lindbergh was least eager to answer the question highest in all other minds: *Who is Charles Lindbergh?*

If Lindbergh was not yet willing to say much about himself beyond the eighteen-line sketch of his childhood in *"We,"* others were more than happy to fill the silence.[8] As people around the world made speeches, preached sermons, composed poetry, and (already) wrote biographies about the "famous unknown," most could only guess at the details of Lindbergh's life, let alone his beliefs, convictions, and values. But that didn't stop them from making the quiet young Minnesotan into an archetype, the embodiment of their highest ideals and the solution to their most pressing problems.

At this point this book necessarily becomes not just a spiritual biography of Charles Lindbergh but also a spiritual biography of the 1920s, a decade whose roaring progress could not disguise the disparities in American society nor drown out the doubts raised by the worst war to that point in history. Until Lindbergh, wrote the third place finisher in a national poetry contest held in his honor,

> An earthen shadow lay on men's endeavor.
> Four years of war, nine years of bitter peace
> Had bred a cynic wisdom in the young.[9]

But Lindbergh "awakened our slumbering confidence in the possibilities of personality," proclaimed Unitarian minister Charles Francis Potter in June 1927. "He has roused our planet's soul."[10] Free of the "taint" of 1914–1918, Lindbergh "represented a future beyond war."[11]

Though he was a member of "the new generation" that his fellow Minnesotan F. Scott Fitzgerald said had "grown up to find all Gods dead," Lindbergh seemed to disprove their assumption of "all wars fought, all faiths in man shaken."[12] Lindbergh became "an avatar of a new breed of Americans," wrote Brendan Gill fifty years later, "one who seemed cheerfully at ease, as most of the rest of us were not, with the intricate technical wonders pouring daily from our laboratories and factories. He stood for the promises of applied science as a young poet might stand for the promises of the word. He had a thrilling gospel to preach and he preached it in good faith, to millions of people throughout the world, both by uttering it in brief speeches and by the example of his little plane in flight."[13]

In a quickie biography for the Boy Scouts of America, educator John H. Finley proclaimed the pilot "the new Crusader Knight of the Air," whose quest "was in a very real sense a 'Via Dei,' a way of God."[14]

Other Americans, though nonreligious themselves, saw Lindbergh as something more than just a preacher of the "winged gospel." Fitzgerald's friend Ernest Hemingway, who wasn't at Le Bourget, called Lindbergh an "angel." Hemingway's publisher, Harry Crosby, who was, went even further: "Running people ahead running people all round us running and the crowd behind stampeding like buffalo and a pushing and a shoving and where is he where is he Lindbergh where is he and the extraordinary impression I had of hands thousands of hands weaving like maggots over the silver wings of the Spirit of Saint-Louis and it seems as if all the hands in the world are touching or trying to touch *the new Christ* and that the new Cross is the plane."[15]

Who was Charles Lindbergh? Less a man than a messiah, standing at the center of what one newspaper called "the greatest event since the Resurrection."[16]

"Literally Worshipped and Adored"

America's ambassador to France was watching "Big Bill" Tilden play tennis when he received a telegram confirming Lindbergh's approach.[17] Recognizing a golden opportunity to improve Franco-American relations, Myron T. Herrick hosted the pilot at the US embassy and began scheduling the first of Lindbergh's almost endless public appearances that year. "I am not a religious man," said Herrick several days later, at the city of Paris's official reception for Lindbergh. "But I believe there are certain things that happen in life which can only be described as the interpretation of a Divine Act."[18]

Though not personally devout, Herrick (a graduate of Ohio Wesleyan University) didn't hesitate to cast Lindbergh's achievement in religious terms. Invited to contribute the foreword to *"We,"* the ambassador started by comparing the twenty-five-year-old aviator to Joan of Arc, the fifteenth-century Christian mystic who "became immortal," and the "Shepherd boy

David," who wrote the psalm that ended up on Lindbergh's gravestone. "One need not be fanatically religious," Herrick reiterated, " to see in [Lindbergh's] success the guiding hand of providence." Indeed, Lindbergh was the "instrument of a great ideal," and his arrival in Paris "seemed exactly prëordained." For the *Spirit of St. Louis*—named for a city that was named for a legendarily pious French king—"brought as from on high a new spiritual message of peace and good will."

Herrick added that Lindbergh had landed not far from the spot where, in 1914, the French had prayed for—and been granted—a miraculous victory over the advancing German army at the first Battle of the Marne. No wonder that an "electrical thrill . . . ran like some religious emotion through a whole vast population"![19] He wasn't the only observer in Paris to connect Lindbergh to the Great War. The day after the landing at Le Bourget, Maurice Rostand composed a poem to Lindbergh, suggesting that it was the dead doughboys buried in France "which had brought you, predestined one, / Through all the risks where others fell."[20]

As Lindbergh began his initial victory tour in Europe, he couldn't stay out of the Christian sanctuaries he had avoided as a child. In London he participated in a Memorial Day service at St. Margaret's Church, then walked next door to Westminster Abbey to lay a wreath at Britain's Grave of the Unknown Warrior.[21] Back in Paris in early June, he attended services at the city's Swedish church, perhaps the first time he had worshiped in his grandfather's native language. ("As the Vikings of old found these shores," preached the pastor of the Swedish Lutheran Church of Hartford, Connecticut, "so this modern son of a Viking race has found his way over the trackless waters.")[22] But as crowds gathered around "the new Christ" and politicians competed to pay him tribute, a new religiosity was born. In Paris, the French "wanted to acclaim him, touch him, hoist him on their shoulders, worship him."[23]

Lest that last verb slip past anyone on first reading, historian Modris Eksteins repeated it: "What nerve had Lindbergh struck in the sensibility of the modern world? He was literally worshipped and adored. People sought relics from his person and his plane as if he were some new god."[24] If the cult of Lindbergh's celebrity bothered those devoted to older deities, none was as irritated as Charles Lindbergh himself. "'They invented me,'" Reeve Lindbergh remembered her father complaining. "And it wasn't him.

I think that's why it bothered him. That man wouldn't like mass worship anyway. Or any kind of worship."[25]

Nonetheless, it's not a reach to say that "Lindbergh loosed the greatest torrent of mass emotion ever witnessed in human history."[26] Hired to craft a more suitably grandiloquent epilogue to the prosaic *"We,"* Arctic explorer Fitzhugh Green added his own gushing to the flood of feeling he described: "Lindbergh's victory was all victory; for it was not internecine, but that of our human species over the elements against which for thousands of centuries man's weakness has been pitted."[27]

As Lindbergh and his plane returned home aboard a naval vessel dispatched by President Calvin Coolidge, Green's hagiography sketched a stark contrast between the humility of Lindbergh and the adoration of his countrymen. "If there was any wild emotion or bewilderment in the occasion" of his arrival in Washington, "it lay in the welcoming crowds, and not in the air pilot they were saluting."[28] Joined by his mother for a formal presidential dinner, Charles sat quietly while Secretary of State Frank Kellogg, who had defeated Lindbergh's father in a Senate race, praised his fellow Minnesotan as exemplifying modern "progress in science, the arts and invention." He addressed Lindbergh: "Truly this is a marvelous age and your daring feat will pass into the pages of history."[29]

The next day was a Sunday. "Under the able guidance of the Chief Executive," Green assured readers, "Lindbergh did the things every good American would expect him to do," starting with worship.[30] The Lindberghs and Coolidges joined two thousand others at Washington's Metropolitan Theatre, the temporary home of the First Congregational Church. (Syndicated political columnist Rodney Dutcher was scandalized that the faithful had to avert their eyes from posters for a silent movie called *Getting Gertie's Garter,* whose star, Marie Prevost, had her "legs and much else exposed.")[31] The next day a local paper reported favorably that Lindbergh "knelt . . . in humble devotion to the God who watched over him and guarded him as he flew to fame over the perils of the deep and through the hazards of the air." The pilot smiled when a child "squirmed" during the sprinkling of baptismal water and listened attentively to a sermon by Rev. Jason Noble Pierce, who only alluded briefly to Lindbergh and instead preached "the same simple doctrine that has been expounded through the ages, the teachings of the One who gave Lindbergh the power to do and dare."[32]

The rest of the day Lindbergh and his mother participated in festivals of civil religion. He laid a wreath at Arlington National Cemetery; "no empty gesture," according to the *Cincinnati Enquirer*, "it was a silent sermon on American ideals."[33] Their motorcade drove past "thousands of Lindbergh worshippers," many of them weeping. Later that afternoon, fifty thousand spectators; two thousand children clad in red, white, and blue; and "a vested choir of 800 colored singers" took part in a "vesper flag service" on the steps of the US Capitol. Sitting next to former Supreme Court chief justice Charles Evans Hughes, Lindbergh bowed his head for opening prayer, "while 300 feet above him the Goddess of Freedom, facing east with the others on Capitol Hill, seemed bowed in reverent reflection while the priest prayed." After Lindbergh left, the service concluded with a speech entitled "The Religion of the Flag."[34] It was a "day well worthy of what Lindbergh had done and what he stood for," concluded Fitzhugh Green, who was inspired "by the spiritual values it comprised."[35]

As Lindbergh's homecoming tour took him across the country, the adoration of the "new Christ" continued to intertwine with the language and symbols of Christianity. His ticker-tape parade in New York City stopped at St. Patrick's Cathedral so that Lindbergh could meet with Cardinal Hayes, who then prayed the invocation at a formal dinner in honor of Lindbergh.[36] Advertising the pilot's visit to the state where he was born, the chamber of commerce in Grand Rapids, Michigan, explained that he "comes here as an apostle of aviation." The following month in Fort Worth, Texas, Congressman Fritz Lanham described Lindbergh's flight to Paris as "indicative of the broadening scope of man's power under his God-given dominion. . . . Colonel Lindbergh is a missionary of this new progress, preaching its possibilities to a skeptical world."[37]

In his hometown, people scavenged the Lindbergh house in search of relics, and high school students claimed that there was "nothing too lofty, too mighty, too daring" for "The Flier of Little Falls," whose "character glows and shines like a light in the desert."[38] Why did Lindbergh inspire such fervent devotion? The British journalist P. W. Wilson suggested that "the religion of the air itself" had emerged to replace the prophets of old, with Lindbergh's plane treated as "a creation as inspired by truth and beauty as any art and any theology." Wilson wasn't ready to call Lindbergh Christlike, but another biblical metaphor seemed apt: "The Middle Ages built Churches. Reformers read the Bible. Our faith is locomotion. We believe with all our hearts in the happiness of going somewhere else. We are elevated upward. We are subwayed at the altitude of a cemetery. On railways we are not only pulled but Pullmanned. We are automobillious. To fly is a supreme mysticism. To fly across an ocean is the beatific vision. Charles A. Lindbergh is our Elijah. Not only can he ascend to heaven in a chariot of fire, but the public permitting, he can alight again."[39]

CHRISTIAN RESPONSES TO "THE NEW CHRIST"

Later that year, Lindbergh's first biographers, Dale Van Every and Morris DeHaven Tracy, went so far as to claim that the flight to Paris effectively made their subject "a demi-god, the personification of human achievement."[40] ("Full of errors," Lindbergh scoffed, after finally reading their book forty years later, "pure imagination in many places.")[41] Such hyperbole inspired journalist Silas Bent to warn the Methodist readers of the *Christian Advocate* against a contemporary form of "idol worship."

Lindbergh, baseball star Babe Ruth, and heavyweight boxers Jack Dempsey and Gene Tunney, Bent wrote, had become "demi-gods . . . outstanding instances in this year of our Lord of the recrudescence of paganism . . . the worship of the flesh in manifestations of strength, beauty, daring, and skill, as contrasted with that moral scrupulousness which, upholding the freedom of the conscience, associates love of the body with original sin."

While he knew that "Uncle Sam does not hesitate to exploit paganism when it serves his purposes," Bent's chief target was his own industry. The author of an exposé of "ballyhoo," Bent warned that "the populace was stimulated to deify Lindbergh by the daily press, which serves as a Bible to a great part of it." If Frederick Allen was right that religion in the 1920s had "become a debatable subject instead of being accepted without question among the traditions of the community," Bent thought it was because the church was too ready to compromise with "the popular morality of to-day . . . a newspaper-bred and newspaper-stimulated paganism."[42]

But his was a minority opinion, at least judging by the letters to the editor published two weeks later. "We need heroes!" complained a woman from Baltimore, for whom Lindbergh evoked the apostle Paul, if not Jesus:

"Has the author forgotten . . . the wave of inspiration that swept around the world as we marveled that in this age of 'taking our ease' there was left one young man who 'counted his life not dear unto himself' [Acts 20:24] as he strove to do the impossible thing?" Astonished that anyone would impugn Lindbergh, "who is as fine a Christian young man as this or any other country ever produced," a reader in Washington, DC, demanded a formal apology. The editors of the *Christian Advocate* didn't quite oblige, but they did reiterate their own admiration for Lindbergh's "extraordinary modesty, simplicity, generosity, and manliness, displayed under most unusual conditions," and asserted that such was "the general feeling of our Methodist people."[43]

Early in the new year, the same magazine published a response to Bent by Florence Emily Cain, a hymn writer and former YMCA worker. As "a humble follower and an increasingly enthusiastic admirer of Jesus Christ," Cain wished, "in the name of 'whatsoever things are true' [Phil. 4:8], to register the strongest protest of which she is capable against the attitude which, in the name of religion, sees evil in what is so beautifully good." Comparing Bent's treatment of Lindbergh to the Pharisees' abuse of Jesus, Cain insisted that admiration of the pilot did not preclude allegiance to the Savior: "If we say 'Rah, rah, rah' instead of 'Hallelujah,' it does not necessarily mean that we are any the less thankful to Almighty God, the giver of every good and perfect gift."[44]

Like Cain, Christians of all denominations not only praised Lindbergh but interpreted his achievement in light of their faith. Given that he arrived in Paris on a Saturday, one imagines thousands of sermons being frantically rewritten back in North America. The next day Father John Quinn told worshipers at St. Patrick's Cathedral that Lindbergh's example should encourage them to support Catholic summer camps that meet the physical and "spiritual needs of the boy." A few blocks away in Manhattan, Rev. Selden Delany encouraged the members of the Church of St. Mary the Virgin to learn from Lindbergh "a practical lesson in mystical religion. While others are paralyzed by doubt and fear the true mystic makes the venture. He today sets forth into the unknown, trusting to God, and he attains his desire while others remain bothering over details and fussing over difficulties." Another Episcopal priest, Russell Bowie, also found "moral and spiritual meaning" in such "heroism of the human spirit." If campaigns as daunting as the eradication of alcoholism or war did not seem possible, Lindbergh's flight reminded humanity that "there is a fund of moral heroism, as well as a fund of physical heroism among men, which thrills to the challenge of the impossible."[45] In the Methodist church at Chicago's Temple Building, John Thompson compared Lindbergh to Daniel in the lions' den: "When he climbed into his cockpit it was like climbing into his coffin and when he reached Paris it was like opening his eyes in paradise."[46] In Kansas City, Congregational minister Clarence Reidenbach likened Lindbergh going to Paris to the apostle Paul going to Rome: both were "God's fools . . . ready to give their blood that the world may get on."[47]

Far from the bright lights of such cities, on a Canadian island off the coast of Maine, a Baptist pastor preached that evening on an Old Testament vision: "And when the living creatures went, the wheels went by them: and when the living creatures were lifted up from the earth, the wheels were lifted up" (Ezek. 1:19). Rev. E. Cameron decided that the prophet had seen not only "a group of air-planes coming, as if in a whirlwind, out of the north," but also "one plane flying alone." The fulfillment of this prophecy in the first transatlantic flight served, Cameron told his congregation, to "arouse our soul and stir our minds to a deeper and more consecrated faith in God and establish clear and true belief."

For Cameron, Lindbergh's flight did not mark the triumph of the "winged gospel"; it put wings on the Christian gospel. The *Spirit of St. Louis* crossing the Atlantic brought to Cameron's mind "great achievements accomplished by missionaries in the ages, and of the opportunities opening up today." Perhaps, he concluded, aviation could be one of the "inspiring new means which shall be used for the forwarding of the gospel to all mankind."[48] That same day, Rev. A. G. Williams preached in Kansas City that "the real power for [Lindbergh's] trip was within the heart of the pilot. Just so in building the kingdom of God we must find the power outside our church and college buildings." His audience: graduates of a Methodist training school for missionaries.[49]

The Episcopal bishop Harry Carson had already used planes to reach remote parts of Haiti. But missionary aviation took further steps in 1927, when a Presbyterian minister named John Flynn launched an airborne medical branch of the Australian Inland Mission and the German Catholic priest Paul Schulte founded the Missionary International Vehicular Association, soon to fly everywhere from Brazil to Korea. Lindbergh himself recognized that, within a few years of his flight, "preachers and Bishops were flying back and forth across the oceans in Stratocruisers."[50]

He would later decry the effects of Christian missions on non-Western peoples, and non-Christians also made their own meaning of the flight. For example, artist Columba Krebs, a Reformed pastor's daughter who embraced occultism, painted the *Spirit of St. Louis* being guided over the Atlantic by a divine torch.[51] But Christian preachers assumed that the Lone Eagle was committed to their faith. A minister in Detroit denied reports that C. A. Lindbergh had been nonreligious, inspiring a Methodist pastor in New York to call his son a follower "of the Great Master's system of life. The ability to stand sweet and strong amid such adulation as has never before in the history of this country come upon one man further demonstrates Lindbergh's Christian attitude toward his gifts and achievements."[52]

Small wonder that a Reformed church in Gary, Indiana, would soon name its new chapel for Lindbergh, or that a Methodist church in Springfield, Massachusetts, would include him alongside Francis of Assisi, Martin Luther, and John Wesley in a series of twenty-four stained glass panels representing "The Light of Christ in the Life of Civilization."[53] Charles Lindbergh "prayed with every muscle of his splendid young body," claimed one Episcopal priest, "prayed with every sacrifice that he made to gain his ends. He is an example that prayer is answered." "What we admire most in him," said another, "is that he is the product of Christian teaching and the Christian religion."[54]

"Clean and Wholesome"

None of that was true. But for all the public scrutiny that would soon make Charles Lindbergh more protective of his privacy, no one was interested in uncovering the more complicated story of their hero's upbringing, influences, and beliefs. Whether politicians or pastors, reporters or their readers, Americans wanted a type, not a person: Lindy, not Lindbergh.

For the shouts of triumph that greeted Lindbergh disguised sighs of relief. Relief that technological innovation matched to human will could produce something more inspiring than industrialized war. Relief that a town not far from the one that raised and disillusioned Sinclair Lewis could produce something greater and purer than the mediocrity and hypocrisy of George F. Babbitt. "In 1927 a widespread neurosis began to be evident," recalled F. Scott Fitzgerald, then "something bright and alien flashed across the sky. A young Minnesotan who seemed to have nothing to do with his generation did a heroic thing, and for a moment people set down their glasses in country clubs and speak-easies and thought of their old best dreams."[55]

Then there was the relief that this "new Christ" was as fair-haired as the Jesus first sketched three years earlier by another Swedish American, Warner Sallman.[56] "Of course, Lindbergh's Nordic blood had also much to do with his triumph," asserted the principal of the Madison junior high school where Evangeline had taught during Charles's brief stay at the University of Wisconsin.[57] Lindbergh was "an approximate composite of the modern eminent American," claimed one writer, who warned that "the Nordic strain [was] showing less influence and the Mediterranean growing stronger."[58] Others joined Calvin Coolidge in emphasizing that Lindbergh came from settler "stock"—"the stuff of which have been made the pioneers that opened up the wilderness," said _Outlook_ magazine.[59] Even at their most implicit, such descriptions made the pilot's whiteness impossible to miss, especially for people of color. "Did you ever stop to wonder what would have happened if Lindbergh had happened to be a member of your race?" the _Chicago Defender_ asked its black readers.[60]

There was no need to suggest an answer, in a decade when white Americans saw racial threats everywhere. Three years before Coolidge welcomed Lindbergh back across the Atlantic, he signed into law the Immigration Act of 1924, which kept Asians from crossing the Pacific to settle in the United States. In 1925, the Ku Klux Klan marched down the same Washington streets where Lindbergh would be cheered two years later. In the heart of American democracy, tens of thousands of unmasked Klansmen trumpeted what one religion scholar calls "a theology of whiteness, in which the divine created divisions within humanity."[61]

Beset by scandal, the KKK soon fell into decline, but violence against African Americans continued in the year of Lindy. The same day that the _Spirit of St. Louis_ left New York, the _St. Louis Argus_ detailed the acquittal by an all-white jury of the killers of three black Texans who had been burned and shot to death. A week later the *Chicago Defender* ran a cartoon: Uncle Sam saluting a *Spirit of St. Louis* emblazoned with the slogan "American Color Prejudice," while Lindbergh waved back with a paper bearing the word "Lynching."[62] As the NAACP (National Association for the Advancement of Colored People) met in Indianapolis that June, writer William Weldon Johnson grieved that two more black men—brothers—had just been lynched in "dark and benighted Mississippi . . . at [the] very hour when millions of Americans, not only white but black, in the city of New York were acclaiming Lindbergh." The flight to Paris "added to the glory of America," agreed Johnson, but ending lynching would mean something more: "the saving of black America's body and white America's soul."[63]

In 1927, however, most of white America worried less about lynching than about the lax morals of their youth. In Oakland, California, Rev. Edgar Lowther would "let pessimists who think the country is headed for ruin because of the failure of the rising generation think of Lindbergh and change their attitude to one of hope for the future."[64] But by making Lindy embody the ideals of their Christendom, many pastors revealed their anxieties about the Jazz Age. In New York, Lowther's fellow Methodist John Davis credited Evangeline Lindbergh with giving Charles his "stalwart character," itself "a rebuke to those youths who think of nothing but necking and drinking parties" in the era of Prohibition. When the pilot arrived in that city for its ticker-tape parade, fundamentalist leader John Roach Straton marked "Lindbergh Sunday" by comparing him to another Old Testament prophet: "Lindbergh's achievement illustrates as well, like the life of Daniel, the advantages of clean living and a pure heart. Like Daniel, this splendid, smiling American boy has refused to defile his body with strong drink, or by smoking, profanity, or other such abuses. Thanks to a noble mother's example, and the influences of her Christian ideals, this young man, in the midst of the temptations and dangers of today, has maintained his life on a clean and wholesome basis."[65]

Two days later, the son of another Baptist preacher gave the keynote address at the New York mayor's dinner for Lindbergh. By lifting "us into the freer and upper air that is his home," said Charles Evans Hughes, Lindbergh "has displaced everything that is petty; that is sordid; that is vulgar." Speaking in an opulent hotel named for Cornelius Vanderbilt, he asked, "What is money in the presence of Charles A. Lindbergh?" The young hero "has driven the sensation mongers out of the temples of our thought. He has kindled anew the fires on the eight ancient altars of that temple. Where are the stories of crime, of divorce, of the triangles that are never equalateral [sic]? For the moment we have forgotten."[66]

Looking back four years later, Frederick Allen agreed. Before the "idolization of Lindbergh," Americans had become a "disillusioned nation fed on cheap heroics and scandal and crime." The sudden appearance of "a modern Galahad" satisfied the hunger of people who had "been spiritually starved . . . by the disappointing aftermath of the war, by scientific doctrines and psychological theories which undermined their religion and ridiculed their sentimental notions, by the spectacle of graft in politics and crime on the city streets, and finally by their recent newspaper diet of smut and murder."

When even "the god of business" was "made of brass," Allen concluded, "is it any wonder that the public's reception of him took on the aspects of a vast religious revival? . . . No living American—no dead American, one might almost say, save perhaps Abraham Lincoln—commanded such unswerving fealty. . . . For Lindbergh was a god."[67] Or at least some kind of heavenly being. In his 1927 play *Paris Bound*, Philip Barry had one of his characters describe an angel he'd met as "a kind of Lindbergh."[68]

No one would outdo Fitzhugh Green in proclaiming the virtues of the man whose memoir he was finishing. "It is one of the cruelties of social lionization," he wrote, "that we search for the peculiarities of our specimen. In Lindbergh's case his peculiarity lay in the fact that neither by word, nor look, nor deed was he in any way grotesque."[69]

Why was it so important that Lindbergh be so pristine—angelic, if not divine? Why this concern with impurity, vulgarity, and the "grotesque"? A clue lies in one of the many gifts that Charles Lindbergh received from a worshipful public.

A SUPERIOR HEREDITY

When Lindbergh returned to his home state in August 1927, a medical professor at the University of Minnesota asked the welcoming committee to present the man of the hour with a bronze medallion inscribed "In Recognition of His SUPERIOR HEDITARY ENDOWMENT." Dr. Charles

Fremont Dight attached a brief note of explanation: "The thing next to his air plane that made possible Col. Lindbergh's flight across the Atlantic Ocean was his possession of strong qualities of mind and character inherited from his ancestors. The Minnesota Eugenics Society wants to arouse in young people a pride in better heredity and thus begin human betterment at its foundation."

The beleaguered committee brushed off Dight, who received no answer when he tried to go through Lindbergh's mother. The medallion had disappeared for fifteen years before it turned up in the state archives.[70]

But Dight was no crank. The founder of the Minnesota Eugenics Society, he was a prime example of a significant movement in the 1920s. Thanks to Dight's lobbying, Minnesota had enacted a eugenics law in 1925 that led to the forced sterilization of more than 2,200 "feebleminded" Minnesotans.[71] Lindbergh's home state was far from unusual in embracing the argument that the human species could be improved through scientific breeding on the one hand and forced sterilization (or worse) on the other. Eugenics drew support not only from nativists, who saw population control as yet another way of preserving white supremacy, but also from progressives (and socialists like Dight) who saw it as a means of addressing social problems like poverty. The same month that Lindbergh flew across the Atlantic, the US Supreme Court ruled in favor of a Virginia sterilization law, with Justice Oliver Wendell Holmes Jr. concluding for the majority that "three generations of imbeciles are enough."

The sole dissenter in that case was a devout Catholic named Pierce Butler. One week before one of Butler's fellow Minnesotans landed in Paris, the Jesuit magazine *America* objected that "every man, even a lunatic, is an image of God, not a mere animal, that he is a human being, and not a mere social factor."[72] But such protests were relatively rare, at a time when historian Christine Rosen says that "eugenics flourished in the liberal Protestant, Catholic, and Jewish mainstream."[73] Her book on the subject starts with one of Charles Dight's allies in Minneapolis: Rev. Phillips Endecott Osgood, rector of St. Mark's Episcopal Church. "We see that the less fit members of society seem to breed fastest and the right types are less prolific," Osgood told parishioners on Mother's Day in 1926. Preaching as part of a contest sponsored by the American Eugenics Society, Osgood warned that "until the impurities of dross and alloy are purified out of our silver it cannot be taken into the hands of the craftsman for whom the refining is done."[74] As the Minnesota legislature debated the appointment of a state eugenics director in 1929, Osgood shared with Dight his agreement that the "ounce of prevention which will make unnecessary the pound of cure, the removal of a sin against posterity, the ideal of a better thoroughfare for the human spirit, for the removal of unfitness in the process of racial development,—all these things would induce us promptly and enthusiastically to pass this measure."[75]

That bill was voted down, but Minnesota's sterilization law stayed on the books until 1975, a year after Lindbergh's death. After its brief introduction here, eugenics will only grow in importance in our story. Troublingly, Lindbergh's interest in heredity and racial characteristics—encoded in his oft-stated preference for "quality" over equality—would increase, in tandem with his interest in spirituality.

"Ghostly Presences"

But at the time, Charles Lindbergh expressed little interest in eugenics, religion, politics, or anything else that might have given larger meaning to his achievement. "In 1927," he reflected a decade later, "aviation was my greatest interest, and the subject closest to my heart. I thought and cared for little else." Abhorring "the froth of politics and . . . invariably disgusted by contact with a crowd of people," he was willing to discuss only what his trip to Paris portended for the future of flight.[76]

Even then, his version of the "winged gospel" was relatively modest. "Other enthusiasts" of airmindedness, wrote Joseph Corn, looked "to aircraft as a means of achieving perfection on earth or even immortality, promises usually identified with more traditional religions."[77] In *"We"* Lindbergh simply hoped to see a more sophisticated network of "suitable airports," with "airlines radiating in every direction."[78] At his most optimistic, he suggested to French lawmakers that the *Spirit of St. Louis* was "the forerunner of a great air service" that would connect the New World to the Old.[79]

In the process, he paved the way for flight—even transoceanic flight—to become anything but transcendent: a routine of both business and pleasure. By the early twenty-first century, as many as three thousand planes were crossing the North Atlantic every day.[80] What Brendan Gill lamented half a century after the *Spirit of St. Louis* touched down on French soil still rings true: that Lindbergh's "valor is hard to keep fresh in our minds when the most that we are asked to face and outwit above the Atlantic is boredom."[81]

At least as he first told the story, it may seem that Lindbergh's flight was itself rather unremarkable, if not boring. From takeoff to landing, its thirty-three and a half hours take up just over eight dry pages in *"We."*[82] Perhaps John Lardner's sarcastic judgment was correct: "It was not a flight that can be spoken of in detail. That was the happy thing about it in the end: nothing happened, except that the plane was sighted now and then, true on its course and making good time. What went on in the flier's mind the flier might have said, but the chances are he could not." Writing in 1949, Lardner decided that it was the "detachment, the cool, scientific preoccupation, the avoidance of bravado or any sense of great adventure, which make *We* the best memento we have of the man who made the flight."[83]

But four years later, Lindbergh produced a rather different account of the flight. Twice as long as *"We"* and infinitely more interesting, *The Spirit of St. Louis* won Charles Lindbergh the Pulitzer Prize for revealing what went on in his mind on that epochal flight. We'll eventually return to the writing of that book; it's a key midlife document of Lindbergh's spiritual journey. But one section bears noting right away.

Lindbergh began to write what became *The Spirit of St. Louis* in March 1939. That first draft's seventy-one pages of straightforward narrative include none of the flashbacks that would distinguish the final manuscript, and little of its philosophical rumination. But about sixty pages in, Lindbergh suddenly mentions an astonishing event that he had never so much as hinted at before: "As I sat in the cockpit with open eyes and resting mind, it seemed that the fuselage behind me was filled with *disembodied beings*, intangible, friendly, vaguely outlined forms, conversing and advising on my flight, riding weightless with me in the plane, pressing closely to be heard above the engines [*sic*] roar."[84]

By the time *The Spirit of St. Louis* came out in 1953, the "disembodied beings" had become "ghostly presences . . . phantoms . . . emanations from the experience of ages, inhabitants of a universe closed to mortal men." He went on, "They're neither intruders nor strangers. It's more like a gathering of family and friends after years of separation, as though I've known all of them before in some past incarnation."[85]

Writing an even longer autobiography near the end of his life, Lindbergh could "still see those phantoms clearly in memory," though he "could not remember a single word they said." He allowed that severe lack of sleep can cause hallucinations but did not take back his earlier recollection: "My visions are easily explained away through reason, but the longer I live, the more limited I believe rationality to be. I have found that the irrational gives man insight he cannot otherwise attain."[86]

If they weren't hallucinations, then the "ghostly presences" suggest at least two things about Charles Lindbergh. First, his interest in the frontiers between physical and spiritual, natural and supernatural was piqued relatively early on, even if it didn't find expression until his fourth and fifth decades of life.

Second, the first man to fly solo across the Atlantic Ocean wasn't really alone.

CHAPTER FIVE

Anne

I would like . . . to be in love with a person—not seeing
them, not particularly wanting to, not asking anything from
them—just knowing that they *are*, and going to them in your
mind as one goes to a hill or a field or a flowering tree, for
worship and peace.

—*Anne Morrow (May 1928)*[1]

THE WEEK CHARLES LINDBERGH FLEW from New York to Paris,
his future wife was writing a college term paper about her favorite
Christian intellectual. A year earlier, Anne Morrow had apologized to her
father for forgetting to ask if she could borrow his biography of Erasmus,
the sixteenth-century humanist scholar and Catholic reformer. "I really
like him better than any man in history that I have read about (although
they aren't many)," she explained. "I am very interested in him but I could
not give you a clear outline of his life or a list of his principal works and
their influence, or give at all accurately his religious views."[2] So as the
1926–1927 academic year came to a close at Smith College, Anne holed up
in Neilson Library to fill in her knowledge of Erasmus.

But before 1927 was out, Anne Morrow would find herself talking with a
man she liked even better, a pilot who took her on her first flight. And before
the twenties were done, she and Charles Lindbergh would be married.

Like Charles, Anne had an intellectually gifted mother and a politically
ambitious father. But their religious, social, and educational backgrounds
could not have been more different. Reeve Lindbergh later sketched a
contrast between her father's lifelong, "courteous indifference to convention, whether it be intellectual, religious, or political," and the values of her

mother's family, "which attended the Presbyterian church regularly, and voted, as they served, according to the traditional Republican guidelines of their day."[3] Charles's formal education was incomplete and forgettable; Anne attended the best schools available and cherished the experience. Charles preferred to "marry a girl who had no strong ties to any church" because he believed freedom of thought to be "essential" in his home; Anne was raised within the Protestant establishment.[4]

But in her lifelong wrestling with what she called her "Puritan" heritage, never entirely to be embraced or abandoned, Anne both influenced Charles's "spiritual but not religious" journey and lived out a contrasting version of it.

"A Good Presbyterian Family"

Famous for wanting to reform Christianity without splitting it among rival churches, Erasmus drew Anne Morrow's attention because of his resemblance to her father, "a moderate and a peacemaker."[5] In fact, it was because Dwight Morrow took up a second career as a diplomat that his daughter met Charles Lindbergh.

Dwight Morrow grew up in Huntington, West Virginia, where his father headed what's now Marshall University and served as an elder in a Presbyterian church. "The religious education of the Morrow children," observed Dwight's biographer, Harold Nicolson, "was thus no less intensive than their instruction in arithmetic." In addition to Sunday worship (morning and evening) and daily prayers (morning and evening) at home, Dwight and his siblings read from the Bible on Wednesdays, "an ordeal rendered the more exacting owing to the inability of their father to understand how any Christian, however small, could fail to possess his own miraculous knowledge of the Concordance." By age six, Dwight was expected to memorize the 107 questions and answers of the Westminster Shorter Catechism—successful completion of which earned a nickel. As the valedictorian of his high school, Dwight elected the challenge of giving a graduation address on Deuteronomy 11:29: "And it shall come to pass, when Jehovah thy God shall bring thee into the land whither thou goest to possess it, that thou shalt set the blessing upon mount Gerizim, and the curse upon mount Ebal."[6]

In adulthood, Morrow remained a committed Presbyterian, but his horizons widened. Attending Amherst College, he shared a mentor with future president Calvin Coolidge: philosophy professor Charles Edward Garman, whose students often became his "devoted personal disciples," as he led them "from truth to truth with the understanding that however unsettling the preliminary part might be the course would leave them finally with a positive religious belief."[7] After law school at Columbia, Morrow joined a firm in New York and attended Fifth Avenue Presbyterian Church. But an earlier experience of Mass at St. Patrick's had helped foster his ecumenical bent, in religion and politics alike. "Nothing," he decided, "dwarfs a man so much as hatred."[8]

In 1901 Morrow became engaged to a young woman from Ohio, whom he described to his mother as "a fine, dear, straightforward little girl . . . brought up not essentially different from the way our little brood was reared—in a good Presbyterian family."[9] Elizabeth Reeve Cutter had been raised within a kind of Presbyterianism that was morally strict but "not bounded by fear, nor important only in the abysses of tragedy. It also answered her need for poetry when life was humdrum, and gave her tranquility when she was harassed."[10] After graduating from Smith College and spending a year at the Sorbonne, she returned to Cleveland, to teach wealthy girls English, French, and history in private schools and "mischievous boys" Sunday school at Calvary Presbyterian Church.[11] Even decades later, Reeve Lindbergh remembered her grandmother "singing a hymn at the Presbyterian church on Sundays—*'Dear Lord and Father of mankind, forgive our foolish ways.'*" She went on, "It was inconceivable that the Lord to whom she lifted her voice, surely a Father with plenty of good humor and common sense—would *not* forgive my grandmother's foolish ways—if she had any. She must have been so useful to Him as an instrument of harmony and order."[12]

Betty Cutter married Dwight Morrow in 1903, in a ceremony officiated by the pastor of Cleveland's Old Stone Church. Anne, their second child, was born three years later. Each day in the Morrow household finished in prayer, and Sundays began early the same way, Anne writes, with the children "kneeling down in a row by our parents' big bed, followed by regular church service." The Lord's Day ended with evening "Bible stories and sometimes sermons on the green sofa in [their mother's] bedroom."[13]

As Anne and her siblings got older, "these prayers became more and more embarrassing and therefore fewer."[14] But that ritual featured in her earliest published diary entry, recording the family's last Sunday before her older sister, Elisabeth, went to college in 1922. After that morning's sermon exhorted the Morrows "to burn one's bridges behind one, to follow a dream," their mother gathered them that evening to read from the book of Ecclesiastes. "Mother was almost crying," Anne wrote, "and told us always to remember that wherever we went in the world, 'Whatever thy hand findeth to do, do it with thy might' [9:10]."[15]

It was the kind of liberal Protestantism that inspired internationalists like Dwight Morrow and Woodrow Wilson, whose promise of "a war to end war" reminded Anne later that, in her upbringing, "'Good works' were prevalent and indiscriminate. No one questioned their value or the inevitable progress to the millennium."[16]

But as importantly, the Morrows' faith made ample room for diverse kinds of learning. "Perhaps it was [their] Puritan energy," Anne speculated, that made her parents, "by temperament as well as tradition, teachers," who put "much stress . . . [on] our education, both moral and intellectual."[17] While he ended up a partner with the banking House of Morgan, Dwight Morrow remained actively involved in the world of elite higher education. He turned down Yale's presidency but served on the boards of both Union Theological Seminary and his undergraduate alma mater. Rather than educate the clergy, he hoped to see Amherst "give an all-around training to men who would take a large part in the business affairs of the nation."[18] According to Harold Nicolson, Morrow was "the first of the trustees to support" the reformist president Alexander Meiklejohn, and "the last to oppose him," when Meiklejohn's modernism finally became too much for Amherst's more conservative alumni and faculty.[19]

For her part, Elizabeth Cutter Morrow was an accomplished poet who later served as acting president of her alma mater, where Anne started classes in 1924. In her first letter home from Smith, Anne thanked her mother for leaving a devotional under her pillow: "I read the first lesson, right away."[20] But such religious references grew much less frequent as her undergraduate studies continued. In her sophomore year's correspondence with her mother, Anne's only biblical allusion comes in a letter that reports getting out of a Christian club on campus: "I have to stop, but I have to tell you that the whole spirit of this place is better—it has entirely changed. I feel differently. Some powers have no hold on me as they seemed to have before—I feel like saying, 'Let them not have dominion over me!' [Ps. 19:13]"[21] A year later she had to confess that she failed an exam in her Bible course, "in which I *have* been doing good work all year."[22]

But Anne continued to enjoy the music and liturgy of Smith's chapel services, and she found intellectual and spiritual inspiration in the history of Christianity. In 1927 she not only wrote her essay about Erasmus that spring but that fall discovered the work of the Lutheran composer Johann Sebastian Bach. "Absolute perfection," she wrote in her diary:

> transporting, pure, clear, unearthly, untouched, and untouchable; escape into a world unbelievably perfect, apart; unattainable perfection caught and held there crystallized. Lucid, faultless, chaste. . . .
>
> It doesn't matter that it can't last, that we don't find it more often. To know that there is such perfection, that there has been such perfection—it is worth living for. It *exists*. It *has been*—*it is*. One can contemplate it and feel a complete peace.[23]

A few weeks later, she was en route to Mexico City, where her father had been appointed the new US ambassador by his college classmate Calvin Coolidge. "Now I know what the Children of Israel felt like when they came to the 'Promised Land,'" Anne wrote, after the long train journey. "Miracle of warmth and sun and color."[24] The next day she met her parents' other guest: Charles A. Lindbergh.

"That Norse God"

After his return from Paris, Lindbergh had taken the *Spirit of St. Louis* on a three-month, twenty-two-thousand-mile tour of all forty-eight states. When he wasn't being paraded and feted, he "inspected sites for airports, talked to engineers and politicians, and tried to convince everyone who would listen that aviation had a brilliant future, in which America should lead."[25] At the conclusion of that tour, Lindbergh met Dwight Morrow, whom Coolidge had also entrusted with heading an investigation of

American aviation. (The last American president never to fly in an airplane, Calvin Coolidge even forbade his wife to go up with the famous pilot. But in 1926 he had backed legislation meant to regulate pilot licensing and airplane safety.)[26] Morrow invited Lindbergh to join him in Mexico City for Christmas.

It would be the first stage in another months-long tour for the _Spirit of St. Louis_ and its pilot, a trip with two related purposes. First, Lindbergh and wealthy backers like Harry Guggenheim hoped to demonstrate the possibilities of long-distance air travel in the Western Hemisphere. At the tour's last stop in Havana, Lindbergh met Juan Trippe, founder of Pan American Airlines; it was the start of a lifelong partnership.

At the same time, Lindbergh served as a goodwill ambassador for a regional power that few Latin Americans viewed as all that good a neighbor. For example, Lindbergh stopped in Nicaragua, where US Marines had intervened in a civil war earlier in 1927. He kept playing this role for several years, helping US diplomats in 1929 to promote Pan Am as an alternative to SCADTA, a South American competitor backed by German investors.[27] "I felt the great superiority of our civilization to the north," Lindbergh remembered of the 1927–1928 tour, but the crowds that greeted him from Costa Rica to Venezuela were as large and fervent as those he'd encountered in Europe and the United States, to the point that he worried he would accidentally kill someone, for "hardly anyone realized that the _Spirit of St. Louis_, like other airplanes of the period, had no brakes."[28] Though his efforts helped build what Jenifer Van Vleck calls the United States's "empire of the air," Dominicans, Hondurans, and others claimed Lindbergh as one of their own: a son of the Americas, plural.[29]

Lindbergh's stop in Mexico City was particularly important because of the religious situation across the border. Dwight Morrow had been dispatched to Mexico in October 1927, both to protect American oil interests and to seek a resolution to the Cristero War, a conflict pitting Mexican Catholics against the fiercely anticlerical regime of Plutarco Elías Calles. After the federal government closed Catholic churches and schools and nationalized church property in 1926, devout Catholics called Cristeros (from their chants of "_Viva Cristo Rey!_," "Christ the King") began a rebellion. After the attempted assassination of former president Álvaro Obregón, the government executed the Jesuit priest Miguel Pro in Mexico

City, just four weeks before Lindbergh's arrival in the capital. Even as he prepared for the aviator's visit, Morrow met with Calles and toured the northern states where the revolt was strongest. He facilitated a settlement in 1929, a year after Obregón himself was killed.[30]

In December 1927 Morrow had not been happy to learn that Lindbergh meant to fly nonstop from Washington to Mexico City, a trip over half the length of that spring's journey from New York to Paris. Lacking detailed maps of Mexico, the flier was soon lost. He arrived at Valbuena Airport more than two hours behind schedule, but, he remembers, Calles still "greeted me as warmly as though my wheels had touched the ground on time," as did the now-familiar crowds that lined the streets of Mexico's capital city.[31] From their car, Elizabeth Cutter Morrow noticed Lindbergh admirers "on trees, on telegraph poles, tops of cars, roofs, even the towers of the Cathedral. Flowers and confetti were flung every moment."[32]

His celebrity complicated Lindbergh's growing desire to marry: "Girls were everywhere, but it was hard to get to know them." Then as he entered the embassy, he noticed the "blue-eyed, dark-haired, extremely pretty" second daughter of the Morrows.[33]

Lindbergh remembered that Anne "stood very much in the background, as though resting in a shadow thrown by the sparkling vivacity of her older sister, Elisabeth." Though he later insisted, "I always liked Elisabeth, but I fell in love with Anne almost as soon as I saw her," his wife recorded their first meeting with all the insecurity of a younger sister overshadowed by the elder: "I saw standing against the great stone pillar . . . a tall, slim boy in evening dress—so much slimmer, so much taller, so much more poised than I expected. A very refined face, not at all like those grinning 'Lindy' pictures—a firm mouth, clear, straight blue eyes, fair hair, and nice color. . . . Why is it that attractive men stimulate Elisabeth to her best and always terrify me and put me at my worst?"[34]

Anne had vowed that she "was *not* going to worship 'Lindy,'" whom she expected to be "not at all 'intellectual' and not of my world at all." But by the second day of his visit—when Evangeline Lindbergh arrived to join her son—she could "see how they all worship him." It wasn't just that he served as a "symbol of the most beautiful, most stupendous achievement of our age—as typical and as beautiful an expression as the cathedral was of the Middle Ages," but that he somehow remained "too clear-headed to fool himself" into believing the mythology surrounding him. Even as she continued to envy Elisabeth, who made Christmas dinner conversation with Charles about the relative merits of Western and Chinese civilizations, Anne came to the end of his weeklong visit having made a decision: "[The] idea of this clear, direct, straight boy . . . has swept out of sight all other men I have ever known, all the pseudo-intellectuals, the sophisticates, the posers—all the 'arty' people. . . . The feeling of exultant joy that there is anyone like that in the world. I shall never see him again, and he did not notice me, or would ever, but there is *such a person* alive, *there is such a life*, and I am here on this earth, in this age, to know it!"[35]

Back at Smith after the new year, Anne Morrow couldn't stop thinking about a man who was "not a *type* of anything, as the newspapers have made him." Knowing that he flew over Northampton one day that February, she dreamed about throwing everything away for someone: "taking my life," she wrote, "everything I have ever loved—all little petty silly things, all the trivial world I stand for: bits of flowers and lace and scraps of silver paper and red ribbons—and throwing it all away for someone." She still didn't expect that "someone" to be Charles Lindbergh. "The things I love," she wrote, "seem just now utterly worthless compared to the world of Elisabeth and Colonel Lindbergh—that world I cannot touch, those people I cannot be like." Nevertheless, he had become "'le seul saint devant qui je brûle ma chandelle' ['the only saint before whom I light my candle'] . . . the last of the gods. He is unbelievable and it is exhilarating to believe in the unbelievable."[36] Almost a year after bursting on the world scene, Charles Lindbergh was still being worshiped and adored.

As graduation neared that spring, Anne yearned to be in love but fretted that she had "more in common with . . . *anyone*—the most distant of distant people—than with" Lindbergh. She moved back to her parents' house in Englewood, New Jersey, and prepared herself for the inevitability of her sister marrying "the *finest, clearest* man" she had ever imagined, and someone "utterly opposite" to her. Anne went on, "So opposite that I don't exist at all for him or in his world."[37]

Then he called her.

"After some months of carrying on my girl-meeting project rather unsuccessfully," Lindbergh wrote, his thoughts had turned back to the quiet college student he remembered from Mexico City. He resolved to use aviation for something other than diplomacy and commerce. "Dating a girl was seldom difficult for the pilot of an airplane," he reasoned. "He simply asked her to accompany him on a flight around the nearby country. Aviation was romantic, adventurous, spectacular, and, except for timid creatures, the invitation seldom had to be extended twice."[38] Having already taken Anne on one flight in Mexico, he now invited her on a second.

The object of his affections told herself that "Colonel L." asked her "out of duty." She continued, "I feel so sorry for him, but not worshipful." Even after they flew near the Guggenheim estate on Long Island, Anne insisted the following to her diary: "*I don't want to marry him*—God forbid."[39] After a second date, they were engaged.[40]

Anne found herself, she said, "in such a daze that I don't know whether I can write clearly." But she tried to explain her feelings to her sister Constance: "I discovered that I could be *perfectly* natural with him, say anything to him, that I wasn't *a bit* afraid of him or even worshipful any more. That Norse god has just gone. I can't understand why I saw what I did before. He's just terribly *kind* and absolutely natural, and (it seems so strange to say it of him but it expresses what I feel so well—the casualness and the normalcy of my feelings): 'He's rather a dear.'"

She closed with the words of a familiar hymn. "When morning gilds the sky / My heart doth wakening cry," she began, then replaced "May Jesus Christ be praised" with "Someday we'll learn to fly!"[41]

The more Anne got to know Charles, the more human he became—and the more devout her descriptions became. "He is not stern or abrupt or feelingless, and he is not divine or all-powerful or Godlike," she told Elisabeth, after another visit to Mexico City, yet "C." struck her as being "amazingly understanding . . . quite seerlike in tremendous outlooks." Despite his limited reading habits, he could see "far outside of his world, even into ours."[42]

They wed on May 27, 1929, at the Morrows' home in New Jersey, with Union Seminary theologian William Adams Brown officiating. ("Dr. Brown fine," Anne reassured her mother, but Charles "*loved* the dress *and* veil.")[43] They slipped away to spend their honeymoon boating along the Atlantic coast, enjoying a few days of peace before the press caught up with them in Massachusetts.

"I did not see my husband-to-be as a Prince," Anne wrote later, "but though it was never put into words, the image was nearer to that of a knight in shining armor, with myself as his devoted page." It wasn't a good basis for marriage, she admitted, but "it was not a bad beginning."[44] Over forty years into what ended up being a turbulent union, Anne looked back gratefully at its start: "The sheer fact of finding myself loved was unbelievable and changed my world. . . . I was given confidence, strength, and almost a new character. The man I was to marry believed in me and what I could do."[45]

"LIKE MONKS AT THEIR PRAYERS"

Marriage changed Charles Lindbergh's life as well, in part because it brought him into extended conversation with the two people who would do the most to shape his spiritual journey. The first, of course, was Anne, to whom we'll return shortly. But becoming part of the Morrow family also led to Charles meeting the man who had the "most stimulating mind" he ever came to know well.[46]

Lindbergh continued to fly frequently, with Anne joining him for long journeys even after learning that she was pregnant with the couple's first child. But the world's most famous pilot began to realize that his passion for aviation could not exhaust his "intuitive interest in life's mysteries." Indeed, all those hours aloft freed his mind to wander back to the existential questions that he had first asked as a child—and to "the unsatisfactory answers grown-ups gave to [his] inquiries." But "if [man] could learn to fly on wings," he now wondered, "why could he not learn how to live forever?" His quest to make the impossible possible now led him into an unlikely second career, as a biological researcher.[47]

Lindbergh was already reading textbooks, touring laboratories, and buying his own equipment when his interest suddenly became more personal. Anne's sister Elisabeth developed heart problems after a bout of pneumonia. "Astounded" that her doctor could not simply operate, Lindbergh began to contemplate a design for a pump that could sustain circulation during surgery on the heart itself. Even as Anne went into labor with Charles Lindbergh Jr. in June 1930, Charles Sr. explained his idea for a "mechanical heart" to his wife's anesthesiologist, Dr. Paluel Flagg.

The founder of the Catholic Medical Mission Board, Flagg arranged for Lindbergh to meet Dr. Alexis Carrel, the head of experimental surgery at the Rockefeller Institute for Medical Research.[48]

Born in Lyon, France, in 1873 and educated in a Jesuit school, Carrel grew more skeptical of his religious upbringing as he studied medicine. Even as Lindbergh knew him later, Carrel never was "conservative in his viewpoint toward religion, at least on Roman Catholic standards," and "did not follow at all closely the established procedures of the Church."[49] But his interest in Christianity had begun to reawaken in 1903, when his investigation of the miraculous healings associated with the shrine of Our Lady of Lourdes led him to reconsider the relationship between science and religion.[50] An iconoclast both to church authorities who found him too skeptical and to scientific peers who saw him as a "credulous pietist," Carrel took a position at the Rockefeller Institute in 1906. His experiments with suturing blood vessels in animals earned him the Nobel Prize for Medicine in 1912.

When Carrel and Lindbergh finally met for lunch in November 1930, it proved to be a monumentally important meal. "Nowhere," Charles later told Carrel's biographer, the Jesuit historian Joseph Durkin, "could I have found as great [an] opportunity to study the aspects of life and death that had intrigued me since I was a child."[51] Over the next few years, Lindbergh developed a perfusion pump that could keep animal tissues and organs functioning for Carrel's ongoing surgical experiments. Though he hadn't completed even two years of college, Lindbergh now published articles in the prestigious journal *Science*.[52] Praising him for his "unique intellectual capacity, versatility, and perseverance," Paluel Flagg felt privileged to have served as Lindbergh's "Virgil in this Purgatorio, where the light of knowledge and sympathy shines through human pain."[53] Meanwhile, Carrel struggled to keep the Lindbergh-crazed press away from his lab. "Men of science should not attract the curiosity of the public," he chastised one reporter. "They should be left at their meditations like monks at their prayers."[54]

As a result of Charles's connection with Carrel, he and Anne would soon be invited to stay at the home of the institute's wealthy benefactor, John D. Rockefeller. Over dinner, the elderly financier mostly wanted to talk about "the high-towered, gray-stone church he had built on the bank of the Hudson river" (now called Riverside Church); at breakfast, "as was his custom, he read a short passage from the bible." Lindbergh could scarcely believe that their devoutly Baptist host was the "fabulous and reputedly ruthless business executive who had built the Standard Oil Company."[55] It was one of many connections that Charles began to cultivate with the capitalists condemned by his father, who had once pointed to the Rockefeller Institute as an example of how such "invisible influencers . . . buncoed" the American public.[56]

Though the scientific mission of that institute brought them together, Carrel's influence on the younger Charles Lindbergh soon extended well beyond biological research. Even in retrospect, Lindbergh could find "no limit to the breadth and depth" of thinking in a man who discussed extrasensory perception with Albert Einstein as easily as he talked to animal trainers about "the difficulty of teaching a camel to walk backward."[57] As their conversations broadened and deepened, the older Frenchman pushed his young American colleague to consider questions of existence and immortality whose answers lay beyond the reach of science. "After five years," Lindbergh recalled, "I placed less and less value on the mechanistic qualities of life."[58]

A God's-Eye View

Charles Lindbergh "could not foresee that marriage"—by putting him in the path of Alexis Carrel—"would result indirectly in transferring aviation from a primary to a secondary interest of life."[59] But Anne Morrow Lindbergh was no less surprised that marriage would make the airplane a primary interest of hers, as she became a flier in her own right and one of aviation's greatest writers.

From her first encounter with Charles Lindbergh, Anne had fallen under the spell of flight. "God, let me be *conscious* of it," she prayed before first going up with him in Mexico.[60] Already searching for experiences that would supplement or supplant the churchgoing piety of her childhood, she learned that Charles was right when he said, "you *never get over* that feeling of serenity and sense of proportion" that flying provides.[61] In the early years of their marriage, she accompanied him on cross-country and even intercontinental flights, serving as his navigator and radio operator.

But she also took flying lessons from her husband and in 1930 became the first American woman to receive a glider pilot's license. "I now think," she wrote in 1973, that some of their adventures were "tempting providence. But I felt young and strong and invulnerable."[62]

Telling her mother about her first glider flight, in the hills around San Diego's Mount Soledad, Anne chose a biblical simile: "I felt like a lamb about to be sacrificed (right on top of a mountain, too!)."[63] But the more she flew, the more Anne realized that flight was not only "beauty, adventure, discovery—the epitome of breaking into new worlds," but also gave her, "for the first time . . . a sense of value in the 'real world' of life and action."[64] By the time she wrote the autobiographical novella *The Steep Ascent* in 1944, her flying alter ego felt "free, all-powerful, all-seeing"—not the sacrificial lamb, but the object of sacrifice: "One felt oneself a god. No wonder Satan tempted Christ from a mountaintop with the world spread out at his feet, like this."[65]

Flying gave pilots like the Lindberghs a God's-eye view of religion itself. After spending part of the summer of 1929 exploring Pueblo ruins in the American Southwest, they devoted five days to flying over Mayan sites on the Yucatán Peninsula, including the temples of Chichén Itzá.[66] As they continued on to the Caribbean, the governor of Saint Kitts asked Anne and Charles to delay their arrival because residents were having a church service and the chaplain felt they would distract the worshipers. As they circled the town and its "erect brown stone (incongruously) Gothic church" again and again, Anne looked down and admitted forgetting what routines were like in "a minute toy world with round wooden trees and Noah's ark people on round stands and a tiny church one could pick up by its steeple."[67]

They may have skipped church that particular morning—and their record-breaking transcontinental flight from Los Angeles to New York in 1930 began on Easter Sunday. But Charles Lindbergh had married a seasoned religious tourist.[68] Again and again, their travels around the world would belatedly start to fill in his previously limited experience of Christianity. For example, their 1931 tour of the Pacific basin started in Canada's Northwest Territories, where Anne recorded meeting the "eager" Anglican priest in Moose Lake, who showed them a Cree hymnal, and the "full-skirted, white-capped" nuns of Aklavik, whose native schoolgirls were "all decorating colored pictures of Christ" and whose boys were fascinated by airplanes like the Lindberghs' Lockheed Sirius.[69]

In Point Barrow, Alaska, the Lindberghs worshiped in a white frame Presbyterian church. Anne found it "so strange, terribly strange to hear" the minister—"a white-haired, active man with the grit and spirit of Calvin"—preach to an Inuit congregation. "Many could not understand English," she explained in her first book, *North to the Orient* (1935). "Even those who had learned it in school were bewildered by psalms sung by a shepherd on a sun-parched hillside." So the preacher turned the sheep who "went astray" into "reindeer who have scattered on the tundras," while "the power of God" was likened to the dynamite whalers used to break up ice. ("For Thine is the Kingdom, 'the dynamite,' and the Glory forever and ever," Anne prayed. "Amen.") As the service ended, the pastor asked Charles to speak through an interpreter, "comparing dog teams and airplane speeds, what the airplane might bring them, and thanking them for all they had done for him."[70]

After they crossed the Bering Strait and followed the Russian coast south, the Lindberghs came to Japan, where Scott Berg describes their arrival as having been "tantamount to a religious experience, thus furthering his cult following. Missionary groups of all sects throughout eastern Asia hoped he might visit them"—to no avail. They continued on to China that September, then began the long journey home. Much as she enjoyed learning about East Asian cultures, Anne was already homesick—and missing their sixteen-month-old son.[71]

CHAPTER SIX

"A Cruel God of Chance"

Like Orpheus, one tries to follow the dead on the beginning
of their journey. But one cannot, like Orpheus, go all the
way, and after a long journey one comes back. If one is lucky,
one is reborn.

–Anne Morrow Lindbergh (1973)[1]

A T A YEAR OLD, Charles Lindbergh Jr. was "a strong independent
boy swaggering around on his firm little legs," his mother reported
to his grandmother in November 1931. After his parents' months-long
journey to Asia, Anne wrote, "He did not know us but was not afraid of
us—not at *all* afraid of C. which pleased C. tremendously."[2] Anne was
writing to thank Evangeline Lindbergh for coming to the funeral of her
father; Dwight Morrow had died on October 5, 1931, as the Lindberghs
flew back across the Pacific. "I can only try to look at it as some kind of
great cycle turning in the earth," Anne told her sister Constance, "a broad,
impersonal, cycle of birth, life, and death."[3]

The next turn would be even crueler. On the evening of March 1, 1932,
the Lindberghs discovered that their son had been taken from his upstairs
bedroom. The kidnappers left behind pieces of a ladder and a ransom note
in broken English demanding $50,000.

"C. is *marvelous*," Anne assured her mother-in-law the next day, "calm,
clear, alert, and observing." He tried to direct the investigation of what was
soon called the "crime of the century," a case that Anne remembered as
inspiring "both evil and good. Greed, madness, cruelty, and indifference
were countered by goodness, devotion, self-sacrifice, and courage." From
the beginning, Anne felt that she and Charles "were upheld by the devotion,
loyalty, hopes, and prayers of many."[4] A Jewish rabbi and Episcopal bishop

joined Father Charles E. Coughlin to broadcast an interfaith appeal to the kidnappers, the Radio Priest suggesting that the baby could be left at a convent or Catholic orphanage.[5] "If God does not have it in mind to prevent such crimes," argued a Congregational minister in Battle Creek, Michigan, "it can do no good to pray for the child's return."[6] Yet not only did American churches of virtually every denomination offer such prayers, but thousands of boxing fans paused for a three-minute moment of silence at Madison Square Garden. "Did you hear," Anne asked Evangeline Lindbergh, "that whole great square full of people stood quiet (just as they did for C.'s flight)? I think it is thrilling to have so many people moved by one thought."[7]

Alas, not even supernatural tactics could locate Charles Jr. When a psychic in Virginia had a vision of the child turning up in Connecticut, the FBI investigated—and found nothing. Anne allowed a medium from New York to hold a séance in the nursery. One man claimed that the kidnappers wanted to work through a Catholic priest, while another lead came to the Lindberghs via the dean of Christ Episcopal Church in Norfolk, Virginia. Neither amounted to anything.[8]

Instead, the kidnappers took up the offer of John Condon, a retired schoolteacher in the Bronx, to serve as a go-between. After multiple contacts and then weeks of waiting, the ransom payment was arranged for Saturday night, April 2, at St. Raymond's Cemetery in New York. With Lindbergh waiting in the car, Condon talked to a man whom Lindbergh remembered speaking "with a definite accent." Condon handed over $50,000 and was given a note indicating that the child was being kept on a boat off the coast of Massachusetts. No such vessel was found.[9]

Six months pregnant with her second child, Anne resumed keeping a journal in early May, recording the "eternal quality of certain moments in one's life. The baby being lifted out of his crib forever and ever, like Dante's hell. C.'s set face, carved onto Time for always."[10] A day later, the body of Charles Lindbergh Jr. was discovered five miles from the family home. His skull had been fractured, most likely during the kidnapping attempt itself.

A Grief Unobserved

Informed that her son's death was likely accidental, Anne realized that she "would rather believe in crueler mankind than in such a cruel god of chance."[11] But a grieving public tried to point her and Charles to a merciful god of resurrection. Total strangers sent the Lindberghs letters bearing Bible passages and pictures of Jesus. While Charles Sr. had been called "the new Christ," one writer now said that Charles Jr. "offered himself as a helper of humanity, as the Christ did when he incarnated in the body of Jesus." A man from Buffalo, New York, wrote a pamphlet lamenting the passion of "the Little Eaglet."[12] A Presbyterian pastor in Cincinnati took heart, for "such an outpouring of sympathy could never have come to pass in a land where the name of Christ was not known."[13]

Such Christians assumed that the Lindberghs took consolation in the faith that was part of their public persona. "Today the distraught father and mother communed silently with the God to whom they are looking for aid in this hour of trial," reported the *Philadelphia Inquirer* the Sunday after the kidnapping, hastening to add that the Lindberghs avoided public worship not out of impiety, but because "attendance at any local church would only make them objects of public curiosity."[14] Anne did turn to her childhood faith, at least in later years. She came to learn from Christian writer C. S. Lewis that "grief is not a place . . . it is a process."[15] The New Testament's story of "the suffering, death, and resurrection of Christ" eventually helped Anne Lindbergh make sense of her "long road of suffering, insight, healing, or rebirth," though so too did a story of the Buddha.[16]

By contrast, Charles seemed to draw no comfort from Christianity or any other religion, in 1932 or the years to come. Perhaps some long-forgotten Scripture or hymn flickered to mind in those dark moments. More likely, not. In the end, we know little of the man's feelings during this time. He kept no diary, was guarded in letters, and did not even cry in front of Anne, who convinced herself that her husband's grief was different from hers. Even later in life, as his wife shared the intimate details of her grief with the reading public, Charles labored over an autobiography that regularly meanders into general interpretation of specific events but dispenses with the kidnapping in two spare pages that describe no emotion, make no meaning.[17]

At his most philosophical that terrible month of May 1932, Charles simply informed his wife that "everything is chance. You can guard against the high percentage of chance but not against chance itself."[18] So cruel a god offered no consolation.

But if there's no evidence that Charles Lindbergh coped with the tragedy by turning to religious belief or practice, we do know that he threw himself more deeply into his work with Alexis Carrel. After he had been drawn into that research by long-gestating questions about mortality, his son's death seemed to open Lindbergh's mind, as he learned from a Catholic collaborator who refused to respect the boundaries between the material and the spiritual, this world and the next.

That August the Lindberghs' second son, Jon, was born. The labor had been difficult; Anne described it as feeling "near death." But having another baby left her feeling that life had been given back to her. She wrote, "A door to life opened. . . . The spell was broken by this real, tangible, perfect baby, coming into an imperfect world and coming out of the teeth of sorrow—a miracle. My faith had been reborn."[19]

Two nights later, she recorded a conversation with her husband in which he sounded themes he would replay the rest of his life. "The more I go into science," Charles told Anne, "the more I feel that one cannot say that everything ends with the death of the body. . . . I think it's very egotistical to say everything ends when the collection of atoms that was you scatters."

She exclaimed, "But I don't want to be separated from *you*."

"Maybe you won't be," he answered.[20]

"A Somewhat Normal Life"

In February 1933, the Lindberghs had supper with a couple that still discussed the death of their daughter, years before. "I went through it last spring," Charles told Anne that night. "I can't go through it again."[21] Hoping to "rebuild a somewhat normal life," he decided to resume his globetrotting, with an epic journey meant to survey the "great overwater distances" of the Atlantic that "constituted the last major barrier to the commerce of the air."[22] For her part, Anne knew that so long a journey "crowded out any possibility of a quiet contemplative coming to terms with grief." But, she added, "[The] feminist in me longed passionately to prove that I could hold my own and take the place of a man" as her husband's radio operator and relief pilot.[23]

They also hoped for a long break from public attention. "At first you can stand the spotlight in your eyes," Charles later told one of his few reporter friends, Lauren "Deak" Lyman (nicknamed for his father's church role). "Then it blinds you. Others can see you, but you cannot see them."[24] Newspapers initially honored the Lindberghs' request to leave their second son alone. But the first anniversary of the kidnapping revived a cycle of publicity that the Lindberghs could only interrupt by taking short trips, and then in disguise. "On the whole," Charles wrote that July, "the press is a very great hinderance [sic] to us and indirectly probably constitutes our most dangerous and certainly most difficult element. It is not possible to care for a plane properly with ten or twenty photographers and reporters around. There may be advantages to publicity but it does make it difficult to work efficiently. It seems that it should be possible to carry news without the turmoil and nuisance which goes with it today."[25]

Anne felt much the same. "Both of us very private individuals," she wrote later, "we were thrown into the glare of publicity and were pursued by newspaper reporters and a public curious for every detail of our private lives. We could not walk the streets, go into restaurants together, or shop like normal people. Experiencing a kind of publicity hitherto known only by royal families, Presidents, or movie stars, we had none of the official protection of public figures."[26]

Ambitious trips like a tour of the Atlantic Basin gave the Lindberghs temporary respites from such attention—and sustained their celebrity.

Leaving Jon to celebrate his first birthday in the care of his grandmothers, Charles and Anne left New York on July 9, 1933. On the way to Europe, they stopped in Labrador, where the Moravian missionary in Hebron reported having "converted 'twenty-five heathen' that year," and Greenland, whose Inuit inhabitants christened the Lindberghs' plane the *Tingmissartoq* ("the one who flies like a big bird").[27] After visiting Charles's ancestral lands in Sweden, he and Anne paid their first visit to Moscow. They found history's first experiment in Communist government dreary and disappointing, save for what Anne described as the "fantastic Arabian Nights Church of St. Basil, its jeweled bubbles looking as if they had just risen from the ground or from the wand of a magician."[28] In Paris the Lindberghs met Alexis Carrel's wife. Anne Carrel struck Anne

Lindbergh as "a marvelous woman—a scientist, and yet a marvelously womanly woman." She went on, "I hope that all she said about C. and the work is true, for it made him happy, especially at that moment when life seemed unreal."[29]

They came home that December by way of Africa and South America, a harrowing journey that became the basis for Anne's book *Listen! The Wind* (1938). On their return to the United States, the Lindberghs received a congratulatory telegram from the new president, Franklin D. Roosevelt. It was a good start to a relationship that soon derailed. Two months later, Roosevelt abruptly canceled mail contracts between the government and aviation companies like Transcontinental & Western Air, which Lindbergh had helped launch in 1930—and in which he still held stock. (A congressional investigation had found evidence of conspiracy in the bidding process, though Lindbergh was soon cleared.) Several military pilots died in the rushed transition to an army-run replacement system, and by May TWA, the so-called "Lindbergh Line," was again delivering the mail. Lindbergh never forgave Roosevelt.[30]

Later that year he and Anne retreated to the Morrows' summer home in Maine. At one point, Charles sat down to write something so philosophical that it would have astonished the readers of *"We."* Having avoided all complicated questions in his first written work, he now asked one that he would spend the rest of his life contemplating: "What is the object of life?"

Lindbergh would not publish a more final answer until after World War II, but the two pages he drafted in 1934 introduced ideas he would never reject: "If one demands an answer conforming to the reasoning ability of the human mind he finds little satisfaction in the passing assertions of religion or science. The most that can be said of the first is that from its chaos and contradiction can be related some of the best philosophic thought regarding human conduct. From the second is obtained the only actual knowledge we have about the group of things which immediately surround us. Except by fable and postulation neither gives us a reason or an object for life."

As he continued, Lindbergh sounded more and more like Alexis Carrel, dissatisfied with conventional understandings of both science and religion:

Religion has described a creation and an hereafter. Science has tried to measure the ultimate—the smallest particle—the extent of the universe. Actually neither has done more than somewhat confusedly describe a middle chapter in human history and in human knowledge.... It is hardly satisfactory, in the light of logic, to place the biblical heaven as the object of life and to proceed toward a mythical hereafter according to some specific dogma which has grown from superstition and desire. Neither can much satisfaction be found in looking for an object in the decaying universe of thermodynamic science—a science which is blithely unwilling to prophesy the future of a universe which it has not yet been able to create.[31]

Meanwhile, Anne both wrote an article about their North Atlantic travels and encouraged her older sister in writing a family memoir. The latter project awakened fond memories of their younger siblings "fighting over who was to be next to Daddy" during family prayers.[32] But Elisabeth, still in poor health, died that December, just thirty years old. Her funeral repeated their father's service. "No one wanted to cry," wrote Anne, "but to sing the hymns gratefully."

But even as she struggled beneath layer after layer of unresolved grief, Anne came to the end of 1934 mostly hoping "not to disappoint C. at the Trial."[33]

"The Biggest Story Since the Resurrection"

There had been a break in the kidnapping in September 1934. A German immigrant named Bruno Richard Hauptmann paid a gas station attendant with a $10 bill whose serial number appeared on a list of the Lindbergh ransom money paid in April 1932. More than a quarter of that payment was soon found in Hauptmann's apartment. After further investigation and interrogation, a New Jersey grand jury indicted Hauptmann for first-degree murder. Staying with the Morrows that fall to research Dwight's biography, British diplomat Harold Nicolson reported to his wife, writer Vita Sackville-West, "The Lindbergh case is still front-page news. It *must* mean something to him. Yet [Charles] never glances at them [the newspapers] and chatters quite happily to me about Roosevelt and the air-mail contracts. It is not a pose. It is merely a determined habit of ignoring the Press."[34] The trial was scheduled to begin on January 2, 1935.

A media spectacle from the start, Hauptmann's trial struck H. L. Mencken as "the biggest story since the Resurrection."[35] Both Lindberghs testified, with Charles identifying Hauptmann's as the accented voice he had heard during the ransom exchange in April 1932. Though the trial continued for weeks, Lindbergh's lawyer, Henry Breckinridge, thought the verdict was sealed in that early moment: "'Jesus Christ' himself had said he was *convinced* this was the man who killed his son. Who was anybody to doubt him or deny him justice?"[36] Hauptmann's pompous attorney, Edward Reilly, began his closing argument by quoting Jesus Christ himself: "Judge not, lest ye be judged" (Matt. 7:1).[37] But the jury quickly reached a guilty verdict, and Hauptmann was immediately sentenced to death. Despite widespread debate about the fairness of the investigation and trial, he was electrocuted on April 3, 1936.

Lindbergh's autobiographical writing says little more about the trial than about the kidnapping.[38] "There are no self-conscious gaps, no glancing references or euphemisms," remarks Brian Horrigan. The kidnapping and its aftermath are "simply omitted."[39] Even as he dictated page after page of corrections to biographies he found lacking, Lindbergh shed little light on how he and his family processed the tragedy, save to praise Anne decades later for bearing "up wonderfully. We were at no time alarmed about her health or mental stability. She was extraordinary."[40]

He knew better. When Anne let him read her 1935 diary six years later, he had to confess that "he did not realize the depth of her depression." He rationalized that it, "of course, covers the worst times rather than the best." He went on, "There were many better days in between, and Anne never let me know how depressed she really was at times." But he did blame himself for not understanding sooner than he did.[41]

When she finally wrote publicly about those days, nearly forty years later, Anne Lindbergh recalled that her husband and mother maintained the "stoic tradition of hiding grief," while she "cried silently at night or sitting on a stump in the scrubby grounds outside the fenced grounds" of the Morrow estate. She was either unable or unwilling to seek out "counseling from doctor, minister, or wise friend." She added, "[I let my] Puritan sense of sin . . . beat down fiercely my rebellious feelings, only to have them balloon at night like monstrous toadstools."[42] ("Do not try to be too brave," she advised another grieving mother in 1948, though she knew that "for us of Puritan background it is hard to do otherwise.")[43]

Anne found some comfort in the "ever renewing face of nature," like the beech trees she walked under, "praying [herself] out through their branches to the clear sky above," and in the sometimes mystical poetry of writers like Rainer Maria Rilke.[44] Both sources would remain central to her spirituality. Later in life, for example, she liked to quote Pope Pius XII's maxim that "feeding the birds is also a form of prayer," and a wooden statue of Francis of Assisi blessing those creatures stood by her window.[45] At her funeral in 2001, one of the readings was a Rilke poem that compared dying to a swan "letting himself fall / into waters."[46]

But in 1935 she also took strength from her own writing, her private diary becoming a refuge and her published work starting to give her a public profile distinct from her husband's. *North to the Orient,* her vivid account of the Lindberghs' 1931 Pacific adventure, entered a third printing within its first week and won Anne a National Booksellers Award.[47] That summer she received an honorary degree from her alma mater. Hearing Smith College president William Allan Neilson read the citation thrilled Anne: "I felt he was speaking right to me, way down into me, like an omniscient father or one's old idea of God. He was praising me not for what the newspapers and what the world saw, but for those inner struggles inside of me."[48]

Much as Charles's refusal to mourn frustrated her—and his fame still threatened to obscure her—Anne also took strength from a husband she continued to adore. Reading through old diaries, Anne decided that she had become stronger, by passing "through the fire of C. and all that C. has meant in [her] life. A kind of change has taken place. The shape is the same but the metal has changed."[49] "At night," she wrote that summer, "C. talks to me—beautifully, so beautifully: that I can do anything I want to do, write anything, do anything I set my mind to. His faith is thrilling although I cannot believe him—what proof is there?"[50]

But the love and support of Charles were not her only source of faith. Back in Maine that fall, Charles took his wife and their three-year-old son on a flight, steering with one hand while taking photographs with the other. Holding her breath as they finally landed, Anne reflected on how much faith she needed in life. "Everybody needs, women especially," she explained, "an absolutely, childlike and perfect faith, that we have laughed at in my generation. The kind of faith that is best illustrated in the Bible, a faith like Gideon's [sic]marching round the walls. In spite of our modern attitude to religion, there are lessons in the Bible better taught there than anywhere, truths that are not found anywhere else but in that symbolism, and now—for me—Faith."[51]

Even as she sought a spirituality more authentic than "one's old idea of God," Anne continued to draw on a Protestant piety she knew from childhood, did not share with her husband, and wondered if she should pass on to their children.

EXILE TO EUROPE

"C. thinks we may go abroad to England or Sweden for the winter, or longer," Anne suddenly told her diary on December 7, 1935. Charles Lindbergh had finally had enough of his native country. "Life for my family," he said, "had become so difficult, disagreeable, and dangerous that I decided to take up residence abroad until such time as we could live in our own country with reasonable assurance." He told his wife to prepare to leave "at twenty-four hours' notice." Anne felt "thrown in a turmoil" but was ready for a new adventure: "Isn't it just another one of those times when life seems to be so exciting that it is impossible to get 'down to business,' *my real* business? (I can't even find out what it is!)"[52] Two weeks later she dashed off a quick letter to her mother-in-law: "We are leaving in an hour. I wish so much we could have seen you before we left. . . . I do feel that we are doing the right thing and will find safety where we go and security during a difficult time, for Jon, and for us all."[53]

Only when it was too late for his friend's departure to make the evening edition did Deak Lyman tell his editor at the *New York Times*. In his Pulitzer-winning exclusive, he told the country about the threatening letters the Lindberghs had received since their wedding and reported that media harassment kept Jon from attending nursery school. Once more, a commentator likened Lindbergh to a pioneer: "It was as though the Lindbergh family were living on a frontier, their home surrounded by savages. In a sense it was worse, for the frontiersman could recognize the savages, but this borderland family had no such protection."

"While it may be a lonely Christmas and New Year for them," Lyman concluded, "it will be free from fear such as the family has never been without since Jon was born in August, 1932."[54]

The Lindberghs' ship docked in Liverpool, England, on December 31. They rang in the new year at the Welsh estate of Aubrey Morgan, Elisabeth's widower. "I am still rather dazed about this whole trip," Anne admitted to her mother ten days later. "I do think we did the right thing and even temporarily in this quiet garden I feel the difference. No fear of the press trespassing on the grounds, or eavesdropping. No fear at night putting Jon up to bed and then running up to see if he is all right."[55] At first it wasn't certain if the Lindberghs would even stay in England; Sweden remained a possibility. But they decided to rent Long Barn, the Nicolsons' country house in Kent, which Vita assured them had hosted no ghosts in twenty years.[56]

"Enjoying more privacy in their marriage than they had ever known," concluded Scott Berg, "Charles and Anne felt that they had awakened from their four-year nightmare."[57] Their exile in Europe, Anne said later, would number "among the happiest years of my life."[58]

CHAPTER SEVEN

The Happiest Years

Somewhere between the extremes of Western science and
Eastern mysticism, I felt, must lie a better answer than we
had yet discovered. If we could not find it in time to prevent a modern struggle, our own hopes and ideals would be
shattered like those Periclean temples and the civilizations
of Europe would be destroyed like that of ancient Greece.

−Charles Lindbergh (ca. 1947)[1]

T HE LINDBERGH FAMILY spent over three years living in England
and France, largely hidden from the prying eyes of an aggressive
press and an insatiably curious public. Though their exile soon entangled
Charles in the origins of World War II, 1936–1939 held a particularly fond
place in Anne Lindbergh's complicated memory of that decade. Forty
years after they arrived in Liverpool, she remained "deeply grateful to the
British and the French for this interim of private peace and happiness."[2]

Those years in Europe were also some of the most intellectually
stimulating in Charles Lindbergh's life, and the first that he amply docu-
mented, through letters, journals, and the autobiographical writing that
he wouldn't stop until his death in 1974. Through correspondence with
his friend Harry Guggenheim, Lindbergh continued to keep an eye on
the development of aviation (and he supported the research of rocketry
pioneer Robert Goddard), and his biological studies turned more and
more to eugenics. Already an ambitious autodidact, he used his quiet
days in Europe to fill in more gaps in his education, reading deliberately
through books by the likes of Plato and Tolstoy.[3] Most strikingly, Lindbergh started to cultivate an interest in the supernatural. But even as he

began to show signs of interest in spirituality, Lindbergh remained wary of organized religion—of one group in particular.

THE OXFORD GROUP

In May 1936 Henry Breckinridge reported to Lindbergh that Harry Guggenheim's wife, Carol, had "'got religion,' and is happy all the day."[4] She had become a follower of an American minister named Frank Buchman.

Though ordained a Lutheran pastor in 1902, Buchman drew on sources ranging from German Pietism to the YMCA. At a 1908 revival in Keswick, England, Buchman had a "poignant vision of the Crucified" and surrendered himself to God. "It was to me as if a strong stream of life suddenly passed through me," he recalled.[5] Buchman's fame grew in the 1920s, as his message of personal transformation through the power of the Holy Spirit attracted followers. Philip Boobbyer describes the Buchmanite movement, commonly called the Oxford Group, as being primarily "concerned with helping people at an individual level. It was also practical rather than theological in orientation, placing emphasis, for example, on confession of sin, listening to God, and absolute moral standards"—namely, the "four absolutes" of honesty, purity, unselfishness, and love.[6] Perhaps the most distinctive practice of Buchman and his followers was to seek guidance from God through regular times of solitary silence.

So, why did Lindbergh tell Breckinridge, "Anne and I are both a little depressed by hearing that Carol has joined the Oxford Group"?[7] He didn't share the concerns of the fundamentalist magazine *Revelation*, whose issue that month warned that "Buchmanism . . . certainly does not have Christ at its center. It unites faith and unbelief." Charles Lindbergh would not have cared that "the Bible has a very secondary place in the movement and the Lord Jesus is not presented as the Saviour of sinners."[8] But he was bothered by Buchman's emphasis on rigid moral behavior and group confession of sin. "Does that mean she confesses Harrys [*sic*] sins too?" he asked Breckinridge. "Or just her own?"[9]

Those practices had attracted notoriety since 1926, when *Time* magazine reported that the "Buchman cult" at Princeton University—including John D. Rockefeller III—was unduly preoccupied with "washing out" sexual impurity. "Like young Buchmanites," the magazine's correspondent gossiped, "Mr. Buchman is a bachelor, though past 40. In what does his influence over them reside?"[10] The group was driven from that campus, and Buchman shifted focus to older adults, especially corporate leaders and members of prominent families.[11] Even as Carol Guggenheim entered the Oxford Group in 1936, its founder appeared on the cover of *Time*, over the title "Cultist Buchman."[12]

In mid-June Lindbergh wrote his friend directly. "I hope you circled the movement at least three times before you got committed," he teased her. "Just remember that your conscience may hurt you more, eventually, if you do confess your sins than if you don't." Though he joked about his friend likely wanting "to come over here and try missionary work on Anne and [him]," Charles insisted that Carol would always be welcome at their home, even if she joined "the Heathen."[13]

Dismissive at first, Lindbergh couldn't long avoid Buchman's movement, for Alexis Carrel would soon introduce him to a young member of the Oxford Group who became one of the Lindberghs' closest friends.

THE UNKNOWN MAN

Even as he continued to mentor Charles Lindbergh, Carrel achieved new fame himself in the midthirties, when he published his most widely read book. *Man, the Unknown* encapsulated Carrel's ongoing efforts to achieve "a much more profound knowledge of ourselves" that would not reduce humanity "to a physiochemical system nor to spiritual entity" but instead fuse empirical, philosophical, and religious ways of knowing into a single "science of man."[14] Johns Hopkins professor Raymond Pearl praised Carrel's achievement in a long review for the *New York Times*: "For probably the first time in history the Soul has taken a duly appointed place in a first-rate professional treatise on biology."[15] Anne Lindbergh said reading *Man, the Unknown* was stretching her mind and making her feel as though she had not been using it enough. "No wonder I can't write," she added.[16] While Carrel is virtually unknown now, his book displaced her *North to the Orient* atop the nonfiction best seller list in 1936.

Rejecting the division of "mental activities into intellectual, moral, esthetic, and religion" as "nothing but an artifact," Carrel exhorted his readers to "have the courage to explore those regions of the self whose horizons, on every side, are shrouded in dense mist." He celebrated medieval mystics like Jan van Ruysbroeck, who recorded divine visions before the Renaissance "arbitrarily" began to privilege the material over the spiritual. But he also urged greater attention to psychic phenomena that Western believers and skeptics tended to reject, such as clairvoyance and telepathy.[17]

Carrel still meant such study to be rigorous. On one of their many visits across the English Channel to the Carrels' house in Brittany, Anne felt sorry for a self-proclaimed clairvoyant Alexis was investigating: "He makes a mistake and then loses confidence, under the penetrating clear burning light of Dr. Carrel's critical observation."[18] But later that year, the Lindberghs listened to Anne Carrel describe psychic auras emanating from Charles ("deep deep violet") and Anne ("pale pale blue"). "What lay beyond the mind's perception?" Charles remembered asking on visits to the Carrels. "How much significance should be accorded to visions, to intuition, to clairvoyance, to prayer? Were subconscious powers manifest through pendulums, divining rods, and trances? Could the miracles of Lourdes be scientifically explained or duplicated?"[19]

Anne watched her husband "race ahead, way way ahead, into 'the far'—new fields, new ideas, new countries, new schemes," and she asked, "Can I follow?"[20] His interest in "new ideas" also led Charles to befriend one of their more unusual neighbors in Kent: Sir Francis Younghusband, a retired British officer who had explored South Asia and served as president of the Royal Geographic Society. Raised as an evangelical Christian, Younghusband experienced a mystical vision in Tibet that led him to explore Eastern religions, pantheism, and what came to be called New Age spirituality. The year Lindbergh flew from New York to Paris, Younghusband published *Life in the Stars: An Exposition of the View That on Some Planets of Some Stars Exist Beings Higher Than Ourselves, and on One a World-Leader, the Supreme Embodiment of the Eternal Spirit Which Animates the Whole.*

He and Lindbergh first met in November 1936, for a ninety-minute conversation that Charles eagerly reported the next day to Carrel: "I was especially interested in some of the phenomena reported by people who had been to India, such as fire walking, levitation, latent life, and hypnotism. . . . I am quite sure that he had expected us to be primarily interested in the geographical aspects of the country [of India], and was unprepared for entry into fields which he is probably reluctant to discuss with people he does not know very well. It is extremely difficult to get people to talk about anything they consider supernatural."[21]

Although a "fire walker" Younghusband knew in London proved to be too much of a self-promoter for Charles's comfort ("I am anxious to avoid the type of publicity which could so easily arise"), he and Anne both hoped to travel to India, meet "even a few of the Indian mystics and religious men," and perhaps live there for a few months.[22]

Asked to lead a session at an international Parliament of Religions in Calcutta in March 1937, Younghusband invited the Lindberghs to join him.[23] Charles agreed but decided to fly instead of joining his new friend on a ship. "In a plane, I feel more a part of the country below me than if I were walking over its ground," he reasoned. "The man I visit means more to me because I know better the country he lives in."[24] Anne decided to accompany her husband on yet another weeks-long aerial journey. "I am sorry to leave Jon," she admitted, "but I think we have given him a good start. I am glad for this year we have all had together."[25] It would also be her last chance for a while to take such a trip; their third child, a boy called Land (Evangeline Lindbergh's maiden name), would be born that May.

"You'd Better Drop This Religion Stuff"

On the long journey from England to India, the Lindberghs passed again and again over what Anne called "the bones of other civilizations." Once more, flight gave them a unique view of religious history. An ancient temple atop a rocky hill in Sicily struck her as "quite perfect and holy . . . pure spirit flowering out of rock. 'The rock whence it was hewn . . .' [Isa. 51:1]." "They _would_ build it just here!" Charles muttered, though he later remembered the temple as a "place where men and gods could meet as never will be conceivable of our day."[26] After the modern buildings in Egypt paled next to the "eternal massive significance" of the pyramids, Anne arrived in Palestine expecting to have "one's Biblical and childlike impressions" disappointed, only to find that "you could understand why it looked like a land 'flowing with milk and honey' to the Israelites."[27]

They managed to reach Calcutta in time for the start of the religious congress, held to honor the centenary of the Hindu mystic known as Ramakrishna. Given prominent seats, the Lindberghs didn't escape unnoticed. Sarojini Naidu, a poet and activist who worked with Mohandas Gandhi, likened Charles to "spiritual figures" like Buddha and Galileo; his many achievements, she claimed, were "part of the world spirit of faith rendered into action." The *New York Times* duly reported that he "blushed with embarrassment."[28]

The secretaries who edited the event's proceedings were pleased to record Lindbergh's attendance, but he saw it as something less than the "phenomenal success" they claimed.[29] Younghusband, who believed in extraterrestrial life on the planet Altair, was "a rock of sanity and logic in this conference of religions," Lindbergh wrote to Carrel. "I wish there were more people like him at the conference, but I do not think it is the type of thing which attracts great men. On the contrary I think the conference has been an indication of the decay of the religions which it represents. The meetings I attended brought to me again the reaction I had in my childhood to the preachings of ministers and the dogma of religious fanaticism."[30]

For her part, Anne had a hard time "keeping a straight face at C., sitting up in the front row of a religious conference facing a large sugary picture of Ramakrishna decked with flowers." She went on, "I nearly died of the incongruity the first day. Also C.'s alarm watch went off in the middle of a prayer!" She thought her husband got "a great kick out of it. The aviation people are seriously worried: 'You'd better drop this religion stuff, you know!'"[31]

Anne feared that they'd "been rather a disappointment to Sir Francis," but Charles assured Carrel that his time in India was "well spent, both interesting and amusing." He found "definite material for study" about Indian practitioners of phenomena like hypnosis and hibernation.[32] (And he found time to kid Harry Guggenheim about his wife's attachment to the Oxford Group: "I wish Carol could have been here. I would like to have had her compare the merits of Buchman and Ramakrishna. They both seem to have believed in 'silent times' but, apparently, Ramakrishna had no sins to confess.")[33] After returning to Europe, Lindbergh read an introduction to yoga by Francis Yeats-Brown, the author of *The Lives of a Bengal Lancer*.[34] Though he agreed with Carrel's assessment that "Christian mysticity [sic] . . . has been influenced by the stricter mental disciplines and the clear intellect of Europe," Lindbergh thought that study of yogic breathing "may form a bridge between Western science and what might be called Eastern phenomena."[35]

But his interest wasn't entirely scientific or spiritual. Ever the fan of practical jokes, Lindbergh taught himself how to stop his own pulse, by wadding up a handkerchief under his armpit. It's not clear if he was more honored or irritated that Carrel (but only Carrel) figured out the trick.[36]

"A Stronger Race"

Other aspects of Carrel and Lindbergh's collaboration were less amusing. In the preface to *Man, the Unknown*, his publisher billed Carrel as "a man of science" who "is acquainted with the poor and the rich, the sound and the diseased, the learned and the ignorant, the weak-minded, the insane, the shrewd, the criminal, etc."[37] While scientific and industrial progress had extended the life spans of moderns and "liberated them from all superstitions," Carrel warned of pervasive intellectual, moral, and spiritual decline in the West.[38] In part, the solution was a more holistic approach to living and learning, for the "happiest and most useful men consist of a well-integrated whole of intellectual, moral, and organic activities." Such a "type" could be found in "a tradesman or a bank president . . . a village mayor or a president of the United States," but Carrel was convinced that "humanity has never gained anything from the efforts of the crowd." Instead, "a few abnormal individuals" drove progress "by the flame of their intelligence, by their ideal of science, of charity, and of beauty."[39]

Carrel certainly saw his experiments with the remarkable Lindbergh in such a light. But he worried that such medical research, though beneficial, also meant that "the weak are saved as well as the strong. Natural selection no longer plays its part." Lamenting the growing population of insane

asylums, Carrel worried about "the future of a race" when "mental dete-
rioration is more dangerous for civilization than the infectious diseases
to which hygienists and physicians have so far exclusively devoted their
attention."[40] Though he decried the "demoralization and the disappear-
ance of the noblest elements of the great races," one particular racial group
was his chief concern. Insanity, feeblemindedness, and other "diseases of
the mind" were "to be feared, not only because they increase the number
of criminals, but chiefly because they profoundly weaken *the dominant
white races.*"[41]

Other advocates of eugenics tended to emphasize sterilization measures, like the law passed in Lindbergh's home state in 1926 and the more
extensive measures adopted a few years later in Nazi Germany. (In 1933
Dr. Charles F. Dight wrote Adolf Hitler a letter complimenting him on his
first months in power; he got a signed card in reply.)[42] Carrel even considered using "small euthanasic [*sic*] institutions" to remove murderers,
kidnappers, and other serious criminals from the gene pool.[43] But the
Frenchman hoped to take more proactive, positive steps. Since the end
of 1936, he had been sending Lindbergh drafts of a proposal for an "Institute of Man, or Institute for Human Betterment," whose first goal would
be the "use of voluntary eugenics in the building up of a stronger race."
From studies into everything from physiology to prayer, Carrel hoped to
promote "the improvement of the spiritual and bodily state of the individual. . . . For the quality of life is more important than life itself."[44]

In general, Lindbergh found the proposal to be "exceptionally well
written and interesting throughout," and he liked the phrase "quality of
life" so much that he would spend much of the rest of his life arguing for
it. But he thought Carrel needed to "enlarge" on one potentially provoc-
ative sentence: the one insisting that the institute "not be especially concerned with sick people. Instead of encouraging the survival of the weak
and the defective, it will attempt to help the normal and to render stronger the strong. For, the creation of an elite is the indispensable condition
of the progress of the masses." Lindbergh didn't disagree with that goal,
but he warned Carrel that "its value may be lost on people who have not
thought along these lines." In particular, he worried that the language of
weakness and strength "might be completely misunderstood and result

in an ignorant antagonism on the part of those who would support such a policy if they understood its broader meaning."[45]

Nevertheless, Lindbergh tried to help Carrel launch his Institute of Man, and his friend Henry Ford offered the use of Ford Hospital in Detroit.[46] Those efforts came to little, but Carrel's language soon began to show up in Lindbergh's own (still private) philosophical writing. Back at Long Barn that fall, Lindbergh began to address a paper "to a minority of people . . . to the men and women who are not willing to accept all others as their equals." His central argument sounded uncannily like Carrel's: "It is based upon the belief that individual character controls the trend and measures the quality of civilization, and that the richness of life is caused by differences and not by similarities. It challenges the doctrine of right based upon the quantity of men and advances the claim of right based upon the quality of men, and in opposition to the attempt to bring the spirit of man within the formulae of Science."[47]

"A Satisfactory Religion"

In December 1937, the Lindberghs visited the United States for the first time in two years. After spending New Year's with his mother, who had returned to teaching in Detroit, Charles took the train back to New York, where he resented having to worry again about newspapers: "Too bad there isn't some way of screening them out like flies."[48] He had a long lunch meeting with Alexis Carrel and several of his wealthy friends, one an "ardent member of the Oxford group" who seemed to Lindbergh to want "to solve every problem by a 'quiet time.' Can't reason with these people."[49] Nevertheless, he agreed to meet another of Carrel's Buchmanite friends: Jim Newton.

An ambitious young businessman who had worked for Thomas Edison and Harvey Firestone and befriended Henry Ford, Newton had experienced a religious conversion in the mid-1920s. During a skiing vacation in Massachusetts, he encountered a Buchman follower who told Newton that he used the Sermon on the Mount as a guide in living out the "four absolutes" of honesty, purity, unselfishness, and love. To that point, Newton said that if he had thought of God at all, it was as someone not that much interested in him, except perhaps when he did something wrong. "Someone with a long beard who says, 'Don't do that.'" But he agreed to conduct a spiritual experiment: he knelt next to the other man and prayed, "I have my ideals, but I can't live up to them. I don't have what it takes. Okay, I've loused things up—If you're there and can call the shots, here's my will and my life. You run it, you fly it." As he increasingly "noticed a new sureness and straightness" in his life, Newton said he began to start each day by being quiet and giving God a chance to show him through his thoughts how God wanted him to live.[50] That practice of surrender to a higher power became one of the key influences of the Oxford Group on Alcoholics Anonymous, whose founder, Bill Wilson, was another of Newton's famous acquaintances.[51]

He soon added Alexis Carrel to that circle. Having avidly read *Man, the Unknown* when it came out, Newton seized the chance to meet its author in January 1937. Like Lindbergh, he admired the Frenchman as "a universal man" with "all encompassing" interests that were hard to categorize but spanned science and religion.[52] In turn, Carrel recommended Newton to Lindbergh. "Although he is a member of the Oxford Group," the surgeon explained carefully that summer, Newton was "not a fanatic. He understands, as we do, the necessity of a new orientation."[53] With the Lindberghs' visit back to the States, Carrel wanted the two Americans to meet in person, so that Newton could tell Lindbergh how God came into his life. "He and I have talked about these things," Carrel said. "He respects my beliefs, but I don't think he's found a satisfying faith himself yet. Possibly you can help him."[54]

Over dinner at a French restaurant in late January 1938, Newton shared his story of praying with one of Buchman's followers. "I had moved from *believing* to *knowing*," he recalled. "That's what happened to me when I made the experiment of asking God to direct my life." Knowing his audience, Carrel emphasized to Lindbergh the notion of following God as an experiment, one that "linked the spiritual with the moral and practical" rather than separating "theology from living."[55] Lindbergh recorded none of that exchange in his diary, but he was pleasantly surprised to enjoy the company of a Buchmanite: "He seems an interesting and intelligent fellow. Would like to see him again but do not understand the great attraction the Oxford movement seems to have on men of his type. It still seems to me to be a rather mediochre [*sic*] religious philosophy. Perhaps the interest in it indicates the need for a satisfactory religion. I believe the lack of religious influence is one of our greatest handicaps today & responsible for much unhappiness and crime."[56]

Anne Lindbergh seemed to have felt a similar "need for a satisfactory religion" during that visit to America. There's a marked increase in spiritual references in her diaries in the winter of 1938, when seeing "the world transformed by snow ... makes one understand better all the big 'conversions' of nature, in oneself, like falling in love, religious conversion, sleep and dying." Likewise, Gerard Manley Hopkins's poem about the Virgin Mary struck her as "one of those poems that does somehow 'convert' you. That is, it makes you wake up (as if from a sleep, or after sickness, or from conversion, or as in falling in love, or after sorrow) to a new world." Listening to Arturo Toscanini conduct Beethoven's Ninth Symphony made her feel transcendent after years of darkness and sorrow: "When one listens to it one can understand, or at least accept, for the moment, the evil in life. The things one has felt unable to understand, to bear, to absorb—all are absorbed, understood, accepted, for one divine moment."[57]

Even more than her husband, Anne was drawn to Eastern religions, such that losing herself in Beethoven put her in the mind of the Buddhist anticipation of the day when "there shall not remain even one particle of dust that does not enter into Buddahood." But it also made her think of Father Zosima, the elderly Orthodox monk in Fyodor Dostoyevsky's *Brothers Karamazov*.[58] She eventually convinced Charles to read the same book, but he was less taken with Dostoyevsky and his countryman Leo Tolstoy: "We do not expect to understand the outlook of the Oriental, but the Russian is sufficiently European to mislead us. We always expect to understand him better than we do."[59]

Charles couldn't remember attending church in England more than once or twice, but Christian practice and symbols hadn't been entirely absent from the Lindbergh family's experience overseas.[60] For Christmas Eve at Long Barn, the Lindberghs listened to the BBC's broadcast of the lessons and carols service from King's College, Cambridge, and Anne used a "kneeling pewter Madonna" to make "the most beautiful centerpiece [Charles] had ever seen!"[61] Before returning to Europe in March 1938, Anne reconnected with her religious upbringing, attending her grand-

mother Cutter's Presbyterian funeral in Cleveland. "The end of her life
and this service about it was *right*," she told her diary. "It was not, as most
of the services in our family, a tragedy, something wrong, cut down, cruel
to bear. No, it was life and death as it always had been, as it should be." In
short, she concluded, "it was Biblical: 'for he flourisheth as a flower of the
field . . . and the place thereof shall know it no more.'"[62]

On the voyage back to England four nights later, she walked the decks
beneath a full moon and thought of another psalm: "The heavens declare
the glory of God; and the firmament showeth his handiwork. Day unto day
uttereth speech, and night unto night showeth knowledge" (Ps. 19:1–2).

"I must teach Jon the Bible," she resolved, but "how?"[63]

She wrote little about her children's religious education the rest of that
year, apart from hiring a nun to serve as their nurse. But just before Christmas she recorded a theological conversation with her six-year-old son.
"I try to explain very generally and broadly that the world is so beautiful
and wonderful that people think *someone* must have planned it."

"Oh no," Jon Lindbergh corrected his mother. "It is much too big for
one person to make."[64]

"THE WORLD FIRST MADE"

Charles returned to Europe ahead of Anne. He wanted to avoid photographers, grumbling, "We can not even bury our dead in peace and without
interference from the ghouls of our American press."[65] But he also needed
to prepare for the family's move to a new home on the coast of Brittany,
whose rocky islands felt like places where, he said, "ghosts were walking
with me . . . where life and spirit could communicate."[66]

The Lindberghs had become familiar with that part of France from regular visits to the Carrels' property on a remote island named for St. Gildas,
a sixth-century British monk who had founded a monastery nearby. From
the start, both Lindberghs were captivated. Perhaps thinking back to the
rural wanderings of his childhood on the Mississippi, Charles loved his
visits to a place where he "could walk over the rocks, or watch the tides."
He added, "To me, it is the most perfect combination of the things I like to
live with that I have ever seen."[67] Anne was taken by the contrast between
the quiet welcome of the Carrels' home—"intensely peaceful . . . like the

garden of a monastery"—and the wild, almost otherworldly beauty of the island's rugged landscape. In the moonlight, the vague shapes of enormous rock formations "seem to merge with the unreality of the world." Brittany seemed both as old as "the world first made" and radically new. Anne wrote, "The island, the rocks, the ideas discussed, the conceptions, plans, beliefs—all new, strange, and cataclysmic to me and yet apparently true, real."[68]

Illiec, a tiny island that felt "more a part of the sea," offered the Lindberghs the proximity to nature and the Carrels—and privacy from most all others—that they craved. It is "even more beautiful than we thought," Charles raved to Alexis Carrel. "It is perfectly located and the sea is marvelous on every side. I do not think the island could be improved upon, unless St. Gildas himself had built a chapel beside one of the rocks."[69] Indeed, there was an aging chapel, whose repair became one of the Lindberghs' many renovation projects. (Built in the 1860s by the composer Ambroise Thomas, their new home was a "scaled-down castle" lacking plumbing, electricity, and heat.)[70] Through Carrel, they also befriended Dom Alexis Presse, a Cistercian monk who had given up his position at the head of a prosperous community in order to restore the nearby abbey of Sainte-Marie de Boquen.[71]

Another of Carrel's religious friends, Jim Newton, got to know both Lindberghs better during a stay at St. Gildas that summer. He impressed Anne as being "a genuine person of integrity and feeling . . . selfless and spiritual," though she shared her husband's assessment of the group to which Newton belonged: "But I somehow feel there is a false simplicity about the Oxford Movement. I am in sympathy with its incentive and many of its beliefs, but the form and expression of it still seems immature and even somehow arrogant in its smugness. (He [Jim] was *not* arrogant or smug, at all.)"[72]

As Newton remembered it, he was sitting with Charles one afternoon as the latter reflected on Carrel's goal of striking "a balance of body, mind, and spirit," to "exercise one's mind and reach into one's spirit—stay open to intuitions and follow one's convictions." As a pilot, said Lindbergh, he was "a materialist—until I get off the ground. . . . What it comes down to is this, Jim: I've found that when you make a deep commitment, unforeseen forces come to your aid." (Perhaps not coincidentally, it was just a few months later that Lindbergh first wrote about the "disembodied beings" who accompanied and advised him on his 1927 flight across the Atlantic.) Whether he called it Carrel's "experiencing spiritual rebirth" or Newton's "listening to the inner voice," Lindbergh said he was "sure this reality is the force at the heart of the universe. That force becomes available to us in some measure, if our spirits are open to it."[73]

CHAPTER EIGHT

"The Nazi Theology"

Nazi Germany, a rising monument to technocracy, was an ideal Lindbergh kept hoping to embrace. So long as he was able to intellectualize his feelings, he was able to believe some new system of government—a new order—might save a degenerating world. . . . Rather than look at the price being paid for that "success," Lindbergh buried his head in the sand when confronted with the crimes of inhumanity that repelled so many others.

–A. Scott Berg (1998)[1]

AS THE SUMMER OF 1938 turned to fall, Charles Lindbergh returned to Alexis Carrel's idea that "the quality of life is more important than life itself." Hoping to replace "present material measures of success" with "the less tangible, but far more valuable measures of health, character, and spiritual satisfaction," Lindbergh added to his unpublished appeal "to a minority of people." Using religious terms that would have seemed foreign to him years before, he refused to sacrifice "the quality of life" to the worst of all "idols set up by man," the "false . . . god of equality."

Men are not equal and should have no desire to be equal. The richness of life lies in its differences, and not in its similarities. A world of equal people would be like a desert of sand.

The doctrine of equality is a doctrine of death. . . . There is no equality in nature, in beauty, or in life. It is a concept of man, and not of God.

What inequality could be so natural, even divine? Lindbergh made it explicit with a rhetorical question: "Shall we submerge the spirit and life of Europe in the Yellow of Asia or the Black of Africa?"[2]

David Friedman suggests that the Lindberghs' 1931 visit to China prepared Charles to embrace Carrel's view that whites needed to unite against "the faster-breeding, less creative races of Africa and Asia, along with the backward races of Eastern Europe."[3] But the roots of Lindbergh's racism may run deeper than that. In 1903, C. A. Lindbergh told a Little Falls reporter that African Americans were "by nature . . . inferior to the white race." According to the future congressman, it had been a mistake to extend the franchise to even the few black Americans then allowed to vote. If that populace could not be given a separate state apart from whites, then the best C. A. Lindbergh hoped for was that interracial marriage "may not elevate the white race" but "will eventually lift the black."[4]

Chastened by the ferocity of World War I, C. A. later hoped for racial reconciliation, but he feared that "too much racial prejudice" existed in the United States for its people to form a single "national human family."[5] Indeed, when Nazi jurists needed guidance in codifying white supremacy after 1933, it was the American legal system they examined most closely. Herbert Kier, for example, found ample "statutory regulation in many areas that grow out of the racial point of view": not just Jim Crow codes in the South, but antimiscegenation laws in thirty states, banning the very marriages C. A. Lindbergh mused about. National Socialists also studied how US legislatures and courts had restricted Asian immigration, kept Filipinos and Puerto Ricans from the full benefits of citizenship, and dispossessed Native Americans of their land.[6]

In Lindbergh's homeland, egalitarianism was the exception, not racism. Even as the United States later waged war against Nazism, someone as progressive as Anne Morrow Lindbergh could praise the Asian and African American speakers at a 1944 civil rights meeting, acknowledge how unjustly her fellow citizens were treated, and yet still recoil from any solution that involved "complete equality, complete intermixture," for "the principle of complete intermingling looks forward . . . to a state of sameness all over the world, as though one grafted peach and pear and apple and plum together and came out with just one fruit in the universe. Would the universe be better off with just one fruit?"[7] Her husband felt even more strongly on this subject. To the end of his life, Charles Lindbergh struggled to understand the "inner drive toward unity and similarity that makes men want to eliminate the differences of race. . . . Is this a result of our Christian ideology? . . . Does it arise from a basic fear of the struggle for survival, or is it grounded in a wisdom that science and education have enhanced?"[8]

Given how Lindbergh framed his disdain for "a state of sameness," it seems that Alexis Carrel was the most immediate influence on his racial views. Lindbergh learned to mimic his mentor's concerns about the "future of the race" that had built Western civilization, while at the same time absorbing some of Carrel's fascination with the mystical and supernatural. Indeed, the more spiritual (if not religious) he became, the more deeply Charles Lindbergh embraced the racialized worldview of eugenics.

"Equal rights exist only among equal people," he wrote in 1938, "equal by their own nature, and not because they simply look similar to other men." Lindbergh prefaced those comments with the proviso that he was engaged in an attempt to clarify his own ideas. He said, "In the present stage, the writing is so incomplete that it may easily give a false, and in some cases opposite conception to that which I hold."[9] In the years to come, he would insist again and again, and more publicly, that the "quality of life" was more important than the equality of the living. Eventually, the phrase would outgrow its eugenicist origins and come to stand for a more balanced approach to modern life. But if such thoughts were "incomplete" in mid-September 1938, Lindbergh was right to worry: for anyone writing such a document that month had to know that one might sound too much like the eugenics-loving German dictator then in the middle of expanding his thousand-year Reich. And Lindbergh had already said and done enough by then to make one close friend conclude that he adhered to "the Nazi theology."

Thirty-six years old that fateful fall of 1938, Lindbergh was at the midpoint of his life. The first half had ended with fame; the second would soon turn to infamy.

BETWEEN NAZISM AND COMMUNISM

Two years before, in 1936, Major Truman Smith, the military attaché at the US embassy in Berlin, had asked Lindbergh for a favor. Nazi air minister Hermann Göring had eagerly agreed to let the famous American pilot inspect German airplane factories and air bases. Would Colonel Charles Lindbergh help the US government assess the air power of the Third Reich?

Just a few months into his European exile, Lindbergh said he was "most anxious to avoid ... the sensational and stupid publicity which we have so frequently encountered in the past; and the difficulty and unpleasantness which invariably accompanies it." Nonetheless, he was "extremely excited," too much to decline.[10] Once again, Anne joined her husband on the trip, which began the last week of July. Though Charles had hoped to avoid "any special entertainment" or "formal functions," Göring hosted a luncheon in their honor and had the famous Americans attend the opening ceremonies of the Berlin Olympics as his special guests.

"I keep thinking of Carrel's book," wrote Anne after touring Olympic facilities. "Of what use is it? Is the emphasis correct? Is the spiritual and mental up to this? Or will it breed a race of tall soft-headed athletes?" She was also put off by a tour of Berlin's Garrison Church, where Adolf Hitler had held a ceremony to reopen the Reichstag after its infamous fire in 1933. "I *can't* place Bach in all this," she wrote. The "clear, perfect, pure, spiritual world" of her favorite Christian composer made for a jarring contrast with a sanctuary so closely associated with the Prussian military.[11] Appalled by Germans' "treatment of the Jews, their brute-force manner, their stupidity, their rudeness, their regimentation," Anne left Germany deeply conflicted. "The energy, pride, and morale of the people—especially the young people," was "thrilling," but also "terrifying in its very unity—a weapon made by one man but also to be used by one man." She added, "Hitler, I am beginning to feel, is like an inspired religious leader, and as such fanatical—a visionary who really wants the best for his country."

In the end, the "strong, united, physical, and spiritual force" she had witnessed could either "be a force for good in the world" or "horribly destructive."[12]

Charles's friend Harry Guggenheim had been glad not to know of the trip in advance. Being left in the dark spared him receiving "overtures from Jewish leaders" who feared Lindbergh's visit would be an indication of Lindbergh's "approval of Nazi anti-semitism and would aid the enemy at home and abroad." He added, "I stated I had every confidence that you would so conduct yourself as to give no aid to anti-semitism."[13] Lindbergh tried to set Guggenheim's mind at ease: "There is no need for me to tell you that I am not in accord with the Jewish situation in Germany." But instead of making clear to his closest Jewish friend just what he disliked about that "situation," Lindbergh was evasive: he was "not in Germany long enough" to "learn very much in this regard" and so to "separate fact from rumour concerning the actual Nazi attitude, and its origin."[14]

If a short visit to the Third Reich was insufficient to let Lindbergh come to a clear conclusion about Nazi race hatred, his stage-managed tour fixed in the pilot's mind the ascendancy of German air power. "There can be no question about the great progress Germany is making along many lines," he told Guggenheim, one of America's strongest advocates for aviation. "Her military strength is growing with inconceivable rapidity, and I think is nowhere more evident than in her aviation."[15] A second tour of Germany in October 1937 left Lindbergh "increasingly impressed with the developments going on in that country in almost every field. Regardless of the reservations one may have concerning some of the actions of the German government, it is impossible to overlook the fact that Germany is rapidly becoming the strongest military power in the world."[16]

Even as that assessment made American officials worry about the Western powers' chances in a second world war, Lindbergh started to think of Germany as a potential ally in a greater fight. On his voyage back from the United States in early 1938, he enjoyed his conversations with German passengers: "They are like our own people. We should be working with them and not constantly crossing swords."[17] That spring he wrote to Truman Smith, "The Germans are our own type of people and . . . as such, they will be to us either a powerful friend or a dangerous enemy. From either standpoint they are entitled to a respect which we do not give them."[18]

Although he still did not agree "with all of the German policies"— without specifying which gave him pause—Lindbergh saw right-wing dictators like Hitler and Benito Mussolini as better partners than the brutal left-wing regime to the east, where Josef Stalin was purging his rivals and imprisoning his people. Lindbergh warned Harold Nicolson that the West could not find "a middle way" between Fascism and Communism; Britain aligning with the Soviet Union against Germany would risk "an end to European civilisation."[19] To Henry Breckinridge, who saw America's "alternatives reduced to a choice between extreme right and extreme left," Lindbergh professed himself "inclined to think that Germany really is a stabilizing factor in Europe today." He went on, "With the present Communistic trend in France, it seems to me quite desirable to have a Nazi Germany between France and Russia."[20] "If it is necessary to choose," he confided to his diary, "I far prefer the systems of Germany and Italy to that of Russia."[21] (That was one of several controversial entries expurgated or abridged when Lindbergh published his *Wartime Journals* in 1970.)

As part of his continuing survey of European air power for the US military, Charles returned in August 1938 to the Soviet Union, which he and Anne had first visited five years earlier. Their second impression of Stalinism was no less negative than their first. "It looks as though the material progress were ahead of the physical and spiritual," Anne wrote after touring Moscow. While she felt "more sympathetic to [Russians] than to Germans, innately," she decided that being "'for them' . . . doesn't mean you are for a system that believes in absolute leveling."[22] No admirer of equality, Charles agreed: "One is almost always surrounded with mediocrity unparalleled in any other place." The Red Air Force paled by comparison to Göring's Luftwaffe, and Lindbergh was astonished to find that the Soviet military trained female pilots, ignoring "a God-made difference between men and women that even the Soviet Union can't eradicate."[23]

Anne explained the overall "mediocrity" of the Soviet population as "what happens in a regime where one takes as a motto 'The last shall be first and the first shall be last' [Matt. 20:16]." But if the Communist outworking of Jesus's saying bothered her, so too did the secularization of the USSR. In Kiev, their staunchly antireligious guide ("Soviet propaganda at its worst," concurred Charles) took the Lindberghs to the Cathedral of St. Sophia, where a mosaic of the Last Supper proved "a relief to look at, to escape into it from this cheap, flamboyant person with no sense of reverence, or beauty, or restraint."[24] Finding images of the Virgin Mary in a Moscow museum left Anne feeling "a kind of passionate pity—why should they be in here? They meant nothing to these people. How far away from a world of Christian grace and holiness was here."[25]

"Anything Seems Preferable"

Anne, at least, could recognize that the "Nuremberg Madonnas . . . look down on a lot of un-Christian things" as well. But her husband simultaneously overestimated German power and understated Nazi iniquity. Harold Nicolson agreed that Britain was likely "outmastered in the air," but he distrusted Lindbergh's advice that the West "just give way and then make an alliance with Germany." First, his English friend suspected that the world's most famous pilot attached too much importance to airpower. (Retrospectively, Anne agreed that her husband's "anti-war stand was in part . . . a last expression of his early faith in the invincibility of aviation.") More disturbingly, Nicolson had come to the conclusion that Charles "believes in the Nazi theology, all tied up with his hatred of degeneracy and his hatred of democracy as represented by the free Press and the American public."[26]

While Nicolson joined Winston Churchill and Anthony Eden in calling for a tougher British response to Hitler's aggressions in central Europe, Lindbergh endorsed Neville Chamberlain's policy of appeasement. The same September 1938 day that the British prime minister left London to discuss the Sudeten crisis with Hitler, Lindbergh told America's pro-appeasement ambassador, Joseph Kennedy, exactly what he wanted to hear:

> Germany now has the means of destroying London, Paris and Prague if she wishes to do so. . . . It seems to me essential to avoid a general European war in the near future at almost any cost. I believe that a war now might easily result in the loss of European civilization. I am by no means convinced that England and France could win a war against Germany at the present time, but, whether they win or lose, all of the participating countries would probably be prostrated by their efforts. A general European war could, I believe, result in something akin to Communism running over Europe and, judging by Russia, anything seems preferable.[27]

"Lindbergh has had unusually favorable opportunities to observe the air establishments of the countries he discusses," Kennedy emphasized to

Cordell Hull, urging the secretary of state to pass along the pilot's assessment to President Roosevelt and his military advisers.[28]

Lindbergh could not believe that the English opponents of appeasement were "ready to fight for their principles, throwing all judgment to the winds, and, in a sense, discarding the more important issues of European civilization itself." Told by David Lloyd George that "the Nazi system was just as bad as the Russian system," Lindbergh concluded that the former prime minister "does not seem to recognize any difference to England between an alliance with European Germany and Asiatic Russia. He apparently does not worry about the effect of Asia on European civilization."[29] As he continued to revise his address "to a minority of people" that fall, Lindbergh warned that "we will not create better children by mating white with Negro, or by throwing America and Europe open to the Asiatic. . . . We must create a democracy . . . built of the best blood and traditions of our western civilization."[30]

Not long after Germany annexed the Sudetenland, Charles paid the last of his prewar visits to the Third Reich. After seeing Junker bombers being built, Lindbergh attended a dinner at the American embassy, where Hermann Göring unexpectedly, but quite publicly, presented him a swastika-emblazoned medal on behalf of the führer. "It is difficult for me to express adequately my appreciation for this decoration," Lindbergh wrote Hitler's deputy a week later. "It is an honor which I shall always prize highly."[31] Anne called the medal "The Albatross" but joined her husband in house hunting; the Lindberghs were considering a temporary relocation to Berlin.[32]

Back in France that November, Anne was dismayed to see Charles criticized in the Western press for accepting the medal from Göring. "How I dislike C. being labeled," she wrote in her diary on November 11—as yet unaware of the massive pogrom called *Kristallnacht*, the Night of the Shattered Glass, that had occurred two nights before. After accounts of thousands of damaged businesses and hundreds of burned synagogues finally reached Illiec, she wrote, "You just get to feeling you can understand and work with these people when they do something stupid and brutal and undisciplined like that. I am shocked and very upset."[33] Charles was confused, too: "I do not understand these riots on the part of the Germans. It seems so contrary to their sense of order and their intelligence in other ways. They have undoubtedly had a difficult Jewish problem, but why is it necessary to handle it so unreasonably? My admiration for the Germans is constantly being dashed against some rock such as this."[34]

With tens of thousands of Jews forced into concentration camps in its aftermath, *Kristallnacht* took Germans one step closer to Hitler's Final Solution to their "difficult Jewish problem."

A week later, Alexis Carrel warned Lindbergh not to exacerbate the "great deal of ill feeling against you." He blamed "Jewish and Russian propaganda" for causing Americans to "go into hysterics" rather than "seeking for a just solution of the Jewish problem."[35] By that point, the Lindberghs had already decided to winter in Paris, rather than in Berlin. At a train station in the French capital, Lindbergh observed a few of the 115,000 Jewish refugees who fled Germany in the months after *Kristallnacht*: "They were a poor looking lot on the whole. I have never been anti-Jewish, and have great respect and admiration for many Jews I know. Some of them are among my best friends. But this group on the station gave me a strange feeling of mixed pity and disgust. These people are bound to cause trouble if many of them go to America."[36]

Many of his fellow Americans apparently agreed. In a Gallup poll conducted that December, two in three respondents were unwilling to allow even ten thousand child refugees to come from Germany to the United States.[37]

As the world moved closer to war, Lindbergh continued to articulate his "strange feeling" regarding Jews—and to deny that it constituted the prejudice that critics were beginning to allege. ("C. is not and never has been antisemitic," Anne insisted to her mother that December.)[38] But whatever genuine pity he felt for Jewish suffering, his disgust at such victims of Nazism was equally authentic. It led Lindbergh to fret that war with Germany would not only abandon Western civilization to "Asiatic Russia," but exacerbate "the Jewish problem" in his own country.

THE LAST MONTHS OF "THE HAPPIEST YEARS"

As war fears abated somewhat during the winter of 1938–1939, the Lindberghs took the chance to renew some of their intellectual and spiritual pursuits. Charles began to draft his autobiography. He called it a record of his life for his children and his friends, and even his enemies—the latter group "a mark of distinction and a measure of character."[39] After Christmas they visited Notre Dame and Sainte-Chapelle, which Charles found "beautiful but somewhat spoiled by a tourist atmosphere."[40] But other religious tourism in France made a deeper impact. While American churches offered nothing but a "shallow, dogmatised religion," the best of those of Europe let him sense "a relationship to God as close as any [he] had ever found in nature." Mont-Saint-Michel, the Gothic cathedral of Chartres, and small Breton chapels alike "seemed to eminate [sic] a mysticism, to have absorbed a quality of spirit from the dedication of craftsmen long since dead."[41]

While in Paris, they also established new relationships with intellectuals and artists. Some were fellow American expats; Anne talked about Jesus with Gertrude Stein, and Charles debated appeasement with Jo Davidson as the sculptor took his likeness. Both Lindberghs also enjoyed the company of philosopher Lin Yutang, a Chinese pastor's son who had embraced Taoism and Confucianism before returning to Christianity. They discussed science and God with Pierre du Noüy, another friend of Alexis Carrel's then developing his argument for a view of evolution that was not purely materialistic. And they met the Jesuit paleontologist and philosopher Pierre Teilhard de Chardin, who discussed with Charles the "physical, mental, spiritual, cultural" nature of race and would become one of Anne's favorite writers.[42]

"We have gained a great deal of wisdom from living in Europe," Charles told Anne on a walk through a Paris park.[43] But moving in such circles still left him dissatisfied. "Why is it," he asked himself, "that Jo [Davidson] and Lin Yutang, and countless other fine and able men, insist on building up a sort of Platonic utopia of their own, in which people, with the nature God gave them, would never be happy?" That kind of idealism, he concluded, led only to failure—"like Russia. . . . Real wisdom is content to walk hand in hand with nature and with life."[44]

But then Davidson didn't share his subject's ostensibly practical view of the situation in Europe.[45] "He is a Jew himself, or at least he is partly Jewish," Lindbergh explained to his diary after one visit to the artist's home, "so it was a little difficult to use words which were accurate and at the same time would not hurt him."[46] Even as his winter in Paris broadened Lindbergh's education, it confirmed his views on "the Jewish problem." Discussing that topic with Pierre du Noüy, for example, made Lindbergh realize "how much anti Jewish feeling there was under the surface" in Europe. As he continued his diary that night, he reflected at length about anti-Semitism:

> Until a few years ago I never considered a Jew differently than any other nationality. I have Jewish friends whom I respect greatly, and whose company I enjoy. I have realized that the average Jew was not a very desirable character, but I felt that the better type made some of the best citizens. I do not like this race feeling which has sprung up. I thoroughly believe in the superiority of some races over others, and I believe in the protection of quality and character in a race, but I dislike the persecution of an entire race of people because a portion, even a large portion, of them have shown themselves to be undesirable and troublemakers. I don't like to think of men like Harry Guggenheim and Abram [sic] Flexner being pushed out of the United States, for instance, because of the "kikes" who line the beaches of New Jersey and Coney Island. Yet if this Jewish movement continues, and, especially if we take a large number of the German Jews into the States, such a thing is not impossible. If an anti-Jewish movement ever gets started seriously in the United States, it may be worse than in Germany.

Though he disliked "the fact that a Jewish problem exists," it's revealing that Lindbergh consistently blamed Jews themselves—at least, the "large portion" who "have shown themselves to be undesirable and troublemakers"—for exacerbating their own troubles.[47]

That "problem" existed both in Europe and "at home," to which the Lindberghs' thoughts increasingly turned. After Hitler's army invaded what remained of Czechoslovakia in March 1939 ("This time you had gone too far," Anne wrote angrily),[48] Charles considered whether it was time to return to the United States. Having experienced significant personal freedom in Europe ("the most . . . in Germany, with England next and then France"), he hesitated to return to a democracy that offered "no freedom for those who have attracted the interest of its public and its press." The threat of war deepened his sense of loyalty to America, but his growing

antipathy to equality made him pessimistic about the future of his homeland, especially if it went to war with Germany:

> What of our ten million negroes? What of our industrial immigration?
> On what stock are we to build? Are we building hatred against an older
> European country because it is facing problems which we ourselves must
> sometime face? . . . One thing is certain—if democracy is to continue
> on this earth it will not be by the blood of its soldiers but only by great
> changes in its present practices. No system based on the equality of the
> strong and the weak—in mind as well as body, in character and spirit, in
> all the qualities of life—can long endure. Democracy can succeed only
> as long as it embraces a relatively small number of comparatively equal
> people—and they must in addition be a superior people. Democracy
> never has and never can encompass the whole of mankind.[49]

Charles soon decided to sail home, leaving Anne to make final arrange-
ments in Europe and follow later with their children.

He boarded a ship for New York that April, believing that "there is
at best an even chance of the year passing without a general war." While
he enjoyed spending time on board with Lin Yutang, he described some
other travelers more negatively, in another passage omitted from his published journals: "The steward tells me that most of the Jewish passengers
are sea sick. Imagine the United States taking these Jews in addition to
those we already have. There are too many in places like New York already.
A few Jews add strength and character to a country, but too many create
chaos. And we are getting too many. This present immigration will have its
reaction. The worst of it is that the good Jews will be carried with it."[50]

"A Christian and a Democrat"

"So long as they performed in separate spheres," observed historian Wayne
Cole, "there was no contest between" Charles Lindbergh and Franklin
Delano Roosevelt. "But when either invaded the domain of the other . . .
the result was a battle of giants."[51] On April 20, 1939, the two men met for
the first time, in the Oval Office. "I liked him," Lindbergh wrote that night,
"and feel that I could get along with him well. Acquaintanceship would

be pleasant and interesting." He preferred that the two work together as long as they could, but he suspected "that it may not be for long."[52]

There were many stumbling blocks. Lindbergh found Roosevelt "too suave, too pleasant, too easy" to trust. The pilot was close with conservative businessmen who despised the New Deal, and he still called FDR's handling of the 1934 air mail investigation "one of the worst political maneuvers" he knew of. In 1938 Pan Am president Juan Trippe had asked if Lindbergh would chair a new commission on civil aviation. Suspecting the idea came from the president, Lindbergh declined; he said, "my past experience leads me to question everything that comes from the Roosevelt Administration."[53]

Most importantly, Roosevelt's view of Nazi Germany fundamentally differed from that of his guest, whom FDR's secretary of the interior, Harold L. Ickes, had publicly condemned for accepting the medal from Göring.[54] At the same time that Lindbergh came to admire aspects of Hitler's leadership, FDR grew increasingly alarmed by the aggressive foreign policies of Germany and its future partners in the Axis. As early as 1937, the president had called for economic sanctions against Germany and Italy. His most recent biographers argue persuasively that Roosevelt, a devout Episcopalian, objected to fascism because his political philosophy stemmed from his basic identity as "a Christian and a Democrat." "When the precepts of religion were not observed," write James Woolverton and James Bratt, FDR concluded that "the most Christian thing to do was to 'quarantine' the rule breakers. If aggression continued, it would have to be stopped by force. Roosevelt sounded like a prophet here in both senses of the term: making predictions about the future and recalling the people to their true tradition, even at the cost of sacrifice."[55]

In his January 1939 State of the Union address, FDR warned that "storms from abroad directly challenge three institutions indispensable to Americans, now as always. The first is religion. It is the source of the other two—democracy and international good faith." Calling on the "God-fearing democracies of the world" not to remain "indifferent to international lawlessness," Roosevelt encouraged Congress to consider the "many methods short of war, but stronger and more effective than mere words, of bringing home to aggressor governments the aggregate sentiments of our own people."[56]

But if the president was a prophet in 1939, his people—and their elected representatives—were not yet ready to heed his call for costly sacrifice. Even after Germany invaded Poland on September 1, 84 percent of Americans opposed sending military forces abroad to join England and France in waging World War II. A majority in that Gallup poll did favor selling the Allies airplanes and other war materiel, but FDR faced stiff opposition in Congress from isolationists unwilling to end the American arms embargo.[57] In the end, all he could secure from a legislature controlled by his own party was "cash-and-carry": Britain and France could purchase American war materiel, but only if they paid up front and used their own ships for transportation.

Even that was too much for Charles Lindbergh, who did "not intend to stand by and see this country pushed into war if it is not absolutely essential to the future welfare of the nation." He continued, "Much as I dislike taking part [in] politics and public life, I intend to do so if necessary to stop the trend which is now going on in this country."[58]

CHAPTER NINE

America First

In just fifteen years he had gone from Jesus to Judas!

—*Constance Morrow Morgan* (1993)[1]

I HAVE COME to a difficult point," Anne Morrow Lindbergh acknowledged in 1976, as she prepared to publish her diaries and letters from the years leading up to World War II. Two years after Charles's death, she still defended him for having worked to avoid war between the United States and Nazi Germany. But Anne knew that anti-interventionists like her husband and herself should have heeded "countering voices of warning," including those of the same Jewish refugees that Charles privately disparaged. Much as World War I had made her loathe any resumption of armed conflict, she "learned—more slowly than most people—that there were worse things. The degradation and horror that was uncovered at Auschwitz, Buchenwald, and Dachau was worse than war." Late in life, Charles had used autobiographical writing to justify his response to Nazi Germany—and edited his published journals so as to deflect charges of anti-Semitism. Anne wanted to resist the temptation "to somewhat falsify and touch up the original picture."[2]

"It would have been easier," she said, "and far kinder to myself and my husband, if I had written a condensed, softened, and retouched autobiography," one that left intact "the desired pleasant image I wanted to remain in the minds of my readers and posterity." But a life lived mostly in the public eye had left her "sickened with images." Quoting the biblical commandment not to "make unto thee a graven image" (Exod. 20:4), Anne said she wanted to avoid creating images as false as those the Nazis made of Jews and those by which "many members of the white race, inside and outside of America, still see the black race."[3]

So, as this biography comes to that same difficult point in time, I want to avoid making a false image of Charles Lindbergh. After all, I'm one of the historians whose task, according to Anne Lindbergh, is "to sort out and unmask the images of another epoch."[4]

If her husband was right, it's likely that I'll arrive at something less than clarity. Starting his memoir in December 1938, Charles Lindbergh observed that the "biographer must base his writing on his own viewpoint and experience in life. Therefore, a biography must confuse to some degree the character of the author with that of his subject."[5] But to the extent that rigorous research and careful interpretation can protect against such confusion, it can also help us see more clearly one of his own blind spots. A worldview shaped by the spirituality of friends like Alexis Carrel left Charles Lindbergh unable to see the image of God in the people Adolf Hitler meant to subjugate or exterminate.

A "Western Wall" and a "Christian Nation"

On September 15, 1939, Charles Lindbergh prepared to give his first speech opposing US intervention in the two-week-old Second World War. That afternoon Truman Smith conveyed a message from the Roosevelt administration: not wanting a public rupture with Lindbergh, the president was willing to offer him a cabinet position ("secretaryship of air") if he called off the address. Lindbergh refused. At 9:45 p.m. Washington time, he began to speak into microphones representing all three major radio networks.[6] "I was not well satisfied with my delivery," Lindbergh admitted afterward, but 95 percent of the responses he read over the next week were "favorable, and most of them are from people of a good type."[7]

That brief radio talk introduced several arguments that would become staples of Lindbergh's anti-intervention campaign. Appealing to Americans as descendants of those who "preferred the wilderness and the Indians to the problems of Europe," the grandson of Ola Månsson argued that the New World had no need to involve itself again in the conflicts of the Old. He denied that American security was at stake; a man best known for flying across the Atlantic now insisted that an "ocean is a formidable

barrier even for modern aircraft." Hearkening back to his father's opposition to American involvement in the First World War, Lindbergh warned
that in fighting a second time "for democracy abroad, we may end by
losing it at home." Most controversially, Lindbergh treated Hitler and his
opponents alike as members of the same civilization, insisting that there
was "no question of banding together to defend the white race against foreign invasion. This is simply one of those age-old quarrels within our own
family of nations.... The gift of civilized life must still be carried on." And
if the European branch of the "family" did tear itself apart, then the United
States had to remain intact, able to "carry on Western civilization."[8]

He fleshed out that last argument in an article that he mailed that same
week to *Reader's Digest* publisher DeWitt Wallace.[9] When "Aviation, Geography, and Race" came out in November, it provided the American
public with its first glimpse into the spiritual and racial worldview Lindbergh had been developing during his European exile. On the one hand,
aviation ("man flung upward in the face of God") seemed "almost a gift
from heaven to those Western nations who were already the leaders of
their era"; the airplane was "a tool specially shaped for Western hands
... one of those priceless possessions which permit the White race to
live at all in a pressing sea of Yellow, Black, and Brown."[10] ("Machines,"
argues historian Michael Adas, had long served as "the measure of men"
for those convinced of white supremacy, with technological superiority
not just enabling the global expansion of Western empire but justifying
it.)[11] But technological progress, in Lindbergh's mind, also risked civilizational decay for "a people too far separated from the soil and from the
sea—the danger of that physical decline which so often goes with a high
intellectual development, of that spiritual decline which seems invariably
to accompany an industrial life, of that racial decline which follows physical and spiritual mediocrity."

That decline of the West—again, both "spiritual" and "racial"—could
only be hastened by "a war within our own family of nations, a war which
will reduce the strength and destroy the treasures of the White race, a
war which may even lead to the end of our civilization." Far from fighting
against Nazi Germany, the time had come for those sharing "our inheritance of European blood"—including Americans—"to turn from our quarrels and to build our White ramparts again," to erect "a Western wall of race

and arms" against the Eastern menace, with "an English fleet, a German air force, a French army, an American nation, standing together as guardians of our common heritage, sharing strength, dividing influence."[12]

Ever loyal, Anne Lindbergh called the article Charles's "deepest, best thinking."[13] Many readers agreed, and some of their letters of thanks and praise echoed his use of religious language. "We can never solve our economic and governmental problems until we as a people return to the old spiritual foundation on which our American tradition rests," preached an insurance salesman from Chicago.[14] Lindbergh reminded one New Jersey reader of John the Baptist; after reading his next anti-intervention article, she "went to sleep last night thinking 'a voice crying in the wilderness' [John 1:23]."[15]

But another Christian reader accused Lindbergh of indulging in "brutal paganism." Katharine Hayden Salter was a feminist writer living in Madison, Wisconsin, where her husband taught political science at the university Lindbergh had briefly attended. "I cannot tell you what a shock of plain horror it has given me," Salter began her impassioned letter to him. As the citizen of "a Christian country (at least in the making)," she found racial supremacy antithetical to the "Christian, and Hebraic" foundations of American life, in which "we have stopped looking at people as bits of races, foreign or non-foreign, and have dealt with each other as human beings." Wanting nothing to do with the "silly, stupid, brutal, dull, inefficient, dishonest, and conceited world that will go on behind the West Wall of the White Race," Salter preferred to "keep the Lord's Prayer, and the Sermon on the Mount, and the parables, and the prophets and the psalms."[16]

In 1939 the notion of America as a "Christian nation" was not a monopoly of the anti–New Deal businessmen who tended to support Lindbergh.[17] For political and theological progressives like Franklin Roosevelt and Katharine Salter, fascism had no place in a country whose aspirations for equality started in Scripture.[18]

St.-Ex.

Lindbergh shared that issue of *Reader's Digest* with a Christian writer who abhorred Hitler, a fellow pilot whose aviation writing had made him a literary sensation. Like Charles Lindbergh, Antoine de Saint-

Exupéry started his flying career by delivering mail, in Africa and then South America. Those experiences inspired his first novels, *Southern Mail* (1929) and *Night Flight* (1931). In 1935 he survived a desert crash, which featured prominently in his memoir, *Wind, Sand, and Stars*. In the excerpt published in *Reader's Digest*, Saint-Exupéry warned that "ancient myths like Pan-Germanism" were "carnivorous idols. The man who dies for the progress of science or the healing of the sick serves life in his very dying. But modern warfare destroys what it claims to foster." In the book's last sentence, he hinted most directly at the Catholic faith that molded his views: "Only the Spirit, if it breathe upon the clay, can create Man."[19]

Saint-Exupéry had written a long preface to the French edition of Anne's second book, so when he visited the United States that August, Charles invited him to spend a couple days at the Lindberghs' home on Long Island. With Anne translating, the three talked until midnight. "He has an exceptional mind," Charles wrote before bed, "a real artist and all that one would expect after reading his books."[20] Anne was even more taken with "St.-Ex." Translating again as he and Charles talked in the car the next day, Anne reflected: "There is a kind of mountain-top, clear, cold-air austerity about him that reminds me of Carrel or of a monk, dedicated to something—what?" As the Lindberghs drove their guest back to the city, they spoke with him "of faith, of the times in a plane when it is black ahead and one must go on only by that patch of green off to the right, like a thread. How one must have faith, like a child. *'Il faut être enfant'* [Anne's French allusion to Matt. 18:3—"Except ye turn, and become as little children, ye shall in no wise enter into the kingdom of heaven"], like the Bible, faith like Gideon [*sic*] at Jericho."[21]

The encounter with the French pilot "had changed everything" for Anne, concludes her biographer, Susan Hertog. "He had done something no one else had done. He saw Anne apart from Charles."[22] Conversation with Saint-Exupéry left Anne's world feeling "almost unbearably beautiful." She went on, "A driving white rainstorm gives me wings, and trees steeped in the drowsy dusk of evening stand up like rooted gods, reaching for the sky." After he departed, she struggled to make conversation at dinner that night with some of Charles's "army friends. . . . They are nice simple people, but it is terribly difficult to talk to them."[23]

After Germany invaded France in May 1940, Saint-Exupéry entered the French air force. As the Wehrmacht neared Paris, he was interviewed by American journalist Dorothy Thompson. A fierce critic of Hitler who had warned readers of her syndicated column that Charles Lindbergh's "inclination toward Fascism is well known to his friends,"[24] Thompson asked Saint-Exupéry why such a great artist needed to risk his life in combat. "Nobody has a right to write a word today," he replied, "who does not participate to the fullest in the agony of his fellow human beings. . . . The Christian idea has got to be served; that the Word is made Flesh [John 1:14]. One must write with one's body." To Saint-Exupéry's mind, the reason "there is a Hitler" is that people "say things and pretend to believe things, but what we say is not translated into the deed. And the deed is divorced from Faith, from the Word." Anne transcribed the interview in her diary, adding, "What he says is so fundamentally true. It is true in its essence. . . . But how, oh God, how to make the Word into Flesh in my own little day-to-day life?"[25]

Her encounter with the French pilot-poet was just one example of how Anne found herself admiring Christians who believed that following the Prince of Peace required them to join the war against Nazi aggression. Even "Carrel feels it is a fight for Christianity," she told her mother, just before reading Saint-Exupéry's interview with Thompson, "as so many people do."[26]

One of those Christian interventionists was Elizabeth Cutter Morrow herself. Then serving as the interim president of Smith College, Anne's mother had publicly criticized Charles for wanting to embargo arms sales to Britain and France and joined an antineutrality committee that included theologian Reinhold Niebuhr.[27] The day that British forces evacuated from Dunkirk, she went on the radio to urge Americans to do everything "short of actually declaring war" to help the Allies defeat Germany, a statement that the New York Times noted was "diametrically opposed" to the most recent speech by her famous son-in-law. "We can hardly help . . . in the spiritual structure of the world," Morrow continued, "without making some sacrifice for its attainment before the end." To those who insisted that "only a miracle can save the Allies now," she urged, "let us go to church and pray." She joined Saint-Exupéry in dismissing belief unmatched by action: "I believe in the power of prayer, and I would turn no one from the church, but who taught us that a miracle is a one-sided effort? We should read our Bibles with more understanding."[28]

"It was a beautiful speech," Anne told her mother, "and courageous and very much like you. . . . There was a fundamental spiritual truth in it that I agree with had I not agreed with a word of the text." But she had decided that "every day they go on fighting, they, their children, their grandchildren and ours will be worse off." Having agonized frequently in her diary since the declaration of war, Anne concluded that the war's swift resolution, whoever the victor, was "the bridge [she] had been forced to build between C.'s logic and factual judgment and [her] own philosophy or religion."[29] The horror of war left her feeling like "a child reading of Christ crucified, Joan of Arc burned at the stake, Catherine crushed on a wheel."

Anne had been praying for peace since the start of the war; that night she woke up suddenly and discovered she was praying as she had not prayed "since little Charles."[30] Though her mother's installation service in Smith's chapel reminded Anne that she no longer had the "perfect faith" of her childhood, she continued to pray "not only that those in power might see some way out of this but also that if there is no way out [she] may learn to understand it and accept it a little."[31] That Christmas, *Reader's Digest* published her "Prayer for Peace," which reiterated Charles's arguments against intervention, quoted Alexis Carrel's warnings of Western collapse, and described Hitler and the Nazi regime as the "embittered spirit of a strong and humiliated people. . . . To exorcise this spirit you must offer Germany and the world not war but peace."[32]

As Philippe Pétain took power and began to negotiate France's surrender, Anne conceded to her diary, "There is some (evil) mystical or spiritual force behind Hitler and I really agree that it will take some equally strong spiritual force to overthrow him. But I do *not* think that the empty gesture of our declaring war on him *is* that force."[33] In the end, she continued to take her husband's side, in public and (more uneasily) in private. "There was only one thing harder to bear than the truth," concludes Hertog, "and that was the thought of separation from Charles." He, "not God, was Anne's bulwark against despair."[34]

MORAL RE-ARMAMENT

On the eve of France's official surrender, Charles Lindbergh wished that "[I] could be either wholeheartedly in the war and fighting for true beliefs and ideals, or else far enough away from it mentally and physically to be able to see the forest when I walk through it, and to feel the beauty of wind rippled water without having part of my mind thinking of politics and bombing planes and plans. Here, at this moment, I feel in contact neither with the world of men nor with the world of God."[35]

Sitting with her husband on the beach as the sun set on June 24, 1940, Anne looked at Long Island Sound, over which Charles's flight to Paris had started. She thought again "how terribly alone C. is. That first symbolic flight of his is still true. He was always, is now, and will always be out there alone over the ocean, alone seeing his destination, alone having faith that he can reach it, with people on the sidelines shouting, 'Flying Fool!'" She added, "And a few holding him blindly in their hearts—like me."

But even as Germany occupied France and prepared for the Battle of Britain, Charles was far from alone in his opposition to America joining World War II. When Gallup surveyed Americans in late June and early July 1940, 86 percent said they would vote against the United States going to war against the Axis.[36] And while Franklin Roosevelt and Wendell Willkie, the Republican candidate seeking to deny FDR a third term, both wanted to increase American aid to Britain, others were organizing to end the war—or at least to keep the United States out of it.

One of those seeking to bring about a reconciliation between Germany and other countries was Frank Buchman. The leader of the Oxford Group had launched a movement called Moral Re-Armament (MRA) in London in May 1938, hoping to avert war by forging an international movement for spiritual renewal. Theologians Dietrich Bonhoeffer and Reinhold Niebuhr both found Buchman's response to fascism naïve, at best.[37] But Buchman succeeded in gaining the public sympathies of the powerful and famous. MRA rally-goers in those years received a pamphlet reprinting endorsements from artists, scientists, labor leaders, industrialists, and thirty-four of America's forty-eight governors.[38] "[If] you're going to change the world," MRA worker T. Willard Hunter explained later, "you need to change the people who run it. So we were out, among other things, to 'make Christians out of Congressmen.'" Most famously, FDR was persuaded to back MRA—at least, to the extent of asking Senator Harry Truman to read a statement on his behalf at a June 1939 rally in Washington's Constitution Hall.[39]

August and Louisa Lindbergh and their children, ca. 1873; C. A. stands behind his mother *(Photo by A. P. Overland, used by permission from Minnesota Historical Society)*

The Charles Lindbergh House in Little Falls, Minnesota, was built in 1906, after its larger predecessor burned *(Photo by author)*

Part of the library in the Lindbergh House in Little Falls
(Photo by author)

Rep. C. A. Lindbergh with his son Charles, ca. 1910 *(Photo by Grand Studios, used by permission from Minnesota Historical Society)*

Bethel Evangelical
Lutheran Church—
spiritual home to
many Swedish-
American residents
of Little Falls, but not
the Lindberghs
(Photo by author)

CONGREGATIONAL CHURCH AND GYMNASIUM, LITTLE FALLS, MINN.

When they went to church in Little Falls, the Lindberghs attended First Congregational. *(Photo by Levis' Book Store, used by permission from Minnesota Historical Society)*

328

Lindbergh with a fellow trainee at Brooks Field, Texas, in 1924 *(Photo by C. A. Lindbergh, used by permission from Minnesota Historical Society)*

The *Spirit of St. Louis*, hanging over the Eagle lunar lander at the National Air and Space Museum *(Photo by author)*

As part of his cross-country tour in 1927, Lindbergh came to Dayton, Ohio, to pay his respects to Orville Wright (in straw hat). *(Photo courtesy of the Library of Congress)*

Lindbergh and his mother after worship at Washington's First Congregational
Church, 1927 *(Photo courtesy of the Library of Congress)*

Dwight Morrow
*(Photo courtesy of the
Library of Congress)*

Alexis Carrel *(Photo courtesy of the Library of Congress)*

Lindbergh testifying at the Hauptmann trial, 1935 *(Photo courtesy of the Library of Congress)*

Frank Buchman
*(Photo courtesy of the
Library of Congress)*

Lindbergh playing with his son Jon at Long Barn in 1937 *(Photo used by permission from Reeve Morrow Lindbergh)*

Anne Morrow Lindbergh and Jim Newton sailing in the Florida Keys, 1941
(Lindbergh Picture Collection [MS 325B], Manuscripts and Archives, Yale University Library)

On the dais for the America First rally in Minneapolis in 1941, Lindbergh sat next to Methodist pastor Richard C. Raines. *(Photo used by permission from Minnesota Historical Society)*

Franklin D. Roosevelt giving a Labor Day address in 1941 *(Photo courtesy of the Roosevelt Presidential Library)*

Henry Ford
*(Photo courtesy of the
Library of Congress)*

"A Grand Canyon of the mechanized world": the Willow Run plant *(Photo courtesy
of the Library of Congress)*

Lindbergh secretly flew fifty combat missions in the South Pacific in 1944.
(Photo used by permission from Minnesota Historical Society)

Charles Lindbergh, left, first man to fly non-stop from New York to Paris, and Neil Armstrong, first man to set foot on the moon, compare notes at 13th Annual Awards Banquet of the Society of Experimental Test Pilots in Beverly Hills, Saturday, Sept. 28, 1969. Center is Mrs. Robert Hoover, wife of the president of the society. Lindbergh and Armstrong received special honors from SETP. *(AP Photo)*

Lindbergh visiting his childhood home at age sixty-nine *(Photo by John Ferguson, used by permission from Minnesota Historical Society)*

The gravestone of Charles A. Lindbergh, inscribed with the words of Psalm 139:9 *(Photo by LuxTonnerre)*

One more Lindbergh legacy: this crater on Mars is named for the *Spirit of St. Louis* *(Photo courtesy of NASA)*

Moral Re-Armament also tried in vain to recruit Charles Lindbergh, through his friendship with Jim Newton. Lindbergh conceded in July 1939 that "if a religious movement can attract enough of [Newton's] type, it will amount to something," but, as usual, he stuck with his first impressions. Even as he encouraged Newton to write about MRA for *Reader's Digest*, Lindbergh remained skeptical of Buchman and his "effervescent, overenthusiastic, impractical disciples": "They all believe in truth and good will and are against sin. They apparently feel that the problems of mankind can be settled by good will, and that Peace on Earth will reign forevermore. But Christ hasn't been able to accomplish that in 2000 years, and I am not sure that Peace and Good will would make men happier if they had to be taken in excess."[40]

He and Buchman finally met that December. Lindbergh was "impressed by him personally" but could not understand "what it is in his 'movement' that brings out such devotion and enthusiasm in his followers."[41] Unlike his friend Henry Ford, Lindbergh never did give a public endorsement of Moral Re-Armament.

While he and Reinhold Niebuhr strongly disagreed about World War II, Lindbergh shared the Christian realist's dim view of MRA idealism. Though Buchman's movement "believes in peace," wishful thinking would not preserve Western civilization. "Even Newton has some of this naïvete about him," Lindbergh wrote in October 1939.[42] He supported neutrality, but the pilot was no pacifist. Later that month, he viewed the filmed version of Erich Maria Remarque's antiwar novel *All Quiet on the Western Front* and found it "terrible. . . . We do not want a nation that is afraid of war if it should become necessary to enter one."[43] As the debate over America's role in the Second World War intensified, Lindbergh both opposed intervention and supported rearmament. "What luck it is to find myself opposing my country's entrance into a war I *don't* believe in," he wrote in 1941, "when I would so much rather be fighting for my country in a war I *do* believe in. . . . If only the United States could be on the *right* side of an intelligent war!"[44]

But Lindbergh's response to MRA also reflected his continuing wariness of religion itself, even when organized as loosely as Buchman's movement. He allowed that "we lack religion in the world today" and continued to hope that MRA could be a helpful force in reversing the spiritual decline he and Carrel had so often lamented. But meeting more of Newton's friends left him convinced that "religion and spirit should be brought into life—innoculated [sic] into life—instead of life being brought to them. Religion is spiritual food and should be taken moderately." His great-grandfather had dunked believers in Orchard Lake, but Lindbergh thought that "nothing is gained by trying to immerse someone in" religion.[45]

Putting America First

Still, Lindbergh continued his own spiritual education as Britain continued the fight against Germany. In late August 1940 he was reading some reflections on the Lord's Prayer by a Russian Orthodox friend, helicopter designer Igor Sikorsky.[46] In September he and Anne met with Quaker leaders in New York; she had just written *The Wave of the Future*, her "*moral* argument for isolationism," and wanted to donate royalties to Quaker relief efforts in Europe, "as they seem to be the only ones living up to the reality of the word *mercy*."[47] The following month, as he read Henry Dwight Sedgwick's essay on contemplative spirituality, *Pro Vita Monastica*, Charles made plans to give a speech at Yale University, where students R. Douglas Stuart Jr. and Kingman Brewster Jr. had organized the America First Committee (AFC).

Brewster would later serve as Yale's president, and Stuart was the son of the founder of Quaker Oats. Their student backers included a future US president (Gerald Ford), vice presidential nominee (Sargent Shriver), and Supreme Court justice (Potter Stewart). But those future elites craved the support of established leaders. Retired general and Sears Roebuck executive Robert Wood became the national chairman, and Stuart and Brewster (an aviation buff) were both eager to add Lindbergh. The pilot declined to take on a formal leadership position in AFC but agreed to give a speech on October 30, the first of many he made for America First over the next twelve months. Passing walls inscribed with the names of Yalies who had died in America's wars, thousands filed into Woolsey Hall to hear Lindbergh give his longest anti-intervention speech to date, about thirty minutes.[48]

After a radio address that summer had inspired more accusations that Lindbergh was a Nazi sympathizer, his speech at Yale ("Impregnable

America") emphasized themes of national security. Gone was the argument that the war was an internal conflict between Germany and fellow members of the West's "family of nations."[49] But racialized concerns of civilizational decline had not disappeared. Lindbergh again argued that democracy could not be saved by foreign adventures, "but by the example of their successful operation at home"; going to war in Europe "would confuse and aggravate *our internal problems*, which are critical enough without war."[50] What he meant became clearer a week later, when he participated in American democracy and proposed limiting who could do likewise.

After casting his vote for Wendell Willkie, Lindbergh went to dinner with Anne, Jim Newton, and Alexis Carrel at the apartment of Carrel's engineer friend Boris Bakhmeteff. In another diary entry sanitized for later publication, Lindbergh recorded saying that he "did not believe a political system based on universal franchise would work in the United States." When the others agreed that restrictions on voting were needed, Lindbergh proposed that a first step "must be to disenfranchise the Negro." Conversation soon turned to "discussing the Jewish problem and how it could be handled in this country with intelligence and moderation." Lindbergh hoped to keep anything like the violent anti-Semitism of Nazi Germany from gathering strength in America, but, he asked, "How is it to be done? The more feeling there is against the Jews, the closer they band together; and the closer they band together, the more feeling rises against them." Driving home that night, Lindbergh heard the *New York Times* call the race for FDR. "The indications," he decided, "are that 'democracy,' as we have known it is a thing of the past."[51]

Anne Lindbergh recorded nothing of that election night conversation in her published diaries, but that month she did report on some of the "strange people" drawn together by shared opposition to the war. More than anything else, she was upset "to find all the right people on the wrong side and—even more appalling—all the *wrong* people on the right side."[52]

That December, for example, Charles had lunch with John E. Kelly, an "unusual and very interesting fellow" who "offered to help organize the Catholic and Irish groups."[53] What Lindbergh did not report (or, perhaps, know) is that his acquaintance was a lobbyist for the Spanish dictator Francisco Franco. Kelly was also a popular speaker with right-wing organizations like the Christian Front, a mostly Catholic group inspired by radio priest Charles Coughlin's call for a "crusade against the anti-Christian forces of the Red Revolution." "I am not content to walk in the footsteps of Christ," Fronters repeated at rallies. "I want to walk ahead of him with a club." In his 1940 exposé of the group, Theodore Irwin described the "sundry hoodlums, crackpots, misguided patriots, and Bundsters" of the Christian Front as "a domestic storm-troop mob running amuck, spewing racial hatred, fomenting violence, staging street scenes never before witnessed in [New York City's] history."[54]

Subsequent meetings with Kelly left him "feeling that it is better not to keep too close contact." But even if Lindbergh was unaware of the Christian Front's history, it nevertheless complicated his work for America First.[55] Despite the bipartisan committee's attempts to distance itself from such anti-Semitic and far-right elements, memories of Christian Front disturbances made Philadelphia's Academy of Music decline to host Lindbergh's AFC address in May 1941, and two radio stations refused to advertise it. "America First had great potential," concludes Philip Jenkins, "as long as it maintained its character as a mainstream pressure group, but it was discredited by the support it received from anti-semitic extremists."[56]

So Anne Lindbergh was relieved to find that the anti-interventionist movement also drew more palatable sorts of Christian support. "At last here are some 'good' people on our side," she wrote of her Quaker partners in international relief, who were "both practical and 'good.' I can go almost 'all the way' with them. But C. cannot."[57] Frederick J. Libby, a Congregational minister who had joined the Friends after World War I, looked, Charles wrote, "very much like a New England preacher. He is apparently rather a pacifist, but showed unusual understanding and intelligence (if one can apply the latter term to a pacifist)."[58] Norman Thomas, who served as a Presbyterian pastor before running six times for president as the candidate of the Socialist Party, got to know Lindbergh as he coordinated joint efforts by America First and the left-wing Keep America out of War Congress.[59] Other prominent Christian anti-interventionists included Methodist peace activist Charles F. Boss Jr. and *Christian Century* editor Charles Clayton Morrison, who defended Lindbergh (but not his racial views) in an August 1940 editorial.[60]

Lindbergh returned to his home state in May 1941 to address an America First rally in Minneapolis, where he was joined on the dais by Richard Raines, pastor of Hennepin Avenue Methodist Church. Recalling his own father's opposition to American involvement in World War I, Lindbergh warned his fellow Minnesotans against heeding the perverse logic of those who would repeat the mistake:

> If only we send our armies abroad once more, they tell us, if only enough people in Europe can be starved and killed, we will be able to spread peace, and democracy, and our way of life over the entire earth. People who have been pacifists all their lives are now saying that peace must be brought by war. Ministers are preaching that Christianity must be spread by famine. Our government asks us to preserve democracy abroad by creating a dictatorship in our own country. And all this in the name of idealism. . . . We do not accept the claim that Christianity will thrive on famine, or that our way of life can be spread around the world by force.[61]

In New York two weeks later, Lindbergh celebrated that the "United States is a nation of mixed races, religions, and beliefs. . . . Why must all this be jeopardized by injecting the wars and the hatreds of Europe into our midst?"[62]

But when Lindbergh returned to the Upper Midwest that fall, he gave a speech that undermined his claims of racial and religious tolerance. What she read of his rough draft horrified Anne, but she couldn't convince her husband to remove or soften its most controversial passage before he took the stage in Des Moines, Iowa, on September 11, 1941. Alongside the British and the Roosevelt administration, Lindbergh identified a third group of "war agitators": Jews, who posed a particular danger, in his mind, because of "their large ownership and influence in our motion pictures, our press, our radio and our government." Lindbergh could easily understand "why Jewish people desire the overthrow of Nazi Germany. . . . No person with a sense of the dignity of mankind can condone the persecution of the Jewish race in Germany." But he argued that their "pro-war policy" was dangerous "both *for us and for them*. . . . We cannot blame them for looking out for what they believe to be their own interests, but we must also look out for ours. We cannot allow the natural passions and prejudices of other peoples to lead our country to destruction."[63]

"It Can't Be You!"

When she read the Des Moines speech in college, Reeve Lindbergh finally understood why some of her friends believed that her father was a "fascist."[64] But it wasn't until she actually heard a recording of that address years later, on a visit to the Lindbergh house in Little Falls, that she felt the full weight of that particular Lindbergh legacy. Hurt, ashamed, and furious, she remembered wanting to cry out to her deceased father: "No! You never said such things! You raised your children never to say, never even to *think*, such things—this must be somebody else talking. It can't be you!"[65]

It can't be you! If not as intensely as his youngest child, that's still how most of us feel when we come to this chapter in the story of Charles Lindbergh. If we have any appreciation for his historic achievements, any admiration for his courage and modesty, any compassion for the tragedies he endured, or if we simply nod along with the honest questions he asked about God, science, and mortality, we don't want to accept that he believed what he said about Jews.

He didn't make things easy for us. To the end of his life, Charles Lindbergh refused to apologize for his Des Moines speech. A man who that summer had defined being "right" as "what a man, in his innermost soul, *believes* should be . . . a thing of God rather than of man" was not a man who would bend to criticism.[66] "Did you think it was enough to ignore the accusers," Reeve wanted to ask her father, "to say briefly, tight-lipped, 'I'm not anti-Semitic!' and ask us with your own silence to do nothing at all, to say nothing at all, forever?"[67] Whether years later, as she first heard her father's recorded voice say those horrifying words, or in the days that followed, as a national outcry mounted, those who loved or supported Charles Lindbergh struggled to explain him.

That fall a Unitarian minister named Leon Birkhead published a pamphlet entitled *Is Lindbergh a Nazi?* Reinhold Niebuhr called on the America First Committee to "divorce itself from the stand taken by Lindbergh and clean its ranks of those who would incite to racial and religious strife in this country."[68] Theodor Geisel, the future Dr. Seuss, drew a cartoon of Lindbergh sitting on "a Nazi Anti-Semite Stink Wagon." Even the conservative papers run by William Randolph Hearst, who had tried to sign Lindbergh to a movie contract in 1927, called his Des Moines talk "intemperate and intolerant."[69]

The best that the best of the anti-interventionists could do was to point out that if Charles Lindbergh was an anti-Semite, so too were some of his accusers. "A hundred clubs and hotel foyers rang with denunciation of Lindbergh on the morning after his Des Moines speech," wrote Charles Clayton Morrison in the *Christian Century*, "clubs and hotels which bar their doors to Jews."[70] An AFC leader in Connecticut condemned the hypocrisy of "smug citizens" who condemned Lindbergh even though they "*practice* anti-Semitism every day of their lives."[71]

As Charles Lindbergh himself had often observed, anti-Semitism was not confined to Germany or Europe. What Kingman Brewster called the "subliminal anti-Semitism" of Yale came out into the open when he struggled to drum up support for Jewish refugees in 1938. (Like other elite universities, Yale maintained a quota system restricting Jewish enrollment until the 1960s.) "I don't often criticize the Lord," said one Baptist pastor and politician a year later, "but I do feel that he drowned the wrong lot in the Red Sea."[72] Even in 1946, more Americans opposed a plan for Jewish refugee resettlement than supported it.[73]

For his part, there can be no doubt that Lindbergh believed he was struggling against Jewish influence in making his case for staying out of the war. He had thought so since the beginning of his public struggle against Roosevelt's foreign policy. In that first radio address in September 1939, Lindbergh vaguely warned of Americans being "deluged with propaganda, both foreign and domestic—some obvious, some insidious . . . we must ask who owns and who influences the newspaper, the news picture and the radio station."[74] Privately, he had already told friends that summer that, while he did "not blame the Jews so much for their attitude," it was necessary to "limit to a reasonable amount the Jewish influence in the Educational agencies in this country. ie., press, radio, and pictures." After meeting with conservative Democratic senator Harry Byrd, he told his diary that they were "both anxious to avoid having this country pushed into a European war by British and Jewish propaganda of which there is already far too much."[75]

Again and again, Lindbergh blamed what he took to be media misrepresentation of his and Anne's messages on Jews, whom he called in May 1941 "the greatest single influence pushing us toward war."[76] In reality, most of the leading interventionists were, like Franklin D. Roosevelt and Elizabeth Cutter Morrow, members of the Protestant establishment. Meanwhile, one of the country's few Jewish newspaper publishers, the New York Times's Arthur Sulzberger, regretted that he had to moderate his public opposition to Hitler for fear of an anti-Semitic backlash.[77]

Precisely because he thought so highly of some Jews, Lindbergh struggled to recognize the deep-seated prejudice that would cause him to distinguish an American "us" from a Jewish "them." So he could genuinely find his friend Abraham Flexner to be "a wonderful old man, and one of those Jews who makes you wonder why the race has been persecuted throughout history—until you remember the other kind, the kind that crowd clothing stores, and refugee ships, and beaches, and New York streets."[78] In February 1941 he could dismiss the conspiracy theorists who handed him a copy of the infamous anti-Semitic forgery known as the Protocols of the Elders of Zion[79] but also see "some reason for" anti-Semitism—even though, he said, "I have never classed myself as anti-semitic, and I think I will be on the side of moderation if an anti-semitic movement gains headway in this country." For he couldn't "help seeing that we have a Jewish and racial problem that is increasing rapidly in seriousness, and which must be faced fairly soon if it is to be met with moderation and influence. This continued Jewish immigration, together with the excessive Jewish influence in certain forms of American life, such as press, radio, motion pictures, finance, etc., is leading to real trouble. In numbers, the Jewish problem is not as serious as our negro problem; but the Jews make up in intellect and solidarity, and internationalism, for whatever they lack in actual numbers."

Notably, he again lumped religious and racial minorities into a single "problem." In the same entry, he also repeated his belief that "the racial problem in America must lead eventually to a limitation of the franchise."[80]

Reading his Des Moines speech just before he delivered it, Anne worried that her husband would be "branded anti-Semitic, Nazi, Führer-seeking, etc." If we want to share her conviction that her husband was actually "a moderate" in his context, we could take Lindbergh at his word that he believed that going to war would actually worsen Jewish suffering, in Europe and in America.[81] We could acknowledge that he made his comments "before the terrors of the Nazi concentration camps" were widely known; perhaps learning those terrors changed him into the father who taught Reeve a fundamentally different attitude.[82] We could agree with John Cowles, the Minneapolis newspaper publisher, who warned Douglas Stuart a month before the Des Moines speech that Lindbergh "is playing the Nazi game unconsciously and unwittingly."[83] But it's hard to be even that charitable when we can also read Lindbergh complain in May 1941 that German Americans were being mistreated while "a Jewish refugee of the worst type from Europe finds a welcome over here."[84]

"WHAT ELSE WAS THERE TO DO?"

He wouldn't apologize, but Lindbergh couldn't escape the fact that his comments in Des Moines had been controversial even among America First's ideologically diverse leadership. On the right, General Wood considered disbanding the committee and former president Herbert Hoover told Lindbergh the speech had been a mistake.[85] From the left, journalist John Flynn could not believe that "Col. Lindbergh without consulting anyone literally committed the America First movement to an open attack on the Jews."[86] "I honestly don't think Lindbergh is an anti-Semite," Norman Thomas concluded, "but I think he is a great idiot."[87] Writing to AFC chapter leaders in late September, Douglas Stuart accused "the war party [of] twisting and distorting what Colonel Lindbergh said in Des Moines" but reemphasized the need "to keep our membership rolls clear of those who seek to promote racial and religious intolerance."[88]

To Wood, Lindbergh insisted that his statements in Des Moines "were true, and that they were moderately worded," and he urged that America First continue its work, noting that Gallup still found most Americans opposed to intervention.[89] In a talk entitled "A Heritage at Stake" given at the Gospel Temple in Fort Wayne, Indiana, on October 3, 1941, Lindbergh started by acknowledging, "It may be my last address," and warned that free speech would soon be curtailed.[90] But he was cheered to hear from a priest that 90 percent of the Catholic hierarchy opposed US entry into the war. At the end of the month, Lindbergh spoke again at Madison Square Garden, "in many ways the most successful meeting we have yet held."[91]

In New York he had largely rehashed old material, but as he prepared for the next rally, scheduled for Boston Garden, Lindbergh drafted his most pointed comments yet about a president whom he accused of taking America up to the brink of a "dictatorial system." Convinced that Franklin Roosevelt had deceived the country in starting his third term as anything other than a committed neutralist, Lindbergh scribbled that "without integrity, freedom and democracy will become only politicians' nicknames for an American totalitarian state." In the end, it was "subterfuge in our political campaigns" that was the greatest danger to America, "not invasion . . . not intervention . . . not Germany or Russia or Japan."[92]

Then Japan attacked Pearl Harbor on Sunday morning, December 7, 1941. Lindbergh urged Stuart to cancel the Boston rally and filed away his undelivered speech. "Well," said Robert Wood, Roosevelt "got us in through the back door." Lindbergh surely agreed, but said, "What else was there to do?" He went on, "If I had been in Congress, I certainly would have voted for a declaration of war."[93]

CHAPTER TEN

The War

Most people remember that Lindbergh . . . opposed our
entry into the war until the day we were attacked at Pearl
Harbor. But how many know the nature of the services he
rendered to our air forces before, during and after the war?

–Deak Lyman (1953)[1]

I F CHARLES LINDBERGH hoped that America's involvement in
World War II could be confined to the Pacific, he was soon disappointed. "We are at war all over the world," he wrote on December 11,
1941, after Germany and Italy declared war on the United States, "and we
are unprepared for it from either a spiritual or a material standpoint."[2] Despite all his dire warnings of insidious British propaganda and the "Asiatic"
threat of Communism, the United States would fight alongside the United
Kingdom and Soviet Union.

"If it were not for the war," he continued in his diary the next day,
"I would like nothing better than to spend a year or two thinking and
reading and writing. But I simply cannot remain idle while my country
is at war. I *must* take some part in it, whatever that may be." Despite his
lingering differences with the Roosevelt administration, Lindbergh professed a patriotic desire to set them aside and help "carry on this war as
intelligently, as constructively, and as successfully as we can."[3] "It seems
to me," he wrote General Wood after the dissolution of the America First
Committee, "that the unity and strength necessary for a successful war,
demand that all viewpoints be represented in Washington."

But he soon found "that definite limits exist to the Administrations
[*sic*] desire for 'unity,' and that those limits do not extend very far into the

group of people who have disagreed with the policies of the President."[4] That wasn't generally true. Robert Stuart served on Dwight Eisenhower's staff, army chief of staff George Marshall hired Truman Smith as an intelligence officer, and AFC vice chair Hanford MacNider was wounded while commanding a unit in the Pacific.[5] But Lindbergh, who openly accused Roosevelt of betraying American democracy, was toxic to an administration that suspected him of Nazi sympathies. He had resigned his army commission in April 1941 after being publicly criticized by FDR, yet he now hoped to return to the military, if only as a civilian adviser. In January meetings in Washington, War Secretary Henry Stimson and army air corps commander Hap Arnold made clear that Lindbergh had burned too many bridges.[6] (It didn't help that the press reported his dinner party comment to America First colleagues that it was "unfortunate that the white race was divided in this war.")[7] Inquiries with Juan Trippe and other friends in the aviation industry were also fruitless. "The companies are all anxious to get him," Anne believed, "but they come back with the same answer: The Administration frowns on it."[8]

Friends suggested that Charles follow his father into politics. But he declined to enter the race for one of Minnesota's US Senate seats; he said, "My mission in life and my duty to my country lie along other lines."[9] What that mission was had never been less clear. It seemed that he might sit out the war "thinking and reading and writing" after all.

In the end, Lindbergh found several ways to serve his country during World War II, both testing warplanes and flying them in combat. He did keep reading and writing, and the experience of war changed his thinking in some ways—and confirmed it in others. Lindbergh continued to see human existence as a divinely ordained competition to produce a higher "quality of life," but his encounters with Japanese troops and Pacific Islanders challenged his assumptions of white supremacy. He refused to second-guess his opposition to intervention, but a visit to a German concentration camp made it impossible for him to ignore the evils of fascism. He worked to improve American air power but was aghast at the devastation rained down by bombers. He mostly stayed away from churches but began to read the Bible seriously for the first time.

World War II, said Anne Lindbergh after her husband's death, was "a great turning point" in his life.[10]

A "Grand Canyon of the Mechanized World"

In March 1942, Lindbergh had to confess to Jim Newton: "[My] plans are still uncertain, and involved in the same political situation I told you about." But he shared a glimmer of hope: he was headed to Detroit to meet with their mutual friend, Henry Ford.[11]

Lindbergh had met the legendary industrialist in the heady days of 1927, when he took Ford for his first flight. Enthusiastic about the future of aviation, America's leading carmaker agreed to build planes for the transcontinental passenger air service that Lindbergh helped get off the ground in 1929. The two Midwesterners came to share other interests as well: support for Alexis Carrel's program of "positive eugenics," admiration for the achievements of German industry under Hitler, and a desire to keep the United States out of World War II. Even more deeply suspicious of Jews than Lindbergh, Henry Ford had published the *Protocols of the Elders of Zion* in the 1920s in his weekly newspaper, the *Dearborn Independent*. When he joined America First in the fall of 1940, the committee tried to head off the inevitable charges of anti-Semitism by simultaneously announcing a Jewish member, Wood's fellow Sears Roebuck executive Lessing Rosenwald. Within a few months Rosenwald resigned, Robert Stuart admitted to making "a grave mistake," and the committee dropped Ford.[12]

But the friendship between Charles Lindbergh and Henry Ford endured. "In their tenacious independence," wrote Wayne Cole, "they were kindred spirits; each felt responsibilities toward others, but neither was prepared to sell his genius for the mess of pottage of personal popularity. Both tenaciously resisted attempts to beat them into conformist molds."[13] Ford invited Lindbergh to work for him, and this time the War Department agreed. "A lank, lonely, youngish man last week found a job," reported *Time*, "and a good one."[14]

In barely a year, Ford had built an enormous factory in rural Ypsilanti Township, near a stream called Willow Run. Over 3,200 feet long and 1,200 feet wide, the L-shaped plant struck Lindbergh as "a stupendous thing—acres upon acres of machinery and jigs and tarred wood floors and busy workmen. It is a sort of Grand Canyon of a mechanized world."[15] Just part of the Ford Motor Company's massive wartime complex, Willow

Run was solely dedicated to the production of one crucially important item: the B-24 bomber.

At first, Lindbergh was "not overly impressed" by the Liberator. With its "awkward" design, clumsy controls, and "inadequate" armament and armor, he "would certainly hate to be in a bomber of this type if a few pursuit planes caught up with it."[16] But he resolved to help Ford improve on its design, using an airfield adjoining the factory. Despite numerous production challenges, the women and men of Willow Run eventually completed a new B-24 every hour, accounting for half of the more than eighteen thousand produced during the war.[17]

"MY GREATEST TEST AT THIS TIME"

Although Lindbergh kept up an intense work and travel schedule during the war, those years also helped him to reconnect with his family. Being so close to Detroit let Charles spend more time with his mother, and he began to explore the Lodge and Land side of his ancestry. He made multiple visits to his great-grandfather's lakeside church and spent time in his grandfather's laboratory, where the old dental instruments, he said, "still 'feel' as they used to in my hand, although I have not touched them for more than twenty years."[18]

Even more importantly, he had decided to give more attention to his wife and children: "My greatest test at this time lies in the type of home I can create for Anne during these years of war." Shortly after taking the job with Ford, he told his diary that he and Anne didn't want to be "too far apart" and that he wanted to be "in close contact" with his children, including their first daughter, a two-year-old named after Anne, and a new baby due that summer.[19] After Anne visited him in April, Charles wrote one of the most passionate letters in the history of their marriage:

> When I think of them, these last four days stand out like posts against the sky. But you—the essence of you—have not remained in that land-scape. I think it is because you do not belong there, because the essence of you is not a part of these routine problems of life—it is something far above and far beyond, and when you touch life you leave a feeling of immortality behind, a feeling that is deeper and stronger than the

memory of your presence. It is what I meant when I wrote you that you had a touch of divinity in your pen. It is what I have felt ever since I have known you. I feel it more strongly with every year that passes.[20]

That summer he rented a house in the suburb of Bloomfield Hills, near the Cranbrook Academy of Art. Though it was "overdone inside, with colors and furniture not well chosen," its "flowers and trees and three acres of ground seem exceptionally attractive after three months of living on the second floor of the Dearborn Inn."[21] By the end of July, the family was reunited.

Anne went into labor two weeks later. Charles arrived at Henry Ford Hospital, bringing along the carving of the Virgin Mary that had been present at Land's and Anne's births. He noticed a postcard on her bedside table of a photo of a Native American image of a deer's head, "with mystical shell eyes inserted in the carved wood. . . . She always has something of the kind around her," he realized. "It may be a seashell, a feather, a painting, or just a post card photograph of a centuries old sculptured head of a deer. The intrinsic value of the object itself is unimportant, but it always holds something that is beyond life, and beyond this world in a sense, just as Anne holds that same element herself. She uses it as a bridge, and on it crosses into a world beyond our own—a world to which she belongs more than anyone I have ever known."

When her doctor asked about the psychological effect of the postcard, Charles "wanted to tell him that the scientifically logical word 'psychology' was inadequate to describe" what the image did for Anne, who "had the physical birth to pass through, but in addition to that, something far greater, something far beyond the science of psychology, something that [the doctor] vaguely recognized but did not understand." It was "something that I can only vaguely indicate with the words I write in this description."

Scott Lindbergh was born at 5:12 a.m. Charles stayed until 6:00, slept an hour, called the happy grandmothers, then went back to work at Willow Run.[22]

"A Year or Two Thinking and Reading and Writing"

When she wasn't parenting four young children or studying sculpture at Cranbrook, Anne tried to find time to write. Charles encouraged her, convinced that her work would be "of more permanent importance to this nation, and to the world," than any contribution he could make building bombers.[23] Reeve Lindbergh (born just after the war) recalled, "My father believed that my mother was not only a great writer, but also a Great Writer, one of the most important writers of the twentieth century." In later years her mother grew "irritated rather than flattered by the sloppy enormity of his praise."[24] But after the intense criticism she had received for her own anti-interventionist writing, that wartime support was invaluable.

Though her novella *The Steep Ascent* received tepid reviews when it came out in 1944, its most autobiographical passages suggest the depth of Anne's love and admiration for Charles, as when her stand-in thought of his stand-in: "Gerald existed. A man like that existed. He lived. God had made him. And she was full of joy merely at the thought of his existence, as one can feel joy at the memory of a Greek temple once seen all alone on a green hillside. One can feel joy at remembering its white flower-like perfection without wishing to own it or be in it. One can feel joy even though one knows one may never see it again."[25]

Even when his work took him away from home—as when he volunteered to serve as a test subject for a high-altitude study at the Mayo Clinic in Rochester, Minnesota—Anne still felt "a spiritual nearness" to her husband during the war.[26]

While he encouraged Anne in her career, Charles was also finding his own literary voice. A month before Pearl Harbor, she had watched him work on his new account of the 1927 flight to Paris, "enviously remembering that fever of absorption with which one works when one has struck a vein of gold."[27] As he continued to add to what he now called *The Spirit of St. Louis*, Charles became more adventurous as a writer. The author of *"We"* was increasingly eager to stretch beyond spare prose into poetic description and philosophical rumination, as when he recalled leaving New England behind and looking down at the frigid waters of the North Atlantic:

That was not a hostile ocean. It had a cold hospitality, a hospitality of the spirit rather than of the body, one that opened more to death than to life. . . . And if I should fall, if I should fall into those green, translucent depths, I would be received with welcome and my spirit would find freedom in its realm. Those waves might seem cold to the flesh and blood of life; but it is escape and freedom (and limitlessness) that the spirit wants in death, not warmth. Those waves took me farther from life and closer to eternity, and that feeling grew with every hour of the flight.[28]

Anne devoured his first draft in a single night in March 1942, "unable to put it down." She went on, "It was so vivid and so moving that I had no words with which to tell him how I felt"—save to assure him that "it was better than St.-Ex."[29]

Separated by the North Atlantic from Alexis Carrel, then living under German occupation in France, Lindbergh used his writing to think more independently about some of their shared interests: the connections between body, mind, and spirit; what lies beyond death; and the realm of the supernatural. While he waited for war work to materialize in January 1942, Lindbergh elaborated on the "disembodied beings" that had accompanied him on the flight to Paris: "These spirits were not of human form, but they spoke with human voice. It seemed that I saw them without my eyes, and heard them without my ears. There were several of them, shapes in the air, without substance, able to vanish or appear at will, to speak or hold silence at their whim, riding crowded comfortable together in the back of the fuselage, one or two of them usually just behind my back, close yet never touching."[30]

At the end of that year, he thought back on flying over Newfoundland, as "one looks down upon the earth with eyes that seem unmortal, as though man had been allowed to rise, for a moment, above his rightful place, and look down to see his earthly life amid a larger sense of values" before the end of a flight took the pilot out of "this realm of the gods" and back down to Earth, whose concerns "envelop you with their triviality and darken the crystal clarity of your heightened vision."[31]

But whenever he contemplated the terrestrial concerns of a war-torn world, Lindbergh continued to sound familiar, troubling notes. Watching another Ford factory churn out war materiel, Anne felt that "one could not stay long there and believe in God or trees or sky or children," but Charles was unshaken in his conviction that strife is "a concept of God."[32] "Since the right to live is based on strife," he wrote in one fragment, "it is inevitable that races clash." In another, he reiterated that "this world was not created on the basis of equality. It was created, and it has always existed on the basis of superiority. . . . God gave competition as a measure of the quality of life. This would be a dull world without it. He did not diversify life so that man might unify it again."

Even as African Americans fought for the "Double V"—victory over fascism abroad and victory over racism at home—and Japanese Americans risked their lives for the same government that interned their families, Lindbergh refined his appeal "to a minority of people" for a "policy based primarily on the quality and improvement of the [white] race."[33]

That letter was never published, but some of its themes would find their way, in more muted form, into Lindbergh's postwar essay, *Of Flight and Life*. The Carrel-inspired critique of equality remained, but it was tempered by the growing influence of another figure: Jesus Christ.

"THE PHILOSOPHY OF CHRIST"

To be sure, Lindbergh had not lost his interest in other religions. Visiting a Washington art gallery in 1940, he came to a "Bodhisattva of the T'ang dynasty—life size" and "thought of the generations of Chinese worshipers who had knelt and bowed before that idol, and how out of place it was there in the center of a modern room in a Modern American museum." He went on, "I wanted to take it back to the gold and laquer [*sic*] decorations of an Oriental temple—to the people in whose life and tradition it belonged." He read and reread Lao Tzu and recommended those books to Jim Newton.[34]

But for the first time, Lindbergh also studied Newton's own faith. One night in late August 1942, as he and Anne listened to Bach, Charles read "Matthew and Plato."[35] It was his first mention of reading the Bible, which now joined William Shakespeare's *Pericles* and Oswald Spengler's *Decline of the West* in his self-designed curriculum. By 1944, the New Testament would be one of his favorite books.

The reasons for this shift, and his evolving response to what he read, remain obscure. During the war, Lindbergh's journal writing tended to focus on the technical details of his work for Ford and other companies, and he stopped keeping the diary altogether between December 1942 and December 1943. But when *Of Flight and Life* came out in 1948, it was studded with references to Jesus and quotations from the Gospels. We'll consider those themes in the following chapter, but it seems most likely that Anne planted the seeds for such writing during the war.

She had never entirely abandoned the faith of her childhood. In a Christmas Eve radio address in 1940, she cast her appeal for European relief in explicitly Christian terms: "I have been saying that humanitarianism is the best policy, that to act in the spirit of Christian mercy is good business. . . . But I believe much more than that. Christianity has never been primarily practical. It has proved to be something more. It has survived a practical world for almost two thousand years, and men still find a transcending power in its message."[36]

Stung to be accused of a "passive acceptance of totalitarianism and all its evils," she entered 1942 reading Fyodor Dostoyevsky, Francis of Assisi, and Blaise Pascal, Christian writers whose poetry and prayers, she said, "can put me in grace."[37] Before the end of the war, she discovered C. S. Lewis, whose *Screwtape Letters* (1942) was "brilliant satire," and T. S. Eliot, whose *Four Quartets* (1943) she revisited throughout her life, even as she was dying of Alzheimer's disease.[38]

But reading a new article from Antoine de Saint-Exupéry in early 1942 left Anne both convinced of the power of grace and dissatisfied by traditional Christian practice and belief:

> One should, I know, get [grace] directly from God, from meditation or prayer, with no intermediary of poet, writer, or musician. But I find myself unable—except rarely—to do this. The language and forms of various religions so often put me off. My Sunday-school pictures of Christ have gotten in the way, the memories of pews, the ugly and unmystical ethics of those Boy-Scout-leader ministers, prayers before horsehair sofas. And the more orthodox faiths, though they appeal to me with their mysticism, again put me off by the language—those capital letters, those blood and wine symbols, those rosaries and colored statues of the Madonna.[39]

That December, the Sunday morning before Christmas, she took Land to worship, perhaps at nearby Christ Church Cranbrook. The "old prayers

[were] lovely," she wrote, but the service "seemed just ritual, with no mysticism and not simple enough. And it was too much a neighborhood-house affair. That is all right, in its place. But its place is *not* in church. The church today, and the Protestant Church particularly, has become simply the Neighborhood House." To Anne Lindbergh's mind, "church . . . should be dark . . . impersonal, anonymous. One should be lost in nameless worship—an unknown soul."[40] Listening to someone play Bach on the piano made her feel like she had entered her own "Kingdom of Heaven," what "church should do for one but doesn't for [her]."[41]

As she wrote *Steep Ascent* the following year, Anne described her character as being embarrassed even to speak of God: "It was too facile, too easy to use a word like that. It smacked of false religions, the purple edges of religion, not the white nameless blaze itself in the center."[42] Yet there was a blazing center, and he had a name.

For all the problems she saw with their "translation" into religious practice, "the words of Christ are crystalline, of course."[43] The sound of spring on Easter Monday no longer struck her—as it did in her childhood—as a literal "sign from heaven," but "it is a sign . . . that beauty still exists and goes on side by side with horror. . . . A morning like this is the morning of Resurrection—when we see and believe, 'Lo, I am with you alway[s], even unto the end of the world' [Matt. 28:20]."[44] One of Jesus's beatitudes—"they which do hunger and thirst after righteousness . . . shall be filled" (Matt. 5:6)—gave her "great hope."[45] She pondered why so many recipients of that blessing remained "such a struggling unhappy lot," but her doubts didn't stop Anne from reading to her children biblical accounts of Jesus's birth at Christmas and his resurrection at Easter.[46]

Her husband doesn't always appear in her descriptions of such holiday rituals, but Charles does figure in Anne's account of the Lindbergh family's Christmas Eve in 1943. Home after a Friday at Willow Run, he set up the Christmas tree while Anne retrieved her mother's crèche and the carved madonna they had picked up in England. With the afternoon sun reflecting off the star atop the tree, "it looks for that instant beautiful beyond words—a miracle of creation." That night, Charles joined Anne and the children as they had their "little service," reading aloud Luke 2 by candlelight and playing carols like "Silent Night." "It was lovely and quiet," Anne wrote contentedly. "The children were hushed and expectant and happy, as though they had shared something secret, and something holy, too . . .

I quote Dostoevsky, 'And even one good memory may be the means of saving us.'" Jon called it "the nicest Christmas Eve [they] ever had!"[47]

"And Charles said so, too," she added. "The best Christmas Eve we have ever had," he confirmed in his own diary.[48] For Lindbergh, such rituals didn't re-create moments from a religious childhood, as they did for his wife; he had no memories of gathering around the nativity story with C. A. and Evangeline. But that time with his family did remind him of happier, prewar days on Illiec.

And that night may have had spiritual, not just familial, significance. On Christmas Eve 1943, he may have thought back to Christmas Day 1940. As baby Anne watched her brothers unwrap their presents that morning, Charles fretted that there were too many gifts. "It dulls appreciation," he wrote, "not only of the presents, but of the day itself." As he continued, he offered his first prolonged reflection on what became an important theme for him: the contrast between Christianity and Christ.

> It seems to me that Christmas has deviated as much from the birth of Christ as Christianity has from his teachings. The keynote at the birth of Christ was simplicity. The keynote of Christmas today is luxury. The birth and life of Christ were surrounded with things mystical. Christmas and Christianity today are surrounded with things material. Sometime I would like to have a Christmas in our home that conforms to the true spirit and significance of that day 2,000 years ago—a Christmas unstuffed by roast turkey and sweet potatoes; a Christmas pure in its simplicity, akin to the sky and the stars, of the mind rather than the body. It should be almost the reverse of a modern Christmas. One should eat too little rather than too much, see no one rather than everyone, spend it in silence rather than in communication. Christmas should be a day that brings one closer to God and to the philosophy of Christ.[49]

If he was interested in Christ's philosophy, Lindbergh didn't seek it out in organized Christianity. He almost never reported attending worship services on his Sundays off. And when religion came to Willow Run, he found it lacking.

In July 1942, Frank Buchman arrived at the factory for a production of the Moral Re-Armament musical play, *You Can Defend America*. Originally written in 1941, it was performed by MRA volunteers for a quarter-million people in twenty-one states over the next two years. The play (and its accompanying book) called on competing factions in American society—including capital and labor—to set aside their differences and put their "Faith in a Wisdom greater than our own." The message may have seemed generically patriotic, but for the MRA presenters, writes historian Daniel Sack, "Christianity remained at the heart of American morale."[50] Lindbergh thought the play was overly sentimental, and "whoever wrote it certainly had 'a tenacious grasp of the obvious.'" He conceded that MRA workers "are definitely on the constructive side of life and deserve encouragement" and tepidly defended them against Henry Ford's criticism. But in the end, Buchman and his followers were just "sincere amateurs. . . . It is not enough to believe in *good* and to advocate *good*; one must develop a philosophy the Buchman movement is lacking."[51]

Anne Lindbergh felt much the same way, about the limits of MRA *and* the need for a "philosophy." As much as the traditional religions "offend me and estrange me," she confessed, so too did "the modern revivalist groups"—by which she meant the MRA—"with its 'quiet times,' 'been changed,' 'absolute purity' and 'guidance.'" But Christ was not Christianity. The month after their Christmas Eve service at home, the Lindberghs were in New York for a visit. Spending time among the diverse faithful streaming into St. Patrick's Cathedral reminded Anne that "there is something to a church that can take in so many different people," but she still struggled to reconcile the spiritual world ("where one can love and trust and have faith") and "another world, as C. sees it—a realer world. . . . What bridge is there, what ladder to throw across?" She thought of Jesus's most famous prayer: "'Thy kingdom come' one throws across, and yet . . ." As they walked together that night through the snow, Charles encouraged her to make such connections: "Yes, he says, there are ladders. *That* was one (Thy Kingdom come). You must try to throw one."[52]

A month later, the couple worshiped at Edwin Lodge's old church on Orchard Lake, where Charles talked to the young pastor about baptism. In April, Charles was back in New York, buying a New Testament from Brentano's: "Since I can only carry one book—and a very small one, that is my choice. It would not have been a decade ago; but the more I learn and the more I read, the less competition it has."[53] Three weeks later he was on a plane to the South Pacific, wearing an insignia-less naval officer's uniform and carrying his Scripture and his journal in his pack. Before May was out, he would see combat.

SOUTH PACIFIC

In October 1943, a young marine flier from Ohio named John Glenn was stationed at El Centro, California, when one day "every pilot's hero" arrived to introduce the squadron to the Corsair fighter-bomber. Carrying his flight helmet under one arm, Charles Lindbergh looked to the future astronaut much older than the ubiquitous old photographs of "Lucky Lindy": "His eyes had seen a lot of horizons. I couldn't say why, but he inspired in me a feeling of kinship. . . . He had lived the best and endured the worst. Now here he was, at forty-one, helping the country produce planes that would help us win the war."

Lindbergh left after a couple of days, but the two men would meet again one year later, when the older pilot joined Glenn's squadron for a couple of bombing runs against Japanese-held positions in the Marshall Islands.[54]

Ostensibly a civilian observer sent to test the Corsair, Lindbergh actually flew fifty combat missions in the South Pacific between May and September 1944. "You didn't fire your guns did you?" an agitated lieutenant colonel asked Lindbergh after a mission against Rabaul in late May. "The Japs would shoot you if they caught you."[55] Thirty years later, as he was dying of cancer, Lindbergh told Jim Newton that his clearest memories of the years before and during World War II were "not the campaign speeches, not even the years in Willow Run on the bombers." He went on, "It's the months of flying in the Pacific I remember best."[56]

Indeed, those memories inspired multiple passages in his never-finished autobiography. If he ever needed to refresh his recollections, he could open his small leather-bound journal from the time and read the tiny writing that filled page after page. Much of his diary records his assessment of the Corsair and the P-38 Lightning, as he helped the military stretch the range and capabilities of those planes. But for our purposes, three other themes stand out.

First, despite having trained in the army and written often about air power, the campaign in the South Pacific was Lindbergh's belated introduction to actual warfare. Reading *Tam O' the Scoots* as a teenager in Little Falls must have seemed impossibly distant as the forty-two-year-old Lindbergh got in a dogfight on the other side of the world. "Good," General Douglas MacArthur replied, when Lindbergh reported shooting down a Japanese observation plane. "I'm glad you got one."[57]

Never a pacifist, Lindbergh was willing to take life, but the nature of his military missions occasionally troubled him. Dropping a bomb on Kavieng from over five thousand feet, he missed the mark (an "area rather than a pinpoint target") and hit other buildings: "You press a button and death flies down. . . . If there is life where that bomb will hit, you have taken it. Yet it is still living, still breathing; the bomb is still falling, there are still seconds before it will hit. . . . The world is the same. The sky is the same. Only that column of smoke, settling now, dissipating. How can there be death down there? How can there be writhing, mangled bodies?"[58]

Combat in closer proximity was no less disturbing. As he strafed a target along a beach, Lindbergh could only "hope there was no one in that building except soldiers—no women, no children." He added, "I will never know." On the same mission, he was about to send a burst into another structure when he saw "a steeple rising through the palms" and took his finger off the trigger. "I learned later in the day that even churches are fired on in this area," he explained that night to his diary, "the Japanese are said to use them for their troops. . . . It seems that both sides can find an excuse to shoot at anything in war."[59]

Flying low over the coast of New Ireland one afternoon, Lindbergh glimpsed a man on the beach. While the standing rule was that "everything is a target—no restrictions—shoot whatever you see," Lindbergh decided that the man's "life is worth more than the pressure of a trigger." Enemy or not, the life of the unknown stranger was "worth a thousand times more to me than his death."[60]

The "unfriendly natives" of New Ireland were just some of the Pacific Islanders whose cultures Lindbergh would later celebrate as he articulated what modern Westerners could learn from "the primitive." His first such encounter, in Tuvalu, had been "both interesting and disappointing," as "close contact with the whites" had resulted in "all kinds of mixtures, from European to Oriental and African, and in most cases, the result has not been good."[61] Lindbergh never got over that concern about racial "mixtures," but visiting another village with a Catholic marine chaplain made him more sympathetic to the non-Western experience of Western empire:

> The natives have lost their natural habits and resourcefulness without gaining enough from western civilization to make up. Their wild, barbaric freedom has been taken away from them and replaced with a form of civilized slavery which leaves neither them nor us better off. The white man has brought them a religion they do not understand, diseases they are unable to combat, standards of life which leave them poverty stricken, a war which has devastated their homes and taken their families away; and they are still supposed to be grateful to us for giving them the benefits of Christianity and civilization.[62]

Before returning to the States that September, he listened to a group of Marshall Islanders sing the hymns they'd learned from Methodist missionaries—plus "two or three new ones from the Marines, including 'Pistol Packin' Mama,' which most of them sing without understanding any of the words they say."[63] While he could be condescending in his descriptions, Lindbergh began to admire peoples who depended more on nature than technology, whose cultures predated their encounter with Western Christians.

Most strikingly, he also found himself sympathizing with the same people he was ordered to kill. Again and again, his combat journals document American brutality against their Japanese enemies. When Lindbergh objected to a story of a sergeant who slit a prisoner's throat, a general responded with "tolerant scorn and pity. . . . 'The sons of bitches do it to us. It's the only way to handle them.'"[64] Before long, Lindbergh was "shocked at the attitude of our American troops. They have no respect for death, the courage of an enemy soldier, or many of the ordinary decencies of life." (One officer told him, "in half apology," that American soldiers usually kill Japanese prisoners first, and only then "kick their teeth in.")[65] "The more I see of this war in the Pacific," Lindbergh wrote after two months, "the less right I think we have to claim to be civilized." In their desire "to exterminate the Jap ruthlessly, even cruelly," his fellow Americans were blind to their own prejudice and hypocrisy:

What is courage for us is fanaticism for [our enemy]. We hold his examples of atrocity screamingly to the heavens while we cover up our own and condone them as just retribution for his acts.

A Japanese soldier who cuts off an American soldier's head is an Oriental barbarian, "lower than a rat." An American soldier who slits a Japanese throat "did it only because he knew the Japs had done it to his buddies." I do not question that Oriental atrocities are often worse than ours. But, after all, we are constantly telling ourselves, and everyone else who will listen to us, that we are the upholders of all that is "good" and "right" and civilized.[66]

Lindbergh was an eyewitness to what historian John Dower called a "war without mercy," but he couldn't fully recognize that the same racialized worldview underpinning his understanding of the "quality of life" also accounted for the brutality of death in the Pacific.[67]

"THE BEAM THAT IS IN THINE OWN EYE"

In a war that killed tens of millions, two individual losses hit the Lindberghs particularly hard. Three days after Charles shot down a Japanese plane while flying a P-38 in the South Pacific, Antoine de Saint-Exupéry disappeared while flying the same type of aircraft over the Mediterranean. "Charles is earth to me," wrote Anne after her husband's return, "the whole world, life. St.-Ex. was not earth but he was a sun or a moon or stars which light earth, which make the whole world and life more beautiful. Now the earth is unlit and it is no longer so beautiful. I go ahead in it stumbling and without joy."[68]

Then in early November, Saint-Exupéry's fellow French Catholic, Alexis Carrel, died of a heart attack in Paris. He had lived to see the Liberation but was dogged by accusations that he had collaborated with the Germans. His widow blamed such critics for his illness: "Mortally wounded by the calumnies of certain envious people, [his heart] could not resist the malice of those who caused his death. He accepted it with full knowledge and with the serenity of a Christian."[69] In words that could have described himself as much as Carrel, Lindbergh penned this about his friend: "[He] loved his country as dearly as any man I have ever met, but whose love did not blind him to its weaknesses and dangers. He foresaw, years in advance, the abyss toward which his country was headed, toward which all European men were headed, and tried in his own way to warn of it. Now, the men he warned, the men who scoffed at him, the men who laughed at him, the men whose indifference, weakness, and corruption caused the downfall of France, these men call him a traitor."[70]

After the war, Lindbergh wrote a preface to Carrel's posthumously published account of the miracles at Lourdes.[71] "While the loss of other friends sensitized Lindbergh," concludes Scott Berg, "Carrel's death spiritualized him, leading him to question, as Carrel had most of his life, the relationship between science and religion."[72]

In April 1945, a more famous death left Lindbergh feeling cold: not Adolf Hitler's suicide, but Franklin Roosevelt's cerebral hemorrhage. "I have not been one of those, of whom there are so many, who wished the President to die," Lindbergh insisted to his diary. But if he hadn't longed for such an end to the longest presidency in American history, it wasn't out of any fondness for FDR: "I had hoped he might live long enough to see clearly the disastrous results of his intrigues and his dishonesty. After a man is dead, you try to forgive his weaknesses and remember his strengths—the things you admire about his life. Every man, I believe, has certain qualities you can respect. Usually, they are not too difficult to discover. But it is difficult for me to find these qualities in the Presidents [*sic*] background. It will take time and more tolerance than I am yet able to feel."[73]

Walking with Truman Smith a few days later, Lindbergh hoped that future leadership would reverse aspects of the New Deal and "encourage the reproduction of the best Americans. . . . But if our policies encourage the reproduction of our less able groups, nothing we do can save our race and civilization."[74]

Whatever he thought of its other policies, Lindbergh found the Truman administration much more willing to call upon his services. Four days after V-E Day, he flew across the Atlantic once more, this time as a passenger: a civilian member of the Naval Technical Mission sent to investigate German military technology.

Lindbergh had hoped that his first flight across the Atlantic would pave the way for greater international cooperation. Not even twenty years later, he now saw another legacy of the airplane, as he toured a country devastated by years of strategic bombing. The "ruined walls and rubble" of Mannheim reminded him "of a Dali painting, which in its feel of hellish death so typifies the excessive abnormality of our age—death without dignity, creation without God."[75] In Nuremberg's "gutted" cathedral, Lindbergh noticed a carving of Jesus intact, "looking down on the rubble which covers the benches where people once came to worship." He felt "surrounded by death. Only in the sky is there hope; only in that which man has never touched and God forbid he ever will."[76]

A visit to Hitler's headquarters at Berchtesgaden made Lindbergh think of the dictator "who in a few years threw the human world into the greatest convulsion it has ever known and from which it will be recuperating for generations. . . . Hitler, a man who controlled such power, who might have turned it to human good, who used it to such resulting evil."[77] But Lindbergh didn't begin to grasp the extent of Nazi wickedness until he visited Nordhausen, where V-2 rockets were produced in an underground factory. (Members of the Naval Technical Mission interviewed Wernher von Braun and other German rocket scientists who would go on to help the United States compete in its "space race" with the Soviet Union.) The factory relied on slave labor from Dora-Mittelbau, which started as a satellite of Buchenwald but grew into an independent concentration camp. One-third of Camp Dora's sixty thousand prisoners died in the process, victims of starvation, disease, overwork, beatings, and torture. Hundreds were executed for trying to sabotage the factory, and others perished on forced marches to Bergen-Belsen. One of Dora's SS officers, Auschwitz veteran Hans Möser, was hanged after a war crimes trial; seven others were sentenced to life imprisonment.

Lindbergh toured Dora on June 11 and was immediately overwhelmed by "the depressing mass-production horror of the place." Seeing the "walking skeleton" of a Polish survivor and a pit filled with ashes from the two cremation furnaces prompted Lindbergh to opine: "Of course, I knew these things were going on; but it is one thing to have the intellectual knowledge, even to look at photographs someone else has taken, and quite another to stand on the scene yourself, seeing, hearing, feeling with your own senses."[78]

But if Lindbergh could no longer avoid the true nature of the Nazi regime, he could deny that it was *particularly* evil. Even the ash pit "is not a thing confined to any nation or to any people. What the German has done to the Jew in Europe, we are doing to the Jap in the Pacific." His diary records images of Camp Dora alongside recollections of the brutality he had seen in the Pacific, then his mind reaches back through human history and finds that "these atrocities have been going on, not only in Germany with its Dachaus and its Buchenwalds and its Camp Doras, but in Russia, in the Pacific, in the riotings and lynchings at home, in the less-publicized uprisings in Central and South America, the cruelties of China, a few years ago in Spain, in pogroms of the past, the burning of witches in New England, tearing people apart on the English rack, burnings at the stake for the benefit of Christ and God."[79]

As he read it during the war, the Bible didn't give Lindbergh a way of explaining, changing, or redeeming such sinful behavior. But he did find in the New Testament an excuse not to judge the perpetrators of the Holocaust. For the first time, his diary quoted Jesus: "And why beholdest thou the mote that is in thy brother's eye but considerest not the beam that is in thine own eye?" (Matt. 7:3).

CHAPTER ELEVEN

Beyond Flight

Can we do what no people have done before; can we pass
the test of the Christian code? That requires charity, humility
and compassion that are lacking all over this post-war world
. . . without these qualities, there can be no security, as the
Germans learned. Without them, we simply sow the wind
with our aircraft and our bombs.

–Charles Lindbergh (December 17, 1945)[1]

AVIATION HAD MADE A DIFFERENCE in the war, just not the one
that Charles Lindbergh predicted. Thanks to prewar reports like
his, the American military believed that the Luftwaffe was many times as
strong as it actually was, and American industry responded accordingly,
producing tens of thousands of cutting-edge planes. By the last year of
the war the Allies ruled the skies, their aircraft covering armies advancing
toward cities bombed into rubble. "Air power did not win the war on its
own," concluded historian Richard Overy, "but it proved to be the critical
weakness on the Axis side and the greatest single advantage enjoyed by
the Allies."[2]

As the United States prepared for conflict with its former ally, the Soviet Union, the airplane remained a symbol of both national strength and
international reconciliation. In 1949, during the nation's annual celebration of the Wright brothers' first flight, a letter from President Truman
declared that "it is for us to use the instrument they gave us as a force for
peace; to make the peoples of the world spiritual neighbors as well as
physical neighbors." Planes would still carry bombs—far more destructive
bombs than those that had demolished Mannheim and Nuremberg—but

Truman yearned to see those same machines used "for travel, for pleasure, for commerce and for all the peaceful pursuits that make up our daily lives."[3]

This hope has never disappeared. Introducing his recent book on Lindbergh's 1927 flight, former air force officer and aviation writer Dan Hampton asserted, "Above all else, Charles Lindbergh believed in the power of aviation: its untapped potential and inherent capacity to join peoples, advance technology, and bring the world closer together. That passion and courage define a spirit that all Americans can claim through Charles Lindbergh and that we, as humans, can collectively share."[4]

Perhaps that was the conviction of the young pilot who flew from New York to Paris, but the middle-aged man who had killed a fellow pilot in the South Pacific and toured the ruins of German cities held a far more complicated assessment of the technology that had made his name. "The war had a great sobering effect on his idealism about aviation," Anne Lindbergh said of her husband on the fiftieth anniversary of the Paris flight. "He was terribly shocked by the destruction aviation had brought to the world."[5]

As he entered the third act of his life, Charles Lindbergh still believed that the airplane could promote peace—and, if necessary, wage war against "godless Communism." "Today," he accepted in 1949, "whether it be for peace or war, we westerners depend on wings."[6] But he now warned of the danger of scientific research and technological development unrestrained by the ethical guidance to be found in the world's religions. He still kept his distance from institutional faith. But having long "regarded the fear of knowledge as ignorant superstition," Lindbergh now repeated a dire Scripture: "But of the tree of knowledge . . . thou shalt not eat of it; for in the day that thou eatest thereof thou shalt surely die" (Gen. 2:17).[7]

"The Monster They Have Created"

Already sobered by his tour of Germany, Lindbergh was horrified to read of the aerial attacks that ended the war with Japan. "Implications staggering," he scrawled in his diary the day an American B-29 dropped an atomic bomb on Hiroshima.[8] Even two years later, as he circled that city in a transport plane, he saw that "a huge gray saucer marks the blasted, radiated, and heat-shrivelled earth of Hiroshima. . . . Within that gray saucer, sixty thousand men, women, and children, were killed; sixty thousand more were burned and mangled. A hundred and twenty thousand casualties, from a single bomb!" How could such "gifts of God, works of men . . . have passed through the excrutiating [sic] horror of that August day, in 1945?"[9]

When Lindbergh returned to Detroit in September 1945 for a meeting with Henry Ford II, he started to articulate how atomic power "might easily bring the end of our civilization."

> This is, I think, the most dangerous and important discovery ever made by man. Some compare it to the discovery of fire, but the discovery of fire was limited in effect by the scientific ignorance of pre-historic man; it took him generations—centuries—to learn its use. His greatest error would result in a forest fire or the cruel death of a handful of his enemies. And what was that in comparison to the atomic bomb, which, in the first crude instance of its use, kills and maims hundreds of thousands of men, women, and children—the control of atomic energy thrust into the midst of a warring, hating, covetous, atheistic world, a world skilled in scientific developments, experienced in killing grasping for new weapons of destruction with which to build more influence and power?

As he recorded University of Chicago president Robert M. Hutchins joining the meeting, Lindbergh again asked himself, "Will this idol of scientific knowledge bring an end to our civilization and atheistic man?" He admitted sometimes thinking that "we deserve such punishment."[10]

But Lindbergh also believed that "the atomic projectile can be combated only by learning more about it," and he didn't want America to leave that tool "for the hands of our enemies." Invited to Chicago by Hutchins for a conference on atomic energy, Lindbergh pondered a Carrel-like question: "Will man finally, in some unforeseen way, gain control of science and use it to enrich his spiritual life? God only knows."[11] The scientists he met in Chicago seemed to grasp the heavy responsibility they carried, but they "feel rather frustrated and helpless in the light of their knowledge of the monster they have created. They themselves are not ammoral [sic], but they are caught in an ammoral force."[12]

That December he began to make public his reservations about the future of flight, in a Wright Day address to the Aero Club of Washington. "It is only 42 years" since the brothers' *Flyer* first took to the skies, but it seemed to Lindbergh "that it must have been centuries ago." Alluding to his experiences in the South Pacific and Germany, he found "something incongruous in picturing that fragile and harmless craft in the same frame with the terrific detonation of bombs and millions of tons of rubble." In the end, he was "fearful of the use of power. . . . History is full of its misuse. There is no better example than Nazi Germany. Power without a moral force to guide it, invariably ends in the destruction of the people who wield it." At a celebration of a bishop's sons, he argued that power must be guided

> by the qualities represented in Christian ideals. To those who say that such ideals are impractical, let us point out the failure of the Hitlerian regime. The philosophy of Christ may have been too intangible for the Nazi government to understand, but the rubble of Berlin is a sufficiently tangible result of their failure. . . . Christian ideals may in one sense seem a far cry from the subject of aviation on which you invited me to speak. But in a deeper sense, they affect every industry and every action. They cannot be left alone to church and clergy. They must live in the philosophy of a nation, in the policies of a world organization, in the use of science and its great inventions. They enter into the pressure of the red button that drops a bomb. They are as essential to the foundations of New York and Washington as they were to those of Berlin and Nurenburg [*sic*].

"We [Americans] are a Christian people," Lindbergh concluded. But the future of his people's civilization depended not "on technical progress" alone, but on how that progress was guided by Christian ideals.[13] Three years later, Lindbergh developed those ideas in print, via a little-remembered book that ran just over fifty pages in length.

OF FLIGHT AND LIFE

At first glance, *Of Flight and Life* is the Cold War artifact that one might expect Lindbergh to have produced in the year of the Marshall Plan and

Berlin Airlift. The same anti-interventionist who had warned that Russia was a greater threat than Germany now declared that there had been no real victory in Europe: "Stalin now holds most of what we fought to keep Hitler from obtaining. . . . We have stamped out the menace of Nazi Germany only to find that we have created the still greater menace of Soviet Russia, behind whose 'Iron Curtain' lies a record of bloodshed and oppression never equalled."[14] Aware of Lindbergh's disdain for Communism, Methodist pastor Abraham Vereide tried to recruit him into the Fellowship, a network of Christian businessmen and politicians he had started in 1935 to stop Washington from becoming "the first Sovietized State of the Union." (The same group later became the subject of Jeff Sharlet's 2008 exposé, *The Family*, and the 2019 Netflix series by the same title.)[15]

The Manichaean overtones of the early Cold War suited Charles Lindbergh. As she listened to her husband talk with diplomat George Kennan in 1954, Anne Lindbergh appreciated that the architect of America's strategy of containing the Soviet Union had a mind that sought "truth in all its shifting subtle gradations of gray." By contrast, she realized that Charles "is looking for a black and white truth—which means that he has a preconceived notion of truth, an axe to grind somewhere (though often it is hidden)."[16] It was a perceptive insight from the person who knew Charles Lindbergh best—and was finding it easier to name his faults.

Committed as he was to containing Communism, Lindbergh served as a consultant to the US Air Force and a test pilot for its Strategic Air Command, whose bombers carried the atomic weapons meant to deter Soviet aggression.[17] But he had not abandoned his concerns about the atomic age. As he explained those fears in *Of Flight and Life*, the book revealed how far Lindbergh had come in his spiritual journey. "While we preached Christian doctrines in our churches," Lindbergh had complained during World War II, "our government allied us with the godless cause of Communism."[18] But from its start, *Of Flight and Life* warned that the capitalist West had entered the Cold War in service to another "godless cause": "We are in the grip of a scientific materialism. . . . I believe the values we are creating and the standards we are now following will lead to the end of our civilization, and that if we do not control our science by a higher moral force, it will destroy us with its materialistic values, its rocket aircraft, and its atom bombs—as it has already destroyed large parts of Europe."[19]

Experimenting with the flashback device that he would use more extensively five years later in *The Spirit of St. Louis,* Lindbergh began *Of Flight and Life* with three wartime vignettes. While his memory of flying a P-38 in a dogfight with Japanese Zeros taught him "that without a highly developed science modern man lacks the power to survive," the memory of losing oxygen during a test flight in Michigan taught him "that in worshipping science man gains power but loses the quality of life." Having once seen Willow Run "as a marvelous feat of engineering," it now "seemed a terrible giant's womb, growling, clanging, giving birth to robots which were killing people by the thousands each day as they destroyed the culture of Europe." Henry Ford's bomber factory had become for Lindbergh "a temple of the god of science at which we moderns worshipped" (9–10, 14).

How to reconcile these two lessons? Lindbergh's third memory—of ruined German cities—taught him "that if his civilization is to continue, modern man must direct the material power of his science by the spiritual truths of his God." In the collapse of German civilization—"one which was basically our own, stemming from the same Christian beliefs"—he saw more clearly the fragility of an empire that had trusted "scientific truth, unbalanced by the truths of religion.... In Germany, the truths of science and the truths of religion had clashed, and religion remained to teach its ancient lesson" (19–21).

Having grown up "as a disciple of science" and having "felt the godlike power man derives from his machines," Lindbergh now asked why humanity should "work for the idol of science when it demands the sacrifice of cities full of children; when it makes robots out of men and blinds their eyes to God" (49–51)? As a child, Lindbergh found "the ever-present truths of God . . . veiled by dogma and convention"; as an adult, Lindbergh decided that the key was not so much belief as balance: "science untempered by religion" was as great a threat to Western civilization as the unscientific religion that "brought the un-Christian tortures of the Middle Ages" (40, 50).

He thought that the wisdom needed to restrain and guide science could be found in many religions, including "the wisdom of Laotzu"— quoted more than once— "the teachings of Buddha . . . the Bible of the Hebrews, in the philosophy of Greece, in the Indian Vedas," and in other mystical and spiritual sources (55). But the central figure in *Of Flight and Life* is Jesus Christ, whom Lindbergh quotes several times: for example, "Seek, and ye shall find" (Matt. 7:7); "They that take the sword shall perish with the sword" (Matt. 26:52). Warning that science uncontrolled by morality risked becoming "the Antichrist prophesied by early Christians," Lindbergh insisted the "spirit of Christ" joined "the mind of science" and "the bodily inheritance of farmers and pioneers" (like Lindbergh's grandfather) in giving "western man . . . a balance unequalled by any civilization in the past" (41, 43). Six years later, accepting the Guggenheim Medal from the Institute of Aeronautical Sciences, Lindbergh reiterated that "the sermons of Christ become as essential as the steel of Bessemer to our power."[20]

Critics were unsure what to make of Lindbergh's fusion of anti-Communism, atomic anxiety, and spiritual rumination. In the *New York Herald Tribune*, where *Of Flight and Life* shared a page with Thomas Merton's *Seven Storey Mountain*, reviewer Harry Baehr affirmed Lindbergh's core critique of uncontrolled science but found his lack of specific religious instruction "disquieting."[21] Describing Lindbergh as "a sort of eclectic in his present phase of religious development," the *Catholic World* lamented "his failure to see the close relationship between moral ideals and doctrines."[22] *Time* concluded that "many Christians may find that Lindbergh's Christianity has a chilling, impersonal, antiseptic quality."[23]

Some Christians did. Paluel Flagg, the Catholic anesthesiologist who had introduced Lindbergh to Alexis Carrel, told Lindbergh he was depressed by the "sweeping generalizations and confusing philosophies which [Lindbergh accepts] under the generic term spirituality."[24] Serge Gluhareff, who designed aircraft with Igor Sikorsky, hoped that Lindbergh, having realized "the present difficulties we have in our scientific and materialistic age," would take the next step: "to admit and to accept the wonderful gift of God in Christ through Whom alone we can be saved, from such present life, for all eternity."[25]

But other followers of Jesus were heartened to hear Lindbergh speaking in even vaguely Christian terms. The editor of a magazine for Methodist clergy thought that *Of Flight and Life* "contains material that should stimulate a number of preachers to write prophetic sermons," and an Indiana pastor with the Disciples of Christ (Lindbergh's great-grandfather's tradition) called it "the book of the year if not the book of our era." He went on, "I have been trying to say many of the same things without the literary genius or practical experience which you possess."[26] A missionary for the United Brethren Church (the Wright brothers' home denomination) wrote, after reading the book, "You live close to God." He was sure that the aviator was "serving Him as truly and perhaps more effectively than many of us who are having credit from our fellowmen for a life of full-time Christian Service."[27]

Among his friends, it was the scientists who found Lindbergh's book most "chilling." Dana Atchley, a physician friend of the Lindberghs, insisted that he didn't "worship science" but did believe that "there is no higher human activity in the intellectual realm than the disinterested search for knowledge and understanding characteristic of most of the scientists" he knew. Though "spiritual seeking" could help humanity cultivate emotional intelligence, Atchley trusted psychiatry more than religion to guide that process.[28] Astronomer Walter Bartky, who had gotten to know Lindbergh from his visits to the University of Chicago, defended science against the pilot's allegation that it had become a false idol: "What better mode of worship than to seek to find out, in order to appreciate the glories of God's handiwork, His creation? That's the chief end of the scientific man." Bartky intentionally echoed the Presbyterian catechism that Dwight Morrow had memorized as a child: *What is the chief end of man? Man's chief end is to glorify God, and to enjoy him forever.*[29] "That's just what the scientist does," said Bartky's wife, Elizabeth, "even though he doesn't postulate a God."[30]

Reading drafts of what became *Of Flight and Life*, Anne Morrow Lindbergh warned her husband that "a lot of men of science are going to feel a fist in the face here" and nudged him to draw a distinction between scientists in general and "the idolatrous scientist—the complete disciple."[31] Perhaps she thought of her own visit to the University of Chicago, where she met physicist Enrico Fermi. "Is the scientist—the true scientist—akin to the artist & the saint?" Anne asked her diary. "In his humility before something greater than himself—in his looking on himself as a tool—a vessel—a road? In his childlikeness—in his simplicity? I had not thought so before, but Fermi makes me think of it."[32]

QUALITY VERSUS EQUALITY

"Don't be offended," Walter Bartky told Lindbergh, "but you sound like Robert Hutchins, who believes in the Antichrist and who sounds awfully like Savonarola"—the fiery Dominican preacher who had sparked a religious revolution in Renaissance Florence. In truth, Bartky's boss had one strong objection to *Of Flight and Life*: not its critique of science, but a different claim buried in the middle of Lindbergh's book. It was a fragment of his unpublished "appeal to a minority" that had survived a decade of rewriting: "We cannot escape the fact that our civilization was built, and still depends, upon the *quality* rather than the *equality* of men."[33]

In *Of Flight and Life*, Lindbergh's older defense of "the white race" gave way to concern for "Western civilization." Yet he still feared that, under a powerful United Nations, "the high birth-rates of ignorance would outvote the low birth-rates of education, and the weapons of western science, from aircraft to the atomic bomb, would be controlled by the desires of the East." (Jim Newton warned his friend that Stalin—"Oriental Georgian Joe"—would take this passage "'out of context'—and circulate [it] widely among the orientals to show 'our' intentions versus 'his' benevolent care and identification for and with them.") For a Western nation like America, Lindbergh still insisted that "the doctrine of universal equality is a doctrine of death." ("Remind you of anything?" asked the *New Yorker*.) "If we ever become an equal people among the other peoples of the world," Lindbergh concluded, "our civilization will fall—and our equality with it."[34]

Warning that America's superpower status in the Cold War had to rest on its "moral and spiritual leadership," Hutchins chided Lindbergh at this point: "I venture to think that you over-simplify the doctrine of equality in your attack on it. . . . It is very hard for me to accept any theory that implies that some nations or some races are better than others. As I have said, some have certainly been luckier than others. But none have been so unlucky or so lucky as to lose its essential likeness to all other branches of the human race."

Hutchins took particular issue with Lindbergh's fears of "the desires of the East." For example, "the reasons why the Chinese are not as powerful and have not as good a form of government . . . seem to me largely accidental, rather than inherent."[35]

The tension between equality and "quality of life" was already a sticking point between the two acquaintances. In 1946 Hutchins had passed along his text for that year's commencement address, in which he argued that "the brotherhood of man must rest on the fatherhood of God. If God is denied, or man's spiritual nature is denied, then the basis of community disappears. . . . Unless we believe that every man is a child of God, we cannot love our neighbors."[36] In response, Lindbergh confessed, "In the interpretation of spiritual truth, I find myself at variance with many of the accepted ideas of the times. I cannot see, for instance, the element of spiritual truth in the concept of human equality. It seems to me that the laws of God are always emphasizing the quality of life, not its equality. Here, I believe, is the basic question facing those of us who believe in God and who search honestly for His way."[37] Before the war or after it, the more that Lindbergh thought about God, the less he celebrated equality.

He finally responded to Hutchins's critique of *Of Flight and Life* in a 1952 letter: "I don't know whether the eyes of God find the Chinese or the Russians equal, better or worse than the Americans. But I do know that the system God created on this earth (unless the devil got the better of him) gives every people a chance to build a better way of life than their competitors."[38] The following week, Lindbergh wrote to the British anthropologist Arthur Keith, whose *New Theory of Human Evolution* came out the same year as *Of Flight and Life*. Among other compliments, Lindbergh thanked Keith for his "emphasis of man's competetive [*sic*] nature" and the skill with which he brought "the word 'race' into the tolerant perspective of its proper meaning." He went on, "I am convinced that our fuzzy ideological thinking along these lines threatens our entire western civilization."[39]

About the same time, Lindbergh began to make regular donations to the American Eugenics Society, hoping to encourage American schools to "teach human genetics and heredity in a manner which will encourage the application of our scientific knowledge to our every-day lives."[40] In 1955 Lindbergh joined the board of an organization that was in the middle of overhauling its image. At the end of that year, the editor of *Eugenics Quarterly* reported an ongoing struggle to distance the science of genetics from "a social movement supporting heredity clinics, etc. The shadows of the racists still inhibit the development of this field."[41] Never more than a passive member of the board, Lindbergh resigned his seat in 1959, but he continued to make donations until his death fifteen years later.

"Home-Churched"

In October 1945, Anne Lindbergh gave birth to a daughter named Reeve. "This is the end," she told herself. "You will never have to do this again." But two years later she discovered that she was pregnant again. Anne agonized over Dana Atchley's suggestion that an abortion, though illegal, would be "completely justified." "Could I say no to a child," she wondered, "to that act of God which had been the greatest experience in my life, from which I learned the most?" It was in bearing children, she thought, that she had most profoundly experienced the Christian idea of incarnation: "The Word was made flesh" (John 1:14). But after deciding to go through with a seventh pregnancy at age forty-one, she miscarried. "I took it as a pure act of mercy from God," she wrote, and "perhaps a warning to me—before it is too late—that 'I must be about my Father's business' [Luke 2:49, KJV]. This is now the task, to find out what it is—for me—my special task."[42]

Anne would soon wrestle with her "instinct as a woman—the eternal nourisher of children, of men, of society."[43] But in the postwar years, she believed that at least part of her "Father's business" was to be a mother, responsible for five children—including their spiritual nurture.

The Lindberghs settled into a house on the Connecticut coast, where her nurse told Reeve that the "stained pink hearts" in the white flowers of a dogwood tree "were left over from the blood of Jesus," but Reeve didn't believe it.[44] More keenly attuned to the spiritual journeys of her parents than any other observer, the Lindberghs' youngest child later reflected that she and her siblings "were raised to be familiar with the spiritual writings and traditions of many religions, but we felt embarrassment about officially attaching ourselves to any religious practice, as if to do so would be pretentious. It may be that for my famous parents during our childhood years, joining a church, like joining a country club, would have risked unwanted attention and publicity. Better to have the Lindbergh children home-churched, as so many children are now homeschooled."[45]

Neither Lindbergh parent thought it appropriate to catechize their children into a particular faith, but being "home-churched" included

Bible stories from Anne, and the family's "little Christmas Eve service" remained a yearly ritual. "I wish Jesus had never grown up," nine-year-old Reeve regretted as she looked at the baby in the crèche in December 1954.[46] Chatting years later with a national guard chaplain who was born to missionaries in China, Reeve realized that that woman's Jesus was the one of her own childhood: "blue-eyed and surrounded by lambs and children, with nothing but love and forgiveness in his message."[47]

In January 1955 the family attended the funeral for Anne's mother, who had sometimes taken the Lindbergh children to the Presbyterian church near the Morrows' summer residence in Maine.[48] Elizabeth Cutter Morrow's memorial service included one of Anne's favorite prayers from Augustine of Hippo: "I behold how some things pass away that others may replace them, but Thou dost never depart, O God, my Father, supremely good. Beauty of all things beautiful, to Thee will I entrust whatsoever I have received from Thee, and so I shall lose nothing."[49]

Reeve's other grandmother had died of Parkinson's disease the year before. We know little of that funeral service, save that it was held at the church on Orchard Lake.[50] But Reeve recorded a different kind of liturgy from not long before, when her father brought her to Michigan for a visit. Hands trembling, Evangeline insisted that Charles feed them each a malted milk tablet. Years later Reeve could still smell the writerly scent of his palm ("pencil shavings and carbon paper"), from which, she said, "in some studied and angular priesthood . . . my father administered communion to three generations of his family that day in Detroit, with malted milk tablets."[51]

She also learned to use Christian language to describe the sensation of flying with America's most famous pilot: "There would be a rushing in my ears, in spite of the cotton, and as I looked over my father's head through the front window of the aircraft I would imagine that we were forcing our way right into heaven, higher and higher through ever more brilliantly white banks of cloud. I sometimes daydreamed of bumping into angels, or startling Saint Peter at his pearly gates, or God Himself in his sanctuary."[52]

But for all such moments of quiet poignance and joyous exhilaration, Reeve chiefly remembered the 1950s as "the iron years. The color of his hair was like iron, and the discipline he administered was like iron: unbending, with stern lectures and occasional spankings." (Her sister Anne called Charles Lindbergh's parental anger the "Ambulatory Wrath of God.") Reeve didn't forget how much she loved him, "always, no matter how scary he sometimes seemed," nor that her family "felt only half complete without him," as his never-ending travels continued. But she also recalled "the relief and relaxation that settled like a kind of warmth over the household when he went away and our mother was once again in gentle command."[53]

FINDING GRACE IN "THE MOST DIFFICULT TIME"

As close as Anne and Charles's marriage had been during the war, it frayed in the years that followed. Anne wrote to her absent husband the week before Christmas 1947, saying, "[I still] would rather have you think me 'a good girl' than be right myself."[54] But just two years later she marked their twentieth wedding anniversary by rewriting her vows as a kind of prayer:

> Since I know you are not perfect, I do not worship you. I have learned that worship of another human being is only a form of shirking one's responsibility, a shifting of the burden to another's shoulders. (I cannot accomplish this difficult task but you, O Superior Being, can do all!) Worship, I believe, is a burden too great for the human frame to bear and in the end is degrading to both the worshipper and the worshipped. On this earth one is permitted only to worship God. . . . I promise then to respect you, to honor you as one of God's representatives on earth. I honor the spark of the divine in you. I will believe in this spark, even when I cannot see it, even when it is obscured, in sickness and in health, in poverty and in riches. I believe in it now and until—and after—Death us do part.[55]

Anne began to see a therapist, and while she destroyed much of the material related to those sessions, they were clearly a source of significant tension between her and Charles. Other letters and diary entries from the time hint at an affair with Dana Atchley.[56] Anne later told Reeve that the most difficult time in her life with her husband was not after the murder of

Charles Jr. but after the war, when she had promised herself that "if things did not get better" by the time Reeve turned ten years old, that is, October 1955, she would leave Charles.[57]

But Anne and Charles Lindbergh stayed together. "Despite my father's frequent disappearances," Reeve concluded, "I have an unmistakable sense of the strong and interdependent partnership my parents shared, however strained their connection at certain periods and however deeply my father's absences impacted their union." She suspected that the time apart "made the marriage and our family life possible," that two such deeply thoughtful individuals needed moments of solitude. But when it came time to put their thoughts in writing, Charles and Anne relied upon each other. As she thought about her parents "sitting side by side, pencils in hand and a manuscript before them, discussing, marking, editing, and proofreading, talking back and forth for hours on end," Reeve recognized that "in this work they were equals, professionals, as they had been a team when they were pilots charting air routes: Charles and Anne Lindbergh, together."[58] The time of greatest crisis for their marriage was also the time when the two Lindberghs wrote their greatest, most deeply spiritual, books.

In 1955, Anne published *Gift from the Sea*, a beautiful meditation on seeking "to live 'in grace' as much of the time as possible." Not grace "in a strictly theological sense," but as an expression "of inner harmony, essentially spiritual, which can be translated into outward harmony," functioning and giving as she was meant to "in the eye of God."[59] Though I found my copy on a bookstore's "Christian Inspiration" shelf, *Gift from the Sea* can sound post-Christian. Anne still regarded the church as "a great centering force for men and women, more needed than ever before," but she doubted that "a single weekly hour of church, helpful as it may be," could stand up to the distractions of modern life. Contemplation was required for balance—even a single, solitary hour to herself "in worship, in prayer, in communion"—but such spiritual practice existed apart from the structures and authorities of religion.[60]

For all her allusions to Christian Scripture, theology, and spiritual tradition, Anne came to believe that grace could be found in the wisdom of multiple religions, in poetry and music, and, maybe above all, in nature. "Beauty of earth and sea and air meant more to me," she realized, after time alone on a beach, whose beauty she described by reimagining Psalm 148: "I was in harmony with it, melted into the universe, lost in it, as one is lost in a canticle of praise, swelling from an unknown crowd in a cathedral, 'Praise ye the Lord, all ye fishes of the sea—all ye birds of the air—all ye children of men—Praise ye the Lord!'"[61]

That sense of melting "into the universe," of experiencing the divine in the mundane and sublime beauty of nature, would feature as prominently in Charles Lindbergh's postwar writing as in his wife's.

Indeed, some suspected that she had ghostwritten his next book. It wasn't true, but in dedicating *The Spirit of St. Louis* to her, he did suspect that she "will never realize how much of this book she has written." Privately, Anne agreed: her editing may have "added to the *perfection* of the book." But, she added, it was "not as important as those twenty years of living with me—slowly changing & opening, sharpening his perceptions, his articulateness, his aesthetic & spiritual sensitivities."[62]

The Spiritual Side of *The Spirit of St. Louis*

Of Flight and Life had sold well enough that its publisher, Charles Scribner, was delighted to hear two years later that Charles Lindbergh "might eventually have another book." In fact, the pilot had been writing *The Spirit of St. Louis* for more than a decade and was nearly finished. When Scribner released it in 1953, Lindbergh's memoir of his flight to Paris became an instant sensation, tapping into what Brian Horrigan calls "a deep reservoir of nostalgia" among readers who had grown up alongside Lindbergh and, like him, "matured through their experiences in World War II."[63]

Though it offered an undeniably exciting account of a still-stunning achievement, *The Spirit of St. Louis* was much more than a page-turner. It revealed "for the first time," said one enthralled reviewer, "the character of this least known and most publicized man of his generation."[64] When Reeve Lindbergh finally read her father's best book, she was surprised to realize that *The Spirit of St. Louis* "wasn't about an airplane, after all. It was about a boy's relationship to the land, where he grew up, and to the sky, where he came of age.... It was the story of a thrilling and dangerous adventure and a revolutionary transformation of vision."[65]

That transformation, and the intellectual adventure of the book, is clearest in what could have been the book's dullest section. As the thirty-three hours from New York to Paris pass by in a series of vivid flashbacks and probing meditations, it becomes clear that the "spirit" of the book's title refers to far more than the name of a plane.

Not quite halfway through the flight, Lindbergh looks around the "weird, unhuman space" of a cloud formation—"this sacred garden of the sky, this inner shrine of higher spirits"—and wonders, "Am I really dead, a spirit in a spirit world? Am I actually in a plane boring through the air, over the Atlantic, toward Paris, or have I crashed on some worldly mountain, and is this the afterlife?"[66] Seven hours later, the appearance of the "ghostly presences"—"emissaries from a spirit world"—confirms for Lindbergh that he's "on the border line of life and a greater realm beyond." As "death no longer seems the final end it used to be," he has to ask, "Am I now more man or spirit?"[67] Such questions would preoccupy him the rest of his life. After Lindbergh finished that memoir and began another, he ruminated on a question raised by Buddhism: "Does the soul look back upon its body as I now look back upon my plane?—as an outer shell—a convenient tool for material accomplishments, but an encumbrance to the essential values of existence."[68]

As surprising as such passages must have been to Lindbergh's fans, _The Spirit of St. Louis_ also echoed the philosophy of the book that preceded it. The preface repeated Lindbergh's now-familiar warning that "the aircraft, to which we devoted our lives, [was] destroying the civilization that created them." And he emphasized that technological advances pose spiritual, not just material, threats: "Is aviation too arrogant? I don't know. Sometimes, flying feels too godlike to be attained by man. . . . Is that true of all things we call human progress—do the gods retire as commerce and science advance?"[69]

But his own experience had followed the opposite trajectory: the more he learned about science, the closer God appeared. In a pair of childhood flashbacks, he revealed how he became what _Of Flight and Life_ had called a "disciple of science" from whom God's truths "were veiled by dogma and convention." But after recounting his uncomfortable first visit to church in Little Falls and then reminiscing about the delights of his grandfather's laboratory in Detroit, Lindbergh finally offered a definitive answer to his earliest theological question: "Is there a God?"

It's hard to be an agnostic up here in the *Spirit of St. Louis*, aware of the frailty of man's devices, a part of the universe between its earth and stars. If one dies, all this goes on existing in a plan so perfectly balanced, so wonderfully simple, so incredibly complex that it's far beyond our comprehension—worlds and moons revolving; planets orbiting on suns; suns flung with apparent recklessness through space. There's the infinite magnitude of the universe; there's the infinite detail of its matter—the outer star, the inner atom. And man conscious of it all—a worldly audience to what if not to God?[70]

In a *Saturday Evening Post* profile meant to help publicize the book, Deak Lyman presented his old friend as "a man of deeply held religious feeling."[71]

Of course, Lindbergh was actually one of "the hundred million" Americans that the Maryknoll Catholic priest James Keller claimed were disconnected from organized religion in the aftermath of World War II. As staunchly anti-Communist as Lindbergh, Keller was dedicated to evangelizing his nonreligious countrymen, who were "living off the benefits of Christianity, but who are becoming less and less conscious of the great Christian fundamentals that make possible their present way of life."[72]

Indeed, in 1954 Lindbergh shared doubts that alarmed some Christian readers, in an article published in the same magazine in which Lyman had testified to his friend's religiosity. Lindbergh's first sustained public reflection on his experience in the South Pacific, "Thoughts of a Combat Pilot," soon arrived at a theological problem that had long bothered Anne: "If God has the power over man claimed by his Disciples, why does He permit the strafing of churches and the atrocities of war? How can one return from battle and believe that an all-powerful God desires 'peace on earth, good will toward men'? One questions the extent of God's power. One questions the very existence of God."

Lindbergh didn't claim to have a solution to the problem of evil, but he did suggest that God might simply be incomprehensible to humans who, in a cosmic sense, were not all that different from "the insects that crawl and buzz around [him].... Maybe God can't be reached by worldly measures; maybe He prefers no shape, no tangibility at all."[73] "Friend— you are lost," wrote a navy veteran who attended an Evangelical Covenant church in Colorado. "There is a vast difference in knowing there *is* a God, and having a personal relationship with him through faith in Jesus Christ." A teenaged girl from Michigan warned Lindbergh that time was running out to decide "whether or not you accept Jesus as your personal Savior."[74] Both correspondents enclosed tracts detailing God's plan for salvation, which their recipient dutifully added to the archive he was assembling at Yale University.

For all his quotations from the New Testament, Lindbergh had already suggested in *Of Flight and Life* that his belief in God still had little to do with "dogma and convention." Putting away childish things, he now realized that while God could not be seen as tangibly as he had demanded in his youth, "His presence can be sensed in every sight and act and incident."[75] Whatever his doubts, Lindbergh remained confident that "whether one attributes them to God, nature or some other name, the power and the plan are there, manifest in the orbits of the heavens, in earth's gravitation, in the existence of human eye and mind."[76] Lindbergh's God did not dwell in any particular religious house; his God was everywhere.

"Overboard with God"

A Lindbergh dabbling in pantheism wasn't going to sell movie tickets in the mid-1950s, however. In the middle of a Cold War against what Lindbergh himself had derided as a "godless" enemy, it wasn't enough for an all-American hero to be "spiritual but not religious."

As writer-director Billy Wilder began to work on the film version of *The Spirit of St. Louis*, he decided to add a vaguely Christian—at least, theistic—arc to the story. At first, "Lindbergh places no value on faith in God," explains a synopsis of the script from Wilder's papers. "He feels that a man must guide his own destiny."[77] So Wilder invented an exchange with Frank Mahoney, president of the San Diego company that built Lindbergh's titular plane. Worried about carrying too much weight, the young pilot decides not even to take a sextant. "How are you going to navigate?" asks Mahoney.

"Dead reckoning," answers Lindbergh—played by a too-old Jimmy Stewart.

"What happens over the water?"

"Over the water, I keep watching the waves, see which direction the wind's blowing, allow for the drift . . ."

". . . and hope the Lord will do the rest," finishes Mahoney.

"No," Lindbergh tells him. "I never bother the Lord. I'll do the rest."

Mahoney is astonished. "Might need a little help up there, don't you think?"

"No, [He'd] only get in the way."[78]

Early in the process, Lindbergh had reassured Wilder that he understood that "a film should have much more freedom of impression than a book." As much as he admired what he took to be the accuracy of Irving Pichel's 1953 biopic of Martin Luther, Lindbergh understood that movies were bound to be more "impressionistic."[79] But while he liked what he read of the shooting script, he hoped Wilder wouldn't "go overboard with God." He went on, "It's awfully tempting to do so at times, but I don't think it's religious—in the deepest sense—and it certainly wouldn't have fit in with my character, then or now. I have a hard enough time keeping in the general Christian category."[80]

He might have been thinking of another flashback scene. Wilder retained Lindbergh's story of giving flying lessons to Father Henry Hussmann, the St. Louis priest, but added some dialogue not present in the original book. "How come I never see you around the church?" Hussmann asks his flight instructor. "You don't believe, hmm?"

"Yes, I believe," replies Lindbergh. "I believe in an instrument panel, a pressure gauge, a compass, things I can see and touch. I can't touch God."

"You're not supposed to. He touches you."

Lindbergh furrows his brow. "Well now, tell me, Father: now suppose you were up in this airplane all alone, and you stalled it. And you fell into a spin; you were dropping like a rock. You believe He would help me out of it?"

"I can't say yes or no," chuckles the priest. "But He'd know I was falling."[81]

Or, as the script's synopsis put it, "the priest tells him that a man can be his own guide up to a point—then a Greater Force will lead the way." As the flight across the Atlantic nears its dramatic conclusion, Lindbergh does indeed realize "that here—at this point in his destiny—a Greater Force has interceded to save his life."[82] As the exhausted, disoriented pilot approaches Le Bourget, we hear him trying to recall what Father Hussmann prayed before landings. "Oh God," Stewart's Lindbergh finally cries out, "help me." The plane lands safely, and Wilder cuts to a close-up of Father Hussmann's St. Christopher medal, dangling in front of the altimeter.[83]

The film came out in 1957, a year after the US Congress added "In God we trust" to American currency. Wilder's version of *The Spirit of St. Louis* received mixed reviews, but Father James Keller was thrilled with it. He arranged for Wilder to receive an award from a group he had named after the patron saint of travel. The Christophers "are not 'earth shaking' to be sure," Keller told Wilder, "but just a little pat on the back to those who, like yourself, are conscientiously using their creative talent in a positive and constructive manner."[84] Already the owner of three Oscars, Wilder assured Keller that the Christopher was "the best award" he had ever received. "An award from a Catholic organization to a man of the Jewish faith is another candle lit in the world. May the precepts of The Christophers gain such momentum that the day of a true Brotherhood of Man will be known to us all."[85]

For his part, Lindbergh congratulated Wilder on "a very difficult task extremely well done." The film's mix of "detailed accuracy juxtaposed with fictional abandon" didn't seem to bother him.[86] But when he took his family to see the movie in New York, Lindbergh's older daughter had one objection to Wilder's fiction: "Little Anne . . . concluded that 'The Spirit of St. Louis' is 'way above average—really a good film—but it does make you seem converted to Catholocism [sic] in the end, Father.'"[87]

CHAPTER TWELVE

Last Years

To me the growing knowledge of science clarifies and supports, rather than refutes, man's intuition of the mystical. Whether outwardly or inwardly, whether in space or in time, the farther we penetrate the unknown the vaster and more marvelous it becomes to us. Far from refuting the existence of divinity, science teaches us to look for it in different forms, in areas minute and huge we did not previously know existed.

–Charles Lindbergh (1966)[1]

THE SAME YEAR HE TOOK HIS KIDS to see *The Spirit of St. Louis*, Charles Lindbergh began a second family. While in Munich, Germany, in 1957, he started an affair with a hatmaker named Brigitte Hesshaimer. He also had sexual relationships with her sister, Marietta, and his German secretary, Valeska. Over the next eleven years, he fathered seven children by the three women. Anne Lindbergh seems not to have discovered the full truth before her death in 2001, the same year Brigitte Hesshaimer passed away. For decades, none of his European offspring even knew their father's true identity, but in 2003, Brigitte's three children with Lindbergh went public.[2]

As when she first listened to his Des Moines speech, Reeve Lindbergh found herself confronting a man who didn't resemble the father she had known and loved. "During all the years when he was the stern arbiter of moral and ethical conduct in our family," she wrote, "he had been leading another life, living according to a whole different set of standards from those he had taught me."[3] As disruptive as that realization was, however, getting to know her half siblings in Europe revealed one constant: "our lives were all marked by our father's perpetual comings and goings, by a brief intensity of presence followed by long absences, over and over again."[4]

I don't mean to linger on yet more evidence that Charles Lindbergh was never as pure as the chaste "Lindy" of earlier sermons and hagiographies. But before we reach the end of a book meant to shed new light on this "famous unknown," the story of his secret European family serves as a startling reminder that there is much about Charles Lindbergh that we simply won't understand. Even beyond the tensions and contradictions that complicate every life, we are trying to get to know someone who wasn't just quiet, didn't just value his privacy, but would go to great lengths to maintain what Reeve called "absolutely Byzantine layers of deception."[5] "There wasn't a single clue," Scott Berg admitted in 2005, when the Hesshaimer children published their book.[6] And if a biographer as diligent as Berg could have complete access to all of Charles Lindbergh's papers and still not pick up on any hint of Brigitte, Marietta, Valeska, and their children, I shudder to think what I've missed in my attempt to tell a smaller version of the same life story.

"I don't know why he lived this way," Reeve concluded, "and I don't think I ever will know, but what it means to me is that every intimate human connection my father had during his later years was fractured by secrecy." This complicates the task of the biographer—to say nothing of what it does to his loved ones—but it also highlights aspects of Lindbergh with important implications for his "spiritual but not religious" journey. Someone who fused intimacy with secrecy might never have been able to commit himself to the relationships central to most religions: those connecting God to humans, and those binding together members of a faith community. (Here we might recall Lindbergh mocking the Oxford Group's practices of individual silent time and corporate confession of sins.) But her father's secretive nature also left Reeve Lindbergh with "a sense of his unutterable loneliness."[7] And someone who felt that alone in this life might naturally give much thought to the life to come.

The Colosseum's Cross

After the success of *The Spirit of St. Louis*, Lindbergh resumed work on a more expansive memoir: not just a sequel chronicling the years after 1927, but an "autobiography of values" spanning his whole life. It would go even further than *Spirit of St. Louis* in departing from a linear story line, flitting from memory to memory to examine the origins and evolution of his deepest convictions.

By August 1957, Lindbergh had completed a partial draft, concluding with a chapter inspired by his visit to Italy twenty years earlier. En route to the world religions congress in India, he and Anne had walked through Roman ruins that now became the setting for Charles to imagine himself an early Christian about to be martyred: "Within the hour, I'll be dead! Those clouds above my head shall not see; I'll no longer shake from fear, and damp of prison walls, and this November air. My ears wont [*sic*] hear the shouts of crowds come to see me killed! Minutes still—no weapon— no refuge—no escape—what beasts will spring—Oh God—I cannot see teeth sinking in my arm—this flesh torn—hanging—pain—more shout- ing—the gate opening . . ."

As imagination faded back into memory, he looked over what remained of "the power, the debauchery, the grandure [*sic*], of ancient Rome," then moved past the arches and columns to notice "a simple wooden cross." He went on, "Life-size and unpainted, it held my eyes, and I began to real- ize its significance. 'The meek shall inherit the earth,' Christ said [Matt. 5:5], and his cross, symbol of meekness and martyrdom, had inherited the Colosseum. The simplicity of Christ survived, not the luxury and power of the Caesars. Over all of Italy, the cross had risen—above the Colos- seum's arena, in the pagan temples, on top of Trajan's column. Everywhere, the living cross of the Martyr, the meek Christian, surmounts the marble bones of arrogant and persecuting Rome."

Fifteen years after he first started to read the New Testament, Lind- bergh still found something compelling about Jesus Christ.

And something still disappointing about Christianity. Against Jesus's meekness, Lindbergh contrasted the "'Christian' civilization that had re- placed pagan Rome. . . . Professing the tenets of Christ, building churches for his worship, and carrying his cross, another civilization had risen, larger, stronger, and more luxurious than Rome's."[8] As he continued to add to his "Colosseum's Cross" chapter, more memories of that 1937 trip inspired more reflection on the difference between Christ and Christi- anity. For example, visiting Pisa reminded Lindbergh of that city's most famous scientist, tried for heresy in 1633: "'Ye shall know the truth,' Christ said, 'and the truth shall make ye free' [John 8:32]. Yet the very church that grew out of Christ's martyrdom in the cause of truth, tried to suppress the truths of Galileo. And just as the truths of Christ overcame the laws of Rome, the truth of Galileo overcame church dogma."

Then flying over the very land where "a man . . . rode through Palestine donkey-back, living in simplicity," made Lindbergh think of the "crusader's armies [sent] to conquer the 'Holy Land' created in his name. . . . From Richard I to Cortez, from Richleau [*sic*] to Rasputin, from the Medici's to the Rockefellers, the Cross has accompanied our western conquests and participated in our luxury and plunder."

Without realizing it, Lindbergh had come close to one of the same conclusions as his Disciples of Christ great-grandfather. A century earlier, Edwin Albert Lodge complained that "the pure primitive love of the lowly Jesus" had been corrupted under the emperor Constantine, who ended the martyrdoms like the one Lindbergh imagined and enlisted Christianity in the service of worldly empire.[9] But Charles Lindbergh had too many objections to that "lowly Jesus" ever to join his ancestor in becoming one of Christ's followers.

Even to the extent that he admired Jesus as a moral philosopher, Lindbergh's worldview could never elevate traits like meekness and mercy. "'Do unto thy neighbor as ye would have him do unto ye,' was a difficult admonition to follow" during the Cold War, when each superpower had "a long record of bloodshed and aggression."[10] Such violence may have been inescapable. "I think the essential value of competition is deplorably lacking in the marvelous philosophy of Jesus," Lindbergh lamented to Harry Guggenheim, "at least as it has been handed on to us."[11] Its "blindness to the competitive qualities of life," he decided, was "one of the greatest weaknesses of Christian theology . . . a highly hypocritical weakness, one might say, in view of the Christian's cruel and bloody record."[12] In a 1961 outline for his autobiography, Lindbergh wrestled with "how [to] combine Christian philosophy with evolution? . . . God, in his laws of evolution, seems indifferent to suffering and death." He went on, "He apparently rewards the killer (like me). . . . Maybe it is part of a greater plan—an entrance to something beyond."[13]

To a degree, Lindbergh regretted that science had "shattered our forbears' religious concepts." But while he recognized that God "entered their lives as a tangible being, intangible though he was," the Word was never made flesh for Lindbergh.[14] He felt he needed no redeemer to reach whatever lay beyond mortal existence; his Christ was no Savior. When he thought of Jesus on the cross, no empty tomb awaited; crucifixion convicted Lindbergh, but bodily resurrection was almost too odd to mention, let alone believe in. And even though "the truths of Christ overcame the laws of Rome," no kingdom of God would really replace an empire of men. Jesus was no Caesar, but neither was he Lindbergh's Lord.

"A Psychiatrist's Paradise"

"Why have I such a resistance to *Jesus*?" Anne Lindbergh asked her sister Constance in 1950. "God is all right, but Jesus comes right out of those Sunday school pictures with the too-sweet glue on the back one pasted into notebooks. It makes me understand Dana [Atchley]'s aversion to religion." Her letter followed a visit in Florida with Jim Newton, whose wife, Ellie, prayed out loud for Charles and her on the beach. "I prayed too—inwardly: Dear God, forgive me for my snobbery and my resentment. Help me to see that this expression is as natural to her as reading poetry is to me—and that her love is real and good, etc."[15] After the two couples had a tense conversation about religion a few years later, Charles Lindbergh wrote a half apology to Ellie Newton: "I'm sorry if I was too much on the devil's side, but I suspect that God smiles on him, at times, at least, with more benevolence than you do. . . . If I didn't think there was a touch of sin and humor in heaven, I'd much prefer to live in hell—I feel sure I'd find plenty of old friends there."[16]

Such differences didn't get in the way of Charles Lindbergh's friendship with Ellie's husband, but he continued to turn down Jim Newton's invitations to learn more about the Moral Re-Armament movement. When it came to MRA, he told his friend in April 1961, "I think it is best to accept the fact that we do not see eye to eye."[17] In his memoir, Newton was philosophical: "I had long ago realized that the adjective 'lone,' which the press often used to describe him . . . was justified. He was no joiner." Not only did his famous friend shy "away from any association except on his own terms," but Lindbergh "was not one readily to relinquish the reins of his life to God or man. So he naturally resisted MRA's challenge to submit one's self to the Almighty."[18]

But later that year, the ever-curious Lindbergh did finally attend an MRA meeting in Switzerland. He and Anne had first summered in that country in 1959, when they met Carl Jung and talked with the psychologist about flying saucers.[19] The Lindberghs returned often in later years, first renting an apartment near Vevey and then building their own chalet. (Meanwhile, Reeve Lindbergh attended St. George's School for Girls in Montreux, where she befriended a Quaker student who refused to kneel for morning prayers and instead sat, legs crossed—as the headmistress put it—"with the heathen.")[20] The June 1961 MRA congress—the last before Frank Buchman's death that August—was held in the nearby village of Caux, so Lindbergh bowed to the Newtons' pressure and attended several sessions.

It made no difference. In a friendly but strained letter, Lindbergh again told Jim Newton, "Your viewpoint and mine toward MRA differ fundamentally and sincerely . . . neither the passage of time nor my visit to Caux have brought them closer together."[21] He was far harsher in private, jotting down in his notes that "MRA is made up largely of people who have been unable to solve their own problems, and who, therefore have gone out to solve the problems of mankind." Deeming arrogance the movement's "fifth absolute," Lindbergh compared MRA to "the Congress of the Soviets in Moscow" and called its meeting "a psychiatrists [*sic*] paradise."[22]

In Search of "the Primitive"

Nonetheless, Lindbergh did thank Newton for making possible a different kind of religious encounter that summer. Frank Buchman had distinguished between the overt Christianity of the Oxford Group and the broader orientation of MRA, which increasingly became a multireligious movement after World War II. (In its obituary for Buchman, *Christianity Today* called MRA "one of the most successful of modern cults . . . though it is Christian-oriented in a broad sense.")[23] At Caux, Newton arranged a conversation with a representative from the Maasai tribe in Kenya. The African delegate told the Americans that his people "had their own God—to which they prayed—a god not in the form of a man, not in any form—but a God—their God."[24]

The following year, Lindbergh traveled to East Africa to stay with the Maasai. In his notes, he again quoted Jesus: "'Go ye into all the world, and preach the gospel to every creature' [Mark 16:15, KJV]. How impossible it seemed, looking down on barren hill-slopes in parts of southern Kenya, that the words of Christ could be connected to such desert ground!" A missionary conceded to him that "these people are still full of superstition and primitive tribal ways. Some of them are very slow in adopting Christianity." But as Lindbergh talked to the Maasai themselves, he found a different story. "Oh, the Christian religion was good," one tribesman told him. "But we had a religion before. We had only one god, too."

"What did you see when you thought of God?" Lindbergh asked him. "Can you describe what your Masai god looks like?"

"Oh, no," the man replied. "The Masai god has no form. Our god is in the trees, in the mountains, in the blades of grass, in the cattle. Our god is in everything. When we sing songs to the dawn and pray to the mountains, we are singing and praying to God because God is in the dawn and in the mountains."[25]

In this period, Lindbergh continued to read Christian Scriptures and explore Eastern religions, attending a 1963 lecture on meditation by Jiddu Krishnamurti and visiting Buddhist temples in Thailand later that year. But he found himself drawn more to the lifestyle and beliefs of people groups like the Maasai. After a return trip to Kenya in 1964, he reported to *Reader's Digest* subscribers that he had become "more aware of the basic miracle of life. Not life as applied humanly to man alone, but life as diversified by God on earth with superhuman wisdom—forms evolved by several million centuries of selection and environment." Rethinking the definition of progress as he lay under an acacia tree at dawn, the pilot of the *Spirit of St. Louis* came upon a realization: "If I had to choose, I would rather have birds than airplanes."[26]

Lindbergh became another of the famous moderns who had gone "in search of the primitive," as anthropologist Stanley Diamond titled his critique of Western civilization. "No mere fantasy or sentimental whim," the civilized man's longing for "the primitive" struck Diamond as being "consonant with fundamental human needs."[27] Lindbergh certainly felt that way. As he returned to writing his autobiography, he considered that "modern war and modern civilization blind you to the importance and strength of the primitive." Though he could "never live long in close contact with primitive conditions" before recognizing their limitations, if he ever left the primitive again, he said, "I will be renouncing God's greatest gift to man."[28]

It wasn't just Africa. His interest in "primitive" societies—and their close relationship with the physical environment—had first been piqued by his 1944 mission in the South Pacific, memories of which kept surfacing in his impressionistic autobiography. In an early fragment, he recalled swimming in the warm waters off New Guinea:

> Naked, on the edge of land, sea, and air, I regain contact with the basic elements of man. . . . I am suddenly stripped of civilization as I am stripped of clothes. . . . It is one of those rare instances in life when body, mind, and spirit are in balance. Here, within this brown covering of skin, is the essential "I," escaped from civilization, in this hour of life, as the soul must escape the body in the moment of death. Here, I am able to look on my civilized life from a frame of values, time, and space that change all of its dimensions.[29]

Twenty years after the war, he returned to that part of the world, visiting American Samoa in 1964–1965. His host was a chief named Tufele, who told his guest that "Civilization is like a weed that grows on our trees. . . . Once it starts it is impossible to get off, and it always kills the tree."[30]

The more time he spent in such settings, the more Lindbergh lamented Christian influence, at least when the religion of Christ had been spread by imperial power. He had first questioned the "benefits of Christianity and civilization" for "wild, barbaric" peoples during the war.[31] In a 1957 draft of early autobiography chapters, he accused Europeans of having "claimed to embrace the ideals of Christianity when they seized America from the Indians."[32] Though missionaries had facilitated many of his first encounters with Native Americans, Africans, and Pacific Islanders, Lindbergh came to agree with Tufele's assessment of such Christians: "They interfere too much with the customs of the people. They think everything American & European is better than anything Samoan, bring in European style homes, dress, even insist that the women wear hats in the church, etc." Lindbergh was particularly disturbed that the missionaries "had brought to their islands, as to other places throughout the world, a shame of nakedness—as though God desired man to hide the beauty of the body His wisdom had created."[33] Visiting the Philippine island of Mindanao in 1970, he was incensed how the Tboli and Agta peoples had lost land and become indebted to an "(encroaching) community of Christians that is constantly attempting to exploit them."[34]

Lindbergh reported on his time in the Philippines in a 1972 article for *Reader's Digest*, "Lessons from the Primitive." He wrote, "Walking back and forth between my plane and the leaf shelter assigned to me was like stepping through time between our modern present and a prehistoric past." The "simplicity and balance" of the Agta contrasted favorably with the "luxury and excess" of civilized peoples who sometimes seemed as "bound to our technologies as an addict is to drugs."[35]

THE SPACE RACE

Lindbergh hoped to combine premodern wisdom and modern discovery—to guide technological advances, not eliminate them. In between his trips to Africa and the Pacific, Lindbergh continued to consult for Pan Am and advise the US Air Force. Most memorably, he served as an ongoing inspiration—and occasional eyewitness—as aviation entered the space age.

Thirty years after Lindbergh's flight to Paris, a Soviet rocket carried *Sputnik* into orbit, at once confirming Lindbergh's prescient support for Robert Goddard's pioneering research in the 1930s, amplifying fears of a global thermonuclear war, and sparking a "space race" between superpowers who measured ideological superiority in terms of scientific and technological achievements. As children, several of the first American astronauts had idolized the first pilot to fly solo across the Atlantic—none more so than Alan Shepard, who read Lindbergh's "*We*" so often that when he was assigned to write an autobiography in grade school, Shepard entitled it *Me*.[36] In 1944 he narrowly missed meeting Lindbergh during his naval service on the island of Biak; we've already seen that John Glenn met the older pilot twice during World War II.

Lindbergh analogies were common on the American side of the space race. *Life* magazine's insider coverage of the astronauts' lives evoked the *New York Times's* exclusive 1927 deal with Lindbergh—save that, as Susan Faludi later complained, Shepard, Glenn, et al. "were heroes not, like Charles Lindbergh, the first man to fly across the Atlantic, because they had done something, but because they were confident they would."[37] When Glenn became the first American to orbit the earth, the resulting ticker-tape parade invited new comparisons to Lindbergh in 1927. As the space race reached its culmination, NASA (National Aeronautics and Space Administration) flight operations director Chris Kraft and his colleagues "knew damn well that . . . the first man on the Moon would be a legend, an American hero beyond Lucky Lindbergh, beyond any soldier or politician or inventor." The astronaut they chose had to be "the Lindbergh type."[38]

Their choice, Neil Armstrong, was Anne and Charles Lindbergh's personal guide when the couple toured Kennedy Space Center in December 1968. Lit up by searchlights on the launch pad, Apollo 8 looked to Anne like "the child of a mechanical womb, of a scientific civilization—untried, but full of promise. Radiating light over the heavens, it seems to be the focus of the world, as the Star of Bethlehem once was. But what does it promise? What new world? What hope for mortal man struggling on earth?"[39] The next morning, Charles was "hypnotized" to watch firsthand as a Saturn V rocket put Goddard's principles into powerful effect, carrying Frank Borman, Jim Lovell, and Bill Anders on the first leg of the first human journey to the moon: "Here, after epoch-measured trials of evolution, earth's life was voyaging to another celestial body. Here one saw our civilization flowering toward the stars. Here modern man had been rewarded for his confidence in science and technology. Soon he would be orbiting the moon."[40] He returned to Cape Kennedy in July 1969. As he waited for Apollo 11 to lift off, the sixty-seven-year-old pilot spent half an hour talking about aviation and celebrity with a starstruck Alan Shepard, who would walk on the moon himself two years later.[41]

Like aviation before it, space flight inspired religious responses. If merely defying gravity gave rise to a "winged gospel," literally leaving the terrestrial realm for the heavenly was bound to make observers think about transcendence. But the people of NASA were rarely given to such language. Historian Kendrick Oliver found that, at most, the astronauts' religious analogue "was not so much the monks of St. Benedict, conceiving their labor to be a prayer to God, but the Zen Buddhist with his quiet, careful reveries: the engineer, utterly absorbed in his machine and in the rational, ordered process by which he will make it work." Those wanting "to reflect on the relation between the exploration of the cosmos and cosmological tradition, to judge whether the space age would be friendly to faith," mostly came from "outside the program."[42]

Two such outsiders were Anne and Charles Lindbergh, both of whom wrote distinctly spiritual reflections on the space program as part of *Life's* continuing coverage in 1969. Meeting the crew of Apollo 8, Anne saw neither "the 'triumph of the squares—the guys with the crew-cuts and slide rules who read the Bible and get things done,'" nor "the 'worship of the dynamo,' that arrogant belief of Western man that now, with his new science and technical powers, he has everything under control and can conquer the universe." Instead, their "new-old sense of mystery and awe" brought to mind words from one of her favorite Christian writers, Pierre Teilhard de Chardin: "Our concept of God must be extended as the dimensions of our world are extended."[43] The month that Apollo 11 launched, Charles used the occasion to call again for humanity to "combine our knowledge of science with the wisdom of wildness." The potential, he thought, was "unbounded. Through his evolving awareness, and his awareness of that awareness, [man] can merge with the miraculous—to which we can attach what better name than 'God'?"

He even dreamed aloud of exploration beyond the physical, as "sensory perception must combine with the extrasensory."[44] A decade earlier, in an autobiography fragment that started with an earlier visit to Cape Canaveral, he had started to muse that the intellect might "evolve until it has no need to travel physically, becoming less and less dependent on the earthly matter that contains it until it extends throughout the universe like space. . . . And in evolving from matter through reason to awareness, will man be approaching an existence close to God?"[45]

Lindbergh developed such themes more publicly in 1974, in his last written work published before his death: a foreword to the memoir by Apollo 11 astronaut Michael Collins. "Relatively inactive and unwatched," Lindbergh wrote of the astronaut who orbited the moon while Armstrong

and Buzz Aldrin walked its surface, Collins "had time for contemplation, time to study both the nearby surface of the moon and the distant
moon-like world. Here was human awareness floating through universal
reaches, attached to our earth by such tenuous bonds as radio waves and
star sights." Lindbergh said it reminded him of his lonely, sleepless flight to
Paris, when "my awareness seemed to be abandoning my body to expand
on stellar scales." Still apprehensive that the twentieth century would end
in a "bleak dead end" rather than "an affluent and spiritual utopia," Lindbergh dreamed of a day when humanity could explore without "vehicles
or matter," as it entered "a stage in evolution when we can discover how
to separate ourselves entirely from earthly life, to abandon our physical
frameworks in order to extend both inwardly and outwardly through lim-
itless dimensions of awareness."[46]

It was an understandable hope for a septuagenarian whose body was
being ravaged by cancer. But Lindbergh was not so much of a gnostic that
he wanted to abandon the physical entirely. Indeed, the last crusade of his
life was not the exploration of space—or extrasensory awareness—but
the protection of the earth.

"Feel the Earth"

Two months after taking his "small step for man," Neil Armstrong was in
Los Angeles for a banquet. He sat next to Charles Lindbergh, who was
being honored as an honorary fellow of the Society of Experimental Test
Pilots. "He told me never to sign autographs," the astronaut remembered.
"Unfortunately I didn't take his advice for thirty years, and I probably
should have."[47] After Lindbergh mounted the dais, he reiterated a varia-
tion on his concerns from *Of Flight and Life*, "that the expanding frontiers
of aviation have overtaken the evolving frontiers of life, and that failure to
integrate the two would almost certainly be catastrophic." As the sixties
ended, one catastrophe was particularly close to his heart: "We cannot escape the fact that while science, industry, and commerce are progressing,
the environment of life is breaking down. We pilots have had an unique
opportunity to watch this breakdown—the stripping of forests, the ero-
sion of land, the pollution of water and air; the destruction of cities at
one time and place, and their megalopolizing at another. Year after year,

we have looked down on such phenomena. The surface of our earth is changing fast, and certainly not for the better."[48]

Lindbergh had started to throw himself into environmental conservation in the mid-1960s, encouraging World Wildlife Fund donors to join the "race between forces of preservation and those of destruction mounting on an exponential scale. The scarcity of eagles in the sky, of whales in the ocean, and of wilderness filled with God's varieties of life warns us clearly of the destructive forces' strength."[49] In 1968, in his first public address since the days of America First, he asked the Alaska state legislature to protect wolves against extinction.[50] The airplane let him travel everywhere from Peru to Indonesia to witness the environmental impact of advancing civilization, but in 1972 Lindbergh helped lead the campaign against an American supersonic transport, warning that it would produce air and noise pollution.[51]

The allusions to "frontiers" in his 1969 test pilots address hint that Lindbergh's latter-day interest in environmental conservation had roots reaching back as far as his boyhood on the Mississippi. ("This love for the living earth was his earliest strength," agreed Reeve Lindbergh.)[52] At the September 1973 dedication of a new interpretive center at the Minnesota state park named for his father, Lindbergh celebrated the "preservation for future generations of the wildness and natural beauty [he] lived in as a child.... In establishing parks and nature reserves, man reaches beyond the material values of science and technology" to regain "the miraculous spiritual awareness that only nature in balance can maintain."[53]

Memories of hiking and hunting with a father who found God in nature had never left him. In 1938 he moved his family to the primeval island of Illiec in part because he wanted to teach his own "children to know and to love the earth itself. If they can keep in contact with the land and the water and the sky, they can obtain all worthwhile that life holds."[54] Modern man was "too far separated from the soil and the sea," he warned in his controversial 1939 article on race and aviation for Reader's Digest, and that concern remained part of Lindbergh's postwar critique of science and technology.[55] Receiving the Wright Brothers Memorial Trophy in 1949, he emphasized that, for all their study of aerodynamics and their tinkering with machines, the Wrights' "bodies were in contact with sun and earth, and weather."[56] As his autobiography draft revisited his memory of swimming in the South Pacific during the war, Lindbergh felt himself "conscious of this sphere called 'Earth.'" He went on, "I take my place, a consciousness of life, under the warm rays of light, amid the coral colors of the sea, near curving trunks of palm on shore, tasting the salt of an ocean's water."[57] Camping in the Alps years later with Anne produced a similar awareness: "Breathe, and you merge with the air around you.... Feel, and you touch the sun at spatial distance.... There are moments when you so identify with your environment that you are conscious of no separate individuality."[58]

"Man and his environment are one," Lindbergh told fellow conservationists meeting in Madagascar in 1970. "Where his environment deteriorates, he himself deteriorates."[59] That he couched his concern for environmental protection in terms of human decay suggests the lingering influence of Alexis Carrel, who was fresh in Lindbergh's memory because of his encounters with two Roman Catholic communities.

First, Lindbergh's connection to Georgetown University developed in the mid-1960s, as he got to know Carrel's biographer, longtime history professor Joseph Durkin, SJ. The Jesuit university awarded the aviator an honorary degree in 1968, then invited him back in 1973 to speak at the centenary celebration of Carrel's birth. Honored to mark the occasion at a Catholic institution where "the educational, the scientific, and the spiritual meet, as they met in him throughout his life," Lindbergh emphasized that "Carrel realized how closely, on this earth, the qualities of body, mind, and spirit interweave and that—looking toward the future—the advance of one is essentially dependent on the others."[60]

In those last years, Lindbergh also spent time at a Benedictine convent whose closeness to nature and "broadness of viewpoint" he had "never encountered before in a religious organization."[61] After World War II, an American-born nun called Mother Benedict Duss left France and established the priory of Regina Laudis on land donated by a Congregational businessman.[62] Just over sixty miles north of the Lindberghs' home in Connecticut, Regina Laudis first became a retreat for Anne, with Charles sometimes joining her to help work the grounds. After a visit in 1971, he began a surprisingly playful correspondence with a nun named for the medieval mystic Hildegard of Bingen. Joking about the possibility of baptizing a frog they'd encountered in the abbey's gardens, Lindbergh wrote to Sister Hildegard: "I've never been present when anything was baptized and I wasn't baptized myself. (Please don't tell the Reverend Mother.) From the heathenish position, I am simply fascinated with what you do as a Benedictine nun and—seriously—I am fascinated and tremendously impressed with your extraordinary approach to and penetration of fields of mysticism."[63] Lindbergh also enjoyed a connection with Mother Benedict herself, a former medical student who shared his admiration for Carrel. In a 1973 letter, he told the prioress that he had "gained much from the spiritual atmosphere you have, rather miraculously, been able to (Carrel-like) keep in contact with the earth."[64]

THE LIFE STREAM

Despite such friendships with environmentally conscious theists, Lindbergh is better understood as a pantheist, or perhaps a panentheist. To his mind, air, water, and land were not parts of a creator's creation; the divine was found everywhere on Earth. "The way of wildness is the way of life," he wrote in Reader's Digest in 1971, "and in the way of life lies the way of God." He told readers that he had learned to see African animals "less as mortal individuals than as temporal manifestations of the immortal lifestreams they contained," a "trail" of living and dying connecting past, present, and future. In the process, he learned to sense "immortality" in himself.[65] He had appealed to the same idea in making the case for environmental conservation to the chair of the US House subcommittee on science, research, and development: "Man must place more value on the human lifestream than on himself as an individual—realizing that he is only a temporary manifestation of that lifestream, that his salvation and immortality lie in it rather than in himself. Possibly this will involve an intellectual religion rooting into intuitive religions of the past."[66]

His interest in "the primitive" and his commitment to wildlife and wilderness dovetailed, not just in wanting to protect parts of the earth where both were threatened, but as he came to share something like the Maasai belief that "god is in the trees, in the mountains, in the blades of grass, in the cattle." If everything in nature wasn't itself God, perhaps God was still "in everything."

"Why does the modern mind so often renounce and refuse to name the mystery to which previous generations applied such terms as 'God'?"

Lindbergh asked his publisher, Bill Jovanovich, in 1971. He hoped to make his friend "both religious and democratic. This may be a more difficult task than flying the Atlantic, but I have hope and I'm embarked on it."[67] When Jovanovich and Yale archivist Judith Schiff edited *Autobiography of Values* after Lindbergh's death, they elected to close with a burst of theological and metaphysical meditation embedded in Lindbergh's memory of spending Christmas camping in the Kimana nature sanctuary, near Mount Kilimanjaro. "Christ's homeland lay closer to Kenya than to New England," he realized, "and the circumstances of his birth corresponded more to a jungle camp's simplicity than to Western civilization's elaborate Christmas rites." In a chapter that quotes Augustine and recalls the ministry of his great-grandfather, Lindbergh decided that "the shape of God we cannot measure, weigh, or clock, but we can conceive a reality without a form." Looking up at Kilimanjaro, he "sensed its divinity in its mass and shifting lights."[68]

In the midst of such reveries, the sound of a lion's roar suddenly makes him conscious of his mortality; he daydreams about being "killed that night and devoured by lions, hyenas, and vultures." What would happen to Lindbergh when his body died? His "life stream" would continue: "I would become part of Kimana, of its earth and its acacia trees, of its grass that hides and feeds the buffalo and therefore of the buffalo themselves. I would return, somewhat more quickly than from civilized life, to what I really am—to the infinite existence in which the unenlightened man thought himself a finite part."

In the end, "death is an entrance to experience rather than an exit from it."[69]

CHAPTER 13

Of Death and Afterlife

Whither shall I go from thy Spirit?
Or whither shall I flee from thy presence?
If I ascend up into heaven, thou art there:
If I make my bed in Sheol, behold, thou art there.
If I take the wings of the morning,
and dwell in the uttermost parts of the sea;
Even there shall thy hand lead me,
and thy right hand shall hold me.

Psalm 139:7–10

THOUGH WE IMAGINE him in the sky, Charles Lindbergh spent much of his life close to water. He was born by the Great Lakes and grew up on the banks of America's greatest river. He made his name crossing one ocean and fought a war in another. His favorite houses had coastlines.

And Lindbergh had long associated the end of his life with the "escape and freedom (and limitlessness)" of water.[1] "If one had to die," he added to a 1943 draft of *The Spirit of St. Louis*, "what better place than the sea? What solitude, what companionship it offered to a restless spirit? Who could prefer a gravestone in a city's crowded cemetery [*sic*] to the unmarked, everchanging, everlasting beauty of the sea?"[2] So when his doctors told him in 1974 that there was no hope he would ever recover from cancer, Lindbergh departed New York one last time: flying not across the Atlantic, but the Pacific, to die at his and Anne's home in Hawaii.

"Death as Death Cannot Be Seen"

The Lindberghs had first visited the Hana coast of Maui in 1968, vacationing at the estate of Pan Am executive Sam Pryor. "It is freer, wilder, and less overlaid than the U.S. or Europe," Anne told their son Scott. "Like Mexico, it seemed to me one of those rare blends of the primitive and the cultured. A man could start a new life here, I felt."[3] Pryor sold them a few acres of his property, and the Lindberghs began building a small A-frame house. "What a romantic C. is!" Anne exclaimed to Dana Atchley. "I suppose we can always get rid of this property if it turns out to be more trouble than it's worth."[4] Two years later, their home was still flooding, but her husband "just loves it. . . . He likes battling with the elements and feeling he is in the wilderness."[5]

Charles gushed to Mother Benedict of Regina Laudis that Maui was ideal for "either the virtuous or sinful . . . one of the most beautiful and attractive areas in the world."[6] He threw himself into local conservation efforts and found new inspiration for the metaphysical musings in his still-unfinished autobiography. Exploring a valley, he thought again of his notion of the "life stream," which he likened to "a mountain river—springing from hidden sources, born out of the earth, touched by stars, merging, blending, evolving in the shape momentarily seen."[7] His experience of combat on islands in the Pacific had first convinced him "that theology's acceptance of a spirit surviving death was more plausible than the nonentity that one infers from science."[8] Now, as he followed that Hawaiian river to its fall over a lava rock formation, Lindbergh "saw death as death cannot be seen." He added, "I stared at the very end of life, and at life that forms beyond, at the fact of immortality."[9]

Death was often on the mind of a man who had been diagnosed with lymphoma in 1972. Radiation treatments caused the seventy-year-old Lindbergh to lose thirty pounds, though family and friends were informed that he was fighting what Anne called "an obscure virus," exacerbated by the "real Job-like affliction" of shingles.[10] She told a friend that their husbands were starting to suffer what Pierre Teilhard de Chardin called the "diminishments" of aging: "Unless one is a saint (and Père Teilhard was a kind of saint), it is difficult to accept the force of diminishment 'as a means of uniting oneself with God.'"[11] The Lindberghs finally told their children the truth in the summer of 1974, as Charles seemed to be on the mend. But by late July Anne reported to Mother Benedict that "it is as if the fire of the disease were raging in him, devouring him."[12] (The nun suggested that she baptize her husband herself: "It's quite simple, really, just a little water.") In one of her last visits, their daughter Reeve noticed something her father had scribbled on a blue airmail pad: "I know there is an infinity outside ourselves. I wonder now if there is an infinity within, as well?"[13]

On Sunday, August 18, Charles Lindbergh checked out of the hospital in New York and flew halfway around the world, occupying a bed specially added to the first-class section of a United Airlines DC-8. His sons Jon and Scott flew with him and their mother; Land met them in Hawaii. Knowing he had days left to live, Charles Lindbergh dedicated himself to planning every detail of his own funeral. "He was really in a terrible state," recalled his local physician, Milton Howell, but Lindbergh was still "the boss, he was in command."[14]

Lindbergh had picked the burial site the year before, while recuperating from radiation therapy. Sam Pryor had shown him a small church overlooking Kipahulu Bay. Established in the mid-nineteenth century by Congregational missionaries, it was called Palapala Ho'omau: the church of the "Everlasting Word."[15] Lindbergh helped Pryor restore the limestone and coral building and secured a small plot on a nearby cliff for his grave.[16] As Charles and his sons now prepared that ground and constructed a coffin for a traditional Hawaiian burial, Anne prayed in the church. When she told him what she'd been doing, "his face contorted with emotion, trying not to cry."[17]

Anne also helped her husband plan his own memorial services: a private ceremony for family and a few friends, and a second one that would be open to reporters. She sang hymns while Charles rested. "That one's too corny," he murmured at one point, when she thought he was asleep.[18] One suggestion he accepted came from Henry Kahula, the local gas station owner who served as the little church's deacon.[19] Written by a Baptist pastor named Robert Lowry and sung to a Hawaiian tune, "Angel's Welcome" begins, "My home is in Heaven, my rest is not here. / Then why should I murmur when trials appear?"[20] The rest of the brief service included readings from sources as diverse as Augustine of Hippo, Mohandas K. Gandhi, a Navajo poem ("Let me live in beauty, let me die in beauty"), and the Bible, including one of Anne's favorite Scriptures: "I will lift up mine eyes unto the mountains: from whence shall my help come?" (Ps. 121:1).[21]

Lindbergh had his gravestone inscribed with a verse from another psalm: "If I take the wings of the morning, and dwell in the uttermost parts of the sea" (139:9). Tellingly, a man who distrusted both atheism and organized religion left unfinished the theological thought: "... even there shall thy hand lead me, and thy right hand shall hold me" (v. 10). "I'm not sure he had any concrete notion as to exactly what [the] supreme being was," Milton Howell remembered, but his friend shared his faith "in that Memorial Service, drawing from a great many different segments of the human population."[22] His wife, Roselle, who worked as clerk at their church, accepted that Lindbergh was simply "larger than Christianity."[23]

He died on Monday morning, August 26, 1974. "The first reaction," Anne wrote a few months later, "was one of gratitude to God that he had been taken—that he was no longer imprisoned in the suffering body."[24] Land, who had pushed his father's wheelchair to allow him a last view of the ocean, reassured his younger sister that the last moments were "really quite beautiful, and not painful at all."[25] Officiating the funeral service that same afternoon, John Tincher, a young Methodist pastor from California who happened to be taking his turn in the Ho'omau pulpit that month, asked a final blessing: "We commit the body of Charles A. Lindbergh to its final resting place, but his spirit we commit to Almighty God, knowing that death is but a new adventure in existence and remembering how Jesus said upon the cross, 'Father, into thy hands I commend my spirit' [Luke 23:46]."[26] Reeve cherished the knowledge that her father had died "exactly as he had wanted to do, in quietness, in a place he loved, with his family all around him, and with that immensity of waters, the Pacific Ocean, bearing witness to his fading heartbeat at the last."[27]

THE AFTERLIFE OF CHARLES LINDBERGH

It was the summer after their oldest son's murder when Charles Lindbergh had first thought out loud that "one cannot say that everything ends with the death of the body." When Anne objected that she didn't "want to be separated" from him, her husband answered, "Maybe you won't be."[28] In the months after his death, she did sense his presence, "in a not at all spiritualistic way." She said she may have felt his impatience, even disapproval, at the way she was handling his passing.[29] But just over a decade later, in 1985, the sudden death of her infant grandson, Jonathan, dredged up memories of Charles Jr. and Charles Sr. alike. While some of her friends took comfort in resurrection and others in reincarnation, Anne confessed to her diary that she believed, in her own vague way, that something "goes on." But, she added, "I do not define it. Spirit, surely, is not wasted. Does it merge into the 'great unconscious' or does it remain only—only? Is this not enough?—in the minds and hearts of others? CAL certainly believed something 'went on,' and I do sometimes feel closer to that 'something.'"[30]

Even if he didn't rejoin the "life stream" or proceed to an afterlife as Christians like his great-grandfather understood that stage of existence, Charles Lindbergh certainly "went on" in the contested spaces of memory and history.

Conscious that such a hereafter awaited, Lindbergh had done what he could to shape how future generations would perceive him. He put out an edited version of his wartime journals in 1970 and helped his wife to prepare her own diaries and letters for publication. Lindbergh allowed Wayne Cole access to his still-private papers at Yale but tried to argue that historian out of the mild criticisms included in an otherwise sympathetic account of the anti-intervention campaign.[31] Almost to the last moment, Lindbergh attended to his legacy. In the hospital in New York, he entrusted his autobiography to Bill Jovanovich, who had refused to publish Cole's manuscript until Lindbergh was allowed to comment on it.[32] He also wrote letters to Brigitte, Marietta, and Valeska, asking them to keep his secret, even from their children with him.[33]

As historians and biographers have taken on their task as Anne Lindbergh defined it in 1979—"to test the image of the public man and find out, if possible, what is false and what is true, or what is probable and what is improbable, and what is relevant to the history of mankind"—they've offered a mixed assessment of her husband.[34] The most critical among them can't dispute the enduring significance of Lindbergh's flight to Paris or his later work as a conservationist; the most admiring can't avoid the ugliness of his racial views or his shortcomings as a husband and father. "The Lindbergh name means different things to different people," Reeve acknowledged in 2001, after her mother died of Alzheimer's. "Reactions can be extreme and contradictory."[35] But wherever they've landed on the most famous aspects of Charles Lindbergh's story, few who tell it have emphasized its spiritual aspects.

One notable exception is T. Willard Hunter, who published a short spiritual biography in 1993. "We know a great deal about the *Spirit of St. Louis,*" he explained. "We know a great deal less about the spirit of her pilot."[36] Hunter was a former MRA worker who was later ordained as a Congregational minister. His interest in his fellow Minnesotan was piqued in the late 1970s when he took a turn pastoring the Hawaiian church where Lindbergh is buried.

One Sunday in December 1980, Hunter organized a memorial service at another Congregational church a few miles up the coast. After leading singing of Christmas carols and a responsive reading of Psalm 139, Hunter moderated a conversation about "the faith of the Lone Eagle" with two of Charles Lindbergh's most devoutly Christian friends: Jim Newton and Sam Pryor. Newton remembered Lindbergh as "a man of faith . . . and courage and integrity"; he imagined those flying to Hawaii looking in the direction of the grave under "that little banyan tree where this man with his faith in God, is now." Pryor emphasized the biblical inscription on the headstone: "He wanted that last on his sleeping place here at the little church, showing he believed that God was in all of us." Before closing with the Christmas story and "O Little Town of Bethlehem," Hunter encouraged the congregation to read *Of Flight and Life*, where they would find Lindbergh "talking, not only in terms of a personal faith that meant a great deal to him" but about "the only thing, he says, that will save our planet, . . . to find the kind of thing we are talking about right here in this room every Sunday."[37]

Charles Lindbergh would probably have warned Hunter, Newton, and Pryor not to "go overboard with God." As he had told the producer of *The Spirit of St. Louis* film, he had "a hard enough time keeping in the general Christian category" without Christians trying to talk about his spirituality "in terms of a personal faith" that was idiosyncratic and stubbornly independent of the authority of any particular church, creed, or tradition.[38]

The most winsome articulator of Lindbergh's spiritual legacy has been his daughter Reeve, whom Hunter credited for inspiring him to write his book and whose perspective is a key influence on this book.[39] In 1977, she suggested that her father would have celebrated his flight to Paris by revisiting the themes of *Of Flight and Life*, using the fiftieth anniversary of his most famous achievement to talk about "progress, history and the evolution of the quality of life." Stripped of its origins in the racial theories of eugenicists, the "quality of life" now spoke to Lindbergh's postwar quest for balance: that of body, mind, and spirit, and that "between technologi-cal and natural values."[40] In 1985, Reeve spoke on "the Lindbergh heritage" at Westminster Presbyterian Church in downtown Minneapolis: "I think we come [to Minnesota], we Lindberghs, searching not only for personal history but for some kind of philosophical wellspring, some sense of who we are and what we're all about. . . . I think [my father's] experience here molded his whole philosophy, which had to do with establishing a balance between technology and the natural environment. He spent his whole life with one foot in each of these two very different worlds, which is an unusual and precarious position to put your feet in."[41]

She celebrated the work of the Lindbergh Fund, established in 1977 by Jimmy Doolittle, Neil Armstrong, Jim Newton, and other friends to encourage that balance between technological innovation and environ-mental conservation. Reeve and other family members remain active in a foundation now named for both her parents.

Her 1985 address came just a few months after the sudden death of Reeve's son Jonathan, at roughly the same age as the elder brother Reeve never knew. As part of her own grieving, she began to write children's liter-ature. In 2000, even as she cared for her dying mother, Reeve published an anthology drawing on various religious traditions. Dedicated to Jim and Ellie Newton, *In Every Tiny Grain of Sand* includes some of Anne Morrow Lindbergh's favorite prayers and poems, plus the version of the Lord's Prayer found in the Gospel of Matthew and Reeve's own paraphrases of Francis of Assisi's "Canticle of the Sun" and Psalm 139.[42]

Her version of that psalm was published separately in 2002, as *On Morning Wings*, "in memory of my father and all who love wings."[43] Addressed to a God who understands us, even "if I don't know how to pray," its rendering of the verse on Charles Lindbergh's gravestone seems an appropriate way to end the "spiritual but not religious" story of that complicated man:

> You are with me everywhere . . .
> On morning wings, in oceans deep. . . .

Afterword

This biography was always going to be one Minnesotan's account of the life of another Minnesotan. But I didn't realize that its writing would be haunted by the deaths of two other Minnesotans: Philando Castile, who was killed by police in 2016, just before I got the idea to attempt a Lindbergh biography, and George Floyd, who was killed by police in 2020, as I finished my manuscript. An African American employee of the St. Paul public school system, Castile was shot during a traffic stop on Larpenteur Avenue, just one mile from my house — but impossibly distant from my experience as a white man who has driven the same road a thousand times without ever worrying that I'd be pulled over, let alone shot.

I started my Lindbergh biography knowing that I'd have to address his sympathy for Nazi Germany and his embrace of eugenics; I didn't realize that I'd find him advocating that voting rights be stripped from those few African Americans enfranchised in 1940. But the deaths of black men like Castile and Floyd underlined for me that it was white supremacy, not just anti-Semitism, that made Lindbergh see Adolf Hitler's regime as a potential ally in a civilizational struggle. Although his encounters with Japanese pilots and soldiers in the South Pacific caused him to start rethinking some of those racial views, he still worried that the "reproduction of our less able groups" would imperil "our race and civilization."[1] Even as his experience of war led him to the teachings of Jesus Christ, in whom "there can be neither Jew nor Greek, there can be neither bond nor free, there can be no male and female" (Gal. 3:28), Charles Lindbergh continued to see basic human equality as inimical to "the quality of life."

While his "spiritual but not religious" journey left him free from the hypocrisies of institutional Christianity, it also left him free to ignore whatever teachings of Christ he found inconvenient. Grace, humility, and unqualified love of neighbor simply did not fit within a worldview that took racial difference for granted and turned racial competition into a divine imperative.[2] Having made God in his own image, Charles Lindbergh saw no image of God in people who didn't resemble him.

But, to paraphrase one statement of Jesus's that Lindbergh did endorse, no Christian should ignore the beam in his own eye. For if religionless spirituality provides no inherent defense against bigotry, a faith like mine cannot guarantee that its adherents will love their neighbors or seek justice for them. On the contrary, Charles Lindbergh advocated no evil that Christians hadn't already inflicted on humanity.

In my church, worship often includes a litany that begins with a verse from the New Testament: "If we say that we have no sin, we deceive ourselves, and the truth is not in us" (1 John 1:8). Charles Lindbergh may have pursued spirituality without practicing the spiritual discipline of confession, but if he deceived himself, so too have Christians like me. The "truth was not in us" for generations of Jesus's followers, as deep-seated prejudices caused us to give silent or vocal assent to sins like the sterilization of the "feebleminded," the slaughter of European Jews, and slavery and segregation. Too few American Christians would agree with Robert P. Jones that it is "Christian theology and institutions"—not the ideas of individual skeptics like Charles Lindbergh — that "have been the central tent pole holding up the very idea of white supremacy." To this day, white Christians—whether evangelical Protestant, mainline Protestant, or Catholic—score significantly higher on Jones's Racism Index than do religiously unaffiliated Americans.[3]

So while I hope that this book causes all its readers to reflect on problems like our reliance on technology, our abuse of the environment, and our participation in celebrity culture, I'm most eager that this biography help prompt Christians to seek a deeper, more honest reckoning with the same sins that made infamous the name of its subject. In particular, I pray that a book haunted by the killing of black men challenges my fellow believers not just to confess and repent our complicity in white supremacy but to identify and transform the systems that perpetuate it. May the story of someone as independent-minded as Charles Lindbergh help us understand how hard it is to elude the insidious influence of what theologians call structural sin—and then move us to reform the social, economic, legal, political, and religious systems that are crushing the very life out of God's children.[4]

Abbreviations

AC	Alexis Carrel
AML	Anne Morrow Lindbergh
ASB	A. Scott Berg
BLL	Bruce L. Larson
CAL	Charles Augustus Lindbergh
CLHM	Charles Lindbergh House and Museum, Little Falls, MN
CMM	Constance Morrow Morgan
EAL	Edwin Albert Lodge
ECM	Elizabeth Cutter Morrow
ELC	Eva Lindbergh Christie
ELLL	Evangeline Lodge Land Lindbergh
EMM	Elisabeth Morrow Morgan
FDR	Franklin Delano Roosevelt
FG	Fitzhugh Green
GLN	Grace Lee Nute
HG	Harry Guggenheim
HN	Harold Nicolson
JN	Jim Newton
LFP	Lindbergh Family Papers
LOC	Manuscript Division, Library of Congress, Washington, DC
MNHS	Gale Family Library, Minnesota Historical Society, St. Paul, MN
RL	Reeve Lindbergh
RMH	Robert M. Hutchins
TWH	T. Willard Hunter
Yale	Sterling Memorial Library, Yale University, New Haven, CT
WSC	Wayne S. Cole

Notes

Introduction

1. CAL, diary entry, April 3, 1944, in *The Wartime Journals of Charles A. Lindbergh* (New York: Harcourt Brace Jovanovich, 1970), 775.

2. Liam Hoare, "Commemorative History: MSP Airport Has Its Own Ugly Connection—Charles Lindbergh," *Minneapolis Star Tribune*, September 1, 2017, https://www.startribune.com/commemorative-history-msp-airport-has-its-own-ugly-connection-charles-lindbergh/442514543.

3. Harry A. Bruno and William S. Dutton, "Lindbergh, the Famous Unknown," *Saturday Evening Post*, October 21, 1933, 23–40.

4. See, for example, Michael Lipka and Claire Gecewicz, "More Americans Now Say They're Spiritual but Not Religious," Pew Research Center, September 6, 2017, https://www.pewresearch.org/fact-tank/2017/09/06/more-americans-now-say-theyre-spiritual-but-not-religious.

5. *The Autobiography of Benjamin Franklin* (New York: Holt, 1916), chap. 8, https://www.gutenberg.org/files/20203/20203-h/20203-h.htm.

6. Allen Guelzo, *Abraham Lincoln: Redeemer President* (Grand Rapids: Eerdmans, 2002), 463.

7. RL, *No More Words: A Journal of My Mother, Anne Morrow Lindbergh* (New York: Simon & Schuster, 2001), 14.

8. JN, *Uncommon Friends: Life with Thomas Edison, Henry Ford, Harvey Firestone, Alexis Carrel & Charles Lindbergh* (San Diego: Harcourt, 1987), 313.

9. Flagg to CAL, September 10, 1948, CAL Papers, Series I, Box 10, Yale.

10. Paul Heelas and Linda Woodhead, *The Spiritual Revolution: Why Religion Is Giving Way to Spirituality* (Malden, MA: Blackwell, 2005), 4–6.

11. CAL, autobiography draft, September 17, 1938, CAL Papers, Series V, Box 174, Yale.

12. CAL to RMH, November 25, 1946, CAL Papers, Series I, Box 39, Yale.

13. CAL, "Aviation, Geography, and Race," *Reader's Digest*, November 1939, 66.

14. CAL, diary entry, April 15, 1945, CAL Papers, Series V, Box 213, Yale.

15. CAL, autobiography draft, December 1938, CAL Papers, Series V, Box 182, Yale.

16. CAL, *Autobiography of Values* (San Diego: Harcourt Brace Jovanovich, 1978), 3.

Chapter One

1. CAL, autobiography draft, late 1938, CAL Papers, Series V, Box 182, Yale.

2. AML, diary entry, February 20, 1944, in *War within and Without: Diaries and Letters of Anne Morrow Lindbergh, 1939–1944* (New York: Harcourt Brace Jovanovich, 1980), 409–10.

3. ELLL, "Unvarnished Memories of the Lodge Family" (unpublished manuscript [ca. 1940], CAL Papers, Series VI, Box 259, Yale); CAL, *The Spirit of St. Louis* (New York: Scribner's Sons, 1953), 321.

4. See Douglas A. Foster, *A Life of Alexander Campbell* (Grand Rapids: Eerdmans, 2020).

5. "About Us," Orchard Lake Community Church, Presbyterian, accessed September 17, 2020, https://www.olccp.com/about-us.

6. CAL, *Autobiography of Values* (San Diego: Harcourt Brace Jovanovich, 1978), 384.

7. EAL, "Martin Luther and the Reformation" (undated lecture [1859], CAL Papers, Series VI, Box 274, Yale).

8. EAL, "The Sabbath: Its Perpetual Obligation" (undated lecture [ca. 1860], CAL Papers, Series VI, Box 274, Yale).

9. ELLL, "Unvarnished Memories of the Lodge Family."

10. AML, diary entry, September 5, 1935, in *Locked Rooms and Open Doors: Diaries and Letters of Anne Morrow Lindbergh, 1933–1935* (New York: Harcourt Brace Jovanovich, 1974), 305–6.

11. CAL, "Paris 1938–'39," autobiography draft, CAL Papers, Series V, Box 182, Yale; CAL, *The Spirit of St. Louis*, 321.

12. CAL, undated [1953?], and March 16, 1956, notes on the life of C. H. Land, CAL Papers, Series VI, Box 248, Yale.

13. L. Laszlo Schwartz, *The Doctor of Dexterity: The Life of C. H. Land, Dentist* (unfinished manuscript [1956], CAL Papers, Series VI, Box 249, Yale).

14. ELLL, "For Charles A. Lindbergh, Jr.," undated [1934?], LFP, Box 1, MNHS.

15. CAL, *Boyhood on the Upper Mississippi: A Reminiscent Letter* (St. Paul: Minnesota Historical Society, 1972), 22.

16. That Bible now sits on a shelf in the Lindbergh House in Little Falls, MN. See chap. 2 for further analysis of that library's contents.

17. CAL, March 16, 1956, notes on C. H. Land.

18. ELLL, "Unvarnished Memories of the Lodge Family" and undated notebooks [ca. 1940], CAL Papers, Series VI, Box 259, Yale.

19. CAL, *Autobiography of Values*, 384.

20. CAL, undated [1953?] notes on the life of C. H. Land.

21. Alumni survey response by Sara Chase (class of 1900), quoted by James Tobin, "The First Women," *University of Michigan Heritage Project*, accessed September 17, 2020, https://heritage.umich.edu/stories/the-first-women.

22. ELLL, "For Charles A. Lindbergh, Jr."

23. RL, *Under a Wing: A Memoir* (New York: Simon & Schuster, 1998), 116.

24. AML to ELLL, September 15, 1933, in *Locked Rooms and Open Doors*, 110.

25. See John G. Rice, "Swedes," in *They Chose Minnesota: A Survey of the State's Ethnic Groups*, ed. June Drenning Holmquist (St. Paul: Minnesota Historical Society Press, 1981), 248–76.

26. Perry Lindbergh, interview by GLN, June 16–19, 1936, LFP, Box 1, MNHS.

27. BLL, *Lindbergh of Minnesota: A Political Biography* (New York: Harcourt Brace Jovanovich, 1971), 4–5.

28. ASB, *Lindbergh* (New York: Berkley Books, 1998), 11–13. Grace Lee Nute never did finish her biography of C. A. Lindbergh, but her research into the family's origins disturbed his siblings and daughters—though not his famous son. See Nute's increasingly tense exchange of letters with Eva Lindbergh Christie in December 1939–January 1940, plus CAL's letter to GLN about the matter on February 8, 1940, all in LFP, Box 2, MNHS.

29. "Intelligence from the Mississippi Valley," *Home Missionary* 33 (February 1850): 233–34.

30. BLL, *Lindbergh of Minnesota*, 6–7.

31. CAL to GLN, December 30, 1936, LFP, Box 2, MNHS.

32. [C. S. Harrison], "'Entering into Life, Maimed,'" *Home Missionary* 34 (March 1862): 258.

33. C. S. Harrison, "On Runners," *Home Missionary* 34 (July 1861): 73.

34. CAL, *The Spirit of St. Louis*, 221–22.

35. GLN to ELC, December 2, 1936, and ELC to GLN, December 7, 1936, LFP, Box 2, MNHS. CAL also mentions Rev. Harrison in the first pages of his first book, *"We": The Famous Flier's Own Story of His Life and His Transatlantic Flight, Together with His Views on the Future of Aviation* (New York: Grosset & Dunlap, 1927), 20.

36. Frank Lindbergh, interview by GLN, June 9, 1936, and Perry Lindbergh interview, June 16–19, 1936, both LFP, Box 1, MNHS.

37. Juno (June) Lindbergh Butler, interview by GLN, July 29, 1935, LFP, Box 1, MNHS.

38. CAL, autobiography draft, March 8, 1959, CAL Papers, Series V, Box 186, Yale.

39. Parish book for Trinity Episcopal Church, Melrose, MN, Episcopal Church, Diocese of Minnesota, Parish Records, Box 65, MNHS.

40. Frank Lindbergh and Perry Lindbergh interviews.

41. CAL, *Autobiography of Values*, 48.

42. William Bell Mitchell, *History of Stearns County, Minnesota*, vol. 1 (Chicago: H. C. Cooper, Jr. & Co., 1915), 1293.

43. BLL, *Lindbergh of Minnesota*, 11–12; June Lindbergh Butler and Perry Lindbergh interviews; GLN to CAL, November 19, 1936, LFP, Box 1, MNHS.

44. C. A. Lindbergh, Congressional platform (1914), C. A. Lindbergh Papers, Box 10, MNHS. See also CAL, *Autobiography of Values*, 48.

45. Clara K. Fuller, *History of Morrison and Todd Counties, Minnesota: Their People, Industries, and Institutions*, vol. 1 (Indianapolis: B. F. Bowen & Co., 1915), 198–99; Harold L. Fisher, *The Land Called Morrison*, rev. ed. (St. Cloud, MN: Volkmuth Publishing, 1976), 132.

46. CAL, *Boyhood*, 3.

47. *Little Falls Herald*, October 16, 1893.

48. ELLL, "For Charles A. Lindbergh, Jr."

49. Ellen LaFond Herron, interview with GLN, September 9, 1937, LFP, Box 1, MNHS; ELC to GLN, February 26, 1937, LFP, Box 2, MNHS.

50. ELLL, "For Charles A. Lindbergh, Jr."

51. ELLL, "Unvarnished Memories of the Lodge Family."

Chapter Two

1. RL, *Under a Wing: A Memoir* (New York: Simon & Schuster, 1998), 204.

2. Quoted in FG, addendum to CAL, *"We": The Famous Flier's Own Story*

of His Life and His Transatlantic Flight, Together with His Views on the Future of Aviation (New York: Grosset & Dunlap, 1927), 274.

3. CAL, *Autobiography of Values* (San Diego: Harcourt Brace Jovanovich, 1978), 50.

4. RL, address at St. Cloud (MN) State University, June 17, 1981, LFP, Box 1, MNHS.

5. AML, address to the Minnesota Historical Society, Minneapolis, October 27, 1979; published as "The Changing Concept of Heroes," *Minnesota History* 46 (Winter 1979): 308.

6. CAL, *Autobiography of Values*, 384.

7. Thomas Kessner, *The Flight of the Century: Charles Lindbergh and the Rise of American Aviation* (New York: Oxford University Press, 2010), 17.

8. Brendan Gill, "The Doom of Heroes," *New Yorker*, September 19, 1953, 113.

9. ASB, *Lindbergh* (New York: Berkley Books, 1998), 27.

10. Sinclair Lewis, introduction to *Main Street*, Modern Library Paperback edition (New York: Random House, 1999), xii; ELLL, notes for CAL, part 2, undated, C. A. Lindbergh Papers, Box 14, MNHS.

11. Joyce Milton, *Loss of Eden: A Biography of Charles and Anne Morrow Lindbergh* (New York: HarperCollins, 1993), 11.

12. Clara K. Fuller, *History of Morrison and Todd Counties, Minnesota: Their People, Industries, and Institutions*, vol. 1 (Indianapolis: B. F. Bowen & Co., 1915), 66–67.

13. Emeroy Johnson, *History of the Bethel Evangelical Lutheran Church, Little Falls, Minnesota and Immanuel Evangelical Lutheran Church, Darling, Minnesota* (Little Falls, MN: Bethel Evangelical Lutheran Church, 1942), 1–10.

14. Johnson, *History of the Bethel Evangelical Lutheran Church*, 16, 19; GLN to CAL, December 27, 1938, LFP, Box 2, MNHS.

15. Perry Lindbergh, interview by GLN, June 16–19, 1936, LFP, Box 1, MNHS.

16. Johnson, *History of the Bethel Evangelical Lutheran Church*, 28–29.

17. "History," First Lutheran Church, Little Falls, MN, accessed September 18, 2020, https://www.flclittlefalls.org/history.html.

18. Harold L. Fisher, *The Land Called Morrison*, rev. ed. (St. Cloud, MN: Volkmuth Publishing, 1976), 149.

19. See Matthew Frye Jacobson, *Whiteness of a Different Color: European Immigrants and the Alchemy of Race* (Cambridge, MA: Harvard University Press, 1998).

20. Erika K. Jackson, *Scandinavians in Chicago: The Origins of White Privilege in Modern America* (Urbana: University of Illinois Press, 2019), 3; Dag Blanck, "'A Mixture of People with Different Roots': Swedish Immigrants in

the American Ethno-Racial Hierarchies," *Journal of American Ethnic History* 33 (Spring 2014): 37–54.

21. Fuller, *History of Morrison and Todd Counties, Minnesota,* 119–20.

22. ELLL, notes for CAL, part 1, undated, CAL Papers, Box 13, MNHS.

23. CAL, 1949 draft, *Spirit of St. Louis* Collection, Box 7, LOC.

24. See CAL, *The Spirit of St. Louis* (New York: Scribner's Sons, 1953), 308–10, and *Autobiography of Values,* 5–6, 308. He also mentions it briefly in *Boyhood on the Upper Mississippi: A Reminiscent Letter* (St. Paul: Minnesota Historical Society, 1972), 6.

25. CAL, *Autobiography of Values,* 308; ELLL, notes for CAL, part 1.

26. CAL, *Autobiography of Values,* 308.

27. Robert Grant, "O Worship the King All Glorious Above," in *The Pilgrim Hymnal* (New York: Pilgrim, 1904), no. 1.

28. CAL, 1949 draft, *Spirit of St. Louis* Collection, Box 7, LOC.

29. CAL, "Incidents" notes, September 1966, CAL Papers, Series V, Box 192, Yale.

30. CAL, autobiography draft, January 19, 1968, CAL Papers, Series V, Box 193, Yale.

31. CAL, 1949 draft, *Spirit of St. Louis* Collection, Box 7, LOC.

32. GLN to CAL, April 8, 1938, LFP, Box 2, MNHS.

33. BLL, *Lindbergh of Minnesota: A Political Biography* (New York: Harcourt Brace Jovanovich, 1971), 34.

34. CAL to GLN, July 27, 1937, LFP, Box 2, MNHS.

35. Russell Fridley, director of the Minnesota Historical Society in the last years of CAL's life, summarizes the decades-long restoration of the Lindbergh House in his introduction to *Boyhood,* x–xii. On the house's library, see also BLL, *Lindbergh of Minnesota,* 32–33.

36. CAL, *Autobiography of Values,* 384.

37. David Hume, *Enquiry concerning Human Understanding* (Chicago: Open Court, 1904), 105.

38. ELC, interview by BLL, April 16, 1966, LFP, Box 1, MNHS.

39. Publisher's introduction to Henry Drummond, *The Evolution of Man* (Philadelphia: Henry Altemus, 1893), 19, 24–25.

40. CAL, autobiography draft, December 24, 1966, CAL Papers, Series V, Box 192, Yale; CAL, *Autobiography of Values,* 383.

41. Henry Drummond, *The Ascent of Man*, 4th ed. (New York: James Pott, 1894), 10, 18.

42. Drummond, *Ascent of Man*, 19, 38–39.

43. Henry Drummond, *Natural Law in the Spiritual World* (New York: James Pott, 1893), 350, 357, 364–65.

44. CAL to GLN, March 23, 1938, LFP, Box 2, MNHS.

45. CAL to GLN, May 27, 1937, LFP, Box 2, MNHS.

46. RL, address at St. Cloud (MN) State University.

47. CAL, autobiography draft, July 15, 1963, CAL Papers, Series V, Box 190, Yale.

48. CAL, diary entries, 1912 [1913], CAL Papers, Series V, Box 214, Yale.

49. Mrs. A. M. Opsahl, interview by GLN, undated [1936–1937], LFP, Box 1, MNHS.

50. Quoted by Carl Bolander, interview by Sarah Thorp Heald, June 1937, WPA Oral Histories, Morrison County Historical Society, Little Falls, MN.

51. CAL, *Autobiography of Values*, 5.

52. ELLL, notes for CAL, part 1, undated.

53. CAL, August 4, 1969, remarks on Kenneth S. Davis, *The Hero: Charles A. Lindbergh and the American Dream* (New York: Doubleday, 1959), CAL Papers, Box 11, MNHS.

54. CAL, *The Spirit of St. Louis*, 316–19; see also CAL, *Autobiography of Values*, 309.

55. CAL, August 1968 remarks on Walter S. Ross, *The Last Hero: Charles A. Lindbergh* (New York: Harper & Row, 1967), CAL Papers, Box 11, MNHS.

56. CAL, December 1950 draft, *Spirit of St. Louis* Collection, Box 23, LOC.

57. Milton, *Loss of Eden*, 19.

58. CAL, *The Spirit of St. Louis*, 319–20; CAL, *Autobiography of Values*, 6.

59. CAL, *The Spirit of St. Louis*, 320.

60. ELLL, interview by United Press, May 21, 1927.

61. CAL to GLN, May 27, 1937, LFP, Box 2, MNHS.

62. CAL, *Autobiography of Values*, 53.

63. CAL, November 29, 1968, remarks on Dale Van Every and Morris De-Haven Tracy, *Charles Lindbergh: His Life* (New York: D. Appleton, 1928), CAL Papers, Box 11, MNHS.

64. [Sidwell] Friends School, *1915–1916 Catalog*, in CAL Papers, Box 11, MNHS.

65. CAL, autobiography draft, March 1939, CAL Papers, Series V, Box 182, Yale.

66. *Washington Evening Star*, May 21, 1927, 2.

67. CAL, autobiography draft, March 1939, CAL Papers, Series V, Box 182, Yale.

68. CAL, December 1950–January 1951 drafts, *Spirit of St. Louis* Collection, Box 23, LOC.

69. CAL, *The Spirit of St. Louis*, 312, 313.

70. CAL to GLN, April 20, 1937, LFP, Box 2, MNHS.

71. CAL to BLL, April 7, 1967, CAL Papers, Series I, Box 42, Yale; BLL, *Lindbergh of Minnesota*, 207.

72. C. A. Lindbergh, congressional platform (1914), C. A. Lindbergh Papers, Box 10, MNHS.

73. C. A. Lindbergh, gubernatorial platform (1916), C. A. Lindbergh Papers, Box 10, MNHS.

74. BLL, *Lindbergh of Minnesota*, 191–98.

75. C. A. Lindbergh, "Some Reflections of My Daughter Lillian, 1916," LFP, Box 1, MNHS.

76. Woodrow Wilson, "War Message to Congress," April 2, 1917, *WWI Document Archive*, Brigham Young University, https://wwi.lib.byu.edu/index.php /Wilson%27s_War_Message_to_Congress. On that president's religious biography, see Barry Hankins, *Woodrow Wilson: Ruling Elder, Spiritual President* (New York: Oxford University Press, 2016).

77. Quoted by George M. Stephenson, "The Attitude of Swedish-Americans toward the World War," *Proceedings of the Mississippi Valley Historical Association* 10 (1918–1919): 84n.

78. Stephenson, "The Attitude of Swedish-Americans toward the World War," 92.

79. Jackson, *Scandinavians in Chicago*, 136–37; Madison Grant, *The Passing of the Great Race, or The Racial Basis of European History*, 4th ed. (New York: Scribner's Sons, 1936; originally published, 1916), 27.

80. Samuel Clemens, *The Mysterious Stranger* (New York: Harper & Brothers, 1916), 119; quoted by Carol Jenson, "Loyalty as a Political Weapon: The 1918 Campaign in Minnesota," *Minnesota History*, Summer 1972, 43.

81. William W. Clay, "What For?," quoted in Charles [August] Lindbergh, *Why Is Your Country at War and What Happens to You after the War and Related Subjects* (Washington, DC: National Capital Press, 1917), 11.

82. J. H. Morse, "Red Blood or Yellow?" (1918 flyer), C. A. Lindbergh Papers, Box 10, MNHS.

83. Thomas Pederson, "Charles Augustus [sic] Lindbergh, Sr., As I Knew Him," undated [1936?], LFP, Box 1, MNHS.

84. Opsahl interview. Opsahl alludes to a saying of Jesus recorded in Matthew 13:57 and Mark 6:4.

85. ELLL, notes for CAL, part 1.

86. CAL, *Boyhood*, 33; CAL, remarks on Ross, *The Last Hero*.

87. RL, address at St. Cloud (MN) State University.

Chapter Three

1. Gill Robb Wilson, *The Airman's World* (New York: Random House, 1957), 20.

2. In his first memoir, Lindbergh identified his first encounter with an airplane as taking place in Washington, DC, in 1912; CAL, *"We": The Famous Flier's Own Story of His Life and His Transatlantic Flight, Together with His Views on the Future of Aviation* (New York: Grosset & Dunlap, 1927), 23. But his later, less-hurried autobiographical reflections relocated that event to Minnesota a year earlier; CAL, *Autobiography of Values* (San Diego: Harcourt Brace Jovanovich, 1978), 58.

3. CAL, *The Spirit of St. Louis* (New York: Scribner's Sons, 1953), 244–45.

4. Wilson, *The Airman's World*, 2.

5. Thomas Kessner, *The Flight of the Century: Charles Lindbergh and the Rise of American Aviation* (New York: Oxford University Press, 2010), 20.

6. Wilson, *The Airman's World*, 26.

7. The title of the most complete biography of the Wright Brothers hints at their religious upbringing: Tom Crouch, *The Bishop's Boys: A Life of Wilbur and Orville Wright* (New York: Norton, 1989).

8. William J. Tate, "With the Wrights at Kitty Hawk: Anniversary of First Flight Twenty-Five Years Ago," *Aeronautic Review* 1 (December 1928): 190.

9. Quoted in Joseph J. Corn, *The Winged Gospel: America's Romance with Aviation*, rev. ed. (Baltimore: Johns Hopkins University Press, 2001), 6.

10. David McCullough, *The Wright Brothers* (New York: Simon & Schuster, 2015), 117–22.

11. A. I. Root, "Our Homes," *Gleanings in Bee Culture*, January 1, 1905, 36.

12. Quoted in Corn, *The Winged Gospel*, 4.

13. McCullough, *The Wright Brothers*, 17–18.

14. Corn, *The Winged Gospel*, 27.

15. Corn, *The Winged Gospel*, 46.

16. Quoted in Corn, *The Winged Gospel*, 4.

17. Corn, *The Winged Gospel*, 52–53, 60–61.

18. Quoted in McCullough, *The Wright Brothers*, 174.

19. Quoted in Robert Wohl, *A Passion for Wings: Aviation and the Western Imagination, 1908–1918* (New Haven: Yale University Press, 1994), 27. The CAL quotation is from *The Spirit of St. Louis*, 227.

20. Wohl, *A Passion for Wings*, 27–28.

21. Edgar Wallace, *Tam O' the Scoots* (Boston: Small, Maynard & Co., 1919), 5.

22. CAL, autobiography draft, March 9, 1959, CAL Papers, Series V, Box 186, Yale.

23. CAL, *Boyhood on the Upper Mississippi: A Reminiscent Letter* (St. Paul: Minnesota Historical Society, 1972), 40.

24. CAL, *Boyhood*, 44–45.

25. CAL, "We," 23–24.

26. CAL, November 29, 1968, remarks on Dale Van Every and Morris De-Haven Tracy, *Charles Lindbergh: His Life* (New York: D. Appleton, 1928), CAL Papers, Box 11, MNHS.

27. CAL, *The Spirit of St. Louis*, 247.

28. CAL, "We," 23.

29. CAL, *The Spirit of St. Louis*, 248.

30. CAL, *The Spirit of St. Louis*, 249.

31. CAL, *The Spirit of St. Louis*, 261–62.

32. CAL, "We," 31.

33. Bill Bryson, *One Summer: America, 1927* (New York: Anchor Books, 2013), 45.

34. CAL, *The Spirit of St. Louis*, 254–61.

35. CAL, *The Spirit of St. Louis*, 288–89.

36. Bud Gurney, undated interview, Billy Wilder Papers, Folder 94, Margaret Herrick Library, Beverly Hills, CA.

37. CAL, *The Spirit of St. Louis*, 252.

38. On this phase of Lindbergh's career, see BLL, "Barnstorming with Lindbergh," *Minnesota History* 52 (Summer 1991): 230–38.

39. CAL interviewed Bud Gurney in 1969. That oral history became the ba-

sis for Giacinta Bradley Koontz, "Slim and Bud," *Air & Space Magazine*, January 2010, https://www.airspacemag.com/history-of-flight/slim-and-bud-9461697.

40. CAL, *The Spirit of St. Louis*, 269.

41. CAL, *"We,"* 198–99.

42. CAL, *Autobiography of Values*, 296–97.

43. Wohl, *A Passion for Wings*, 282.

44. Quoted in BLL, *Lindbergh of Minnesota*, 252.

45. CAL, *"We,"* 28.

46. CAL, *"We,"* 60.

47. CAL, *"We,"* 71–76.

48. CAL, *The Spirit of St. Louis*, 448; BLL, *Lindbergh of Minnesota*, 273–74.

49. CAL, *The Spirit of St. Louis*, 449–50.

50. CAL, autobiography draft, March 26, 1968, CAL Papers, Series V, Box 193, Yale.

51. CAL and ELC, interview by BLL, April 16, 1966, LFP, Box 1, MNHS.

52. Undated advertisement [ca. 1920], First Unitarian Society, Minneapolis, John H. Dietrich Papers, Box 2, MNHS.

53. John H. Dietrich, "The God of Evolution," April 13, 1924, Dietrich Papers, Box 2, MNHS.

54. John H. Dietrich, "Shall It Be Again?" November 12, 1922, Dietrich Papers, Box 2, MNHS.

55. CAL, interview by BLL, April 17, 1966, LFP, Box 1, MNHS.

56. CAL, autobiography draft, March 26, 1968, CAL Papers, Series V, Box 193, Yale. The autobiography makes it sound like the "funeral flight" happened soon after C. A. Lindbergh's death, but Charles told Larson that it was several years later. Contrast CAL, *Autobiography of Values*, 389–90, with BLL, *Lindbergh of Minnesota*, 281.

57. Thomas Pederson, "Charles Augustus [*sic*] Lindbergh, Sr., as I Knew Him," undated [1936?], LFP, Box 1, MNHS.

58. CAL, autobiography draft, March 26, 1968, CAL Papers, Series V, Box 193, Yale.

59. CAL, *The Spirit of St. Louis*, 4.

60. Corn, *The Winged Gospel*, xiv.

61. CAL, *The Spirit of St. Louis*, 35.

Chapter Four

1. *New York Times*, May 30, 1927, 18.

2. Quoted in ASB, *Lindbergh* (New York: Berkley Books, 1998), 121–22.

3. CAL, December 1942 draft, *Spirit of St. Louis* Collection, Box 2, LOC. In the published book, Lindbergh mentions carrying such a medal but is less certain where it came from; CAL, *The Spirit of St. Louis* (New York: Scribner's Sons, 1953), 433.

4. Frederick Lewis Allen, *Only Yesterday: An Informal History of the 1920's* (New York: Harper & Row, 1931), 180.

5. CAL, *The Spirit of St. Louis*, 496.

6. Allen, *Only Yesterday*, 180.

7. ASB, *Lindbergh*, 148.

8. On Lindbergh's autobiographical writing, see Brian Horrigan, "'My Own Mind and Pen': Charles Lindbergh, Autobiography, and Memory," *Minnesota History* 58 (Spring 2002): 2–15.

9. "Poems on Lindbergh," *Bulletin of the Carnegie Institute* 1 (June 1928): 20.

10. *New York Times*, June 13, 1927, 22.

11. Thomas Kessner, *The Flight of the Century: Charles Lindbergh and the Rise of American Aviation* (New York: Oxford University Press, 2010), 111.

12. F. Scott Fitzgerald, *This Side of Paradise* (New York: Scribner's Sons, 1920), 213.

13. Brendan Gill, *Lindbergh Alone: May 21, 1927* (New York: Harcourt Brace Jovanovich, 1977), 14.

14. John H. Finley, foreword to James E. West, *The Lone Scout of the Sky: The Story of Charles A. Lindbergh* (Philadelphia: John C. Winston, 1928), [22].

15. Quoted in Modris Eksteins, *Rites of Spring: The Great War and the Birth of the Modern Age* (New York: Random House, 1989), 243 (emphasis added).

16. Quoted in Bill Bryson, *One Summer: America, 1927* (New York: Anchor Books, 2013), 99.

17. Robert Wohl, *The Spectacle of Flight: Aviation and the Western Imagination, 1920–1950* (New Haven: Yale University Press, 2005), 9.

18. Quoted in FG, addendum to CAL, *"We": The Famous Flier's Own Story of His Life and His Transatlantic Flight, Together with His Views on the Future of Aviation* (New York: Grosset & Dunlap, 1927), 246.

19. Myron Herrick, foreword to CAL, *"We,"* 5–9.

20. "Poems on Lindbergh," 20.

21. FG, addendum to *"We,"* 256.

22. *Hartford Courant,* May 23, 1927, 4

23. Eksteins, *Rites of Spring,* 243.

24. Eksteins, *Rites of Spring,* 247.

25. RL, interview by Russell Fridley, October 23, 1977, LFP, Box 1, MNHS.

26. FG, addendum to *"We,"* 236.

27. FG, addendum to *"We,"* 265.

28. FG, addendum to *"We,"* 266.

29. Quoted in FG, addendum to *"We,"* 289.

30. FG, addendum to *"We,"* 294.

31. *Douglas (AZ) Daily Dispatch,* June 21, 1927, 2.

32. *Washington Evening Star,* June 13, 1927, 5

33. *Cincinnati Enquirer,* June 13, 1927, 8.

34. *Washington Evening Star,* June 13, 1927, 5; Bryson, *One Summer,* 149.

35. FG, addendum to *"We,"* 295–96.

36. FG, addendum to *"We,"* 308.

37. New York, Grand Rapids, and Fort Worth programs among other 1927 memorabilia collected in CAL Papers, Box 19, MNHS.

38. *Lindbergh the Flier of Little Falls,* commemorative booklet published by juniors and seniors of Little Falls (MN) High School (1928), CAL Papers, Box 19, MNHS.

39. *New York Times,* June 12, 1927, 4.

40. Dale Van Every and Morris DeHaven Tracy, *Charles Lindbergh: His Life* (New York: D. Appleton, 1927), 197–98.

41. CAL, November 29, 1968, remarks on Van Every and Tracy, *Charles Lindbergh,* CAL Papers, Box 11, MNHS.

42. Silas Bent, "Idol Worship: 1927," *Christian Advocate,* December 8, 1927, 1496–98. (Thanks to Paul Putz for sharing this article and the responses it inspired.) See also Bent, *Ballyhoo: The Voice of the Press* (New York: Boni and Liveright, 1927). The Allen quotation comes from *Only Yesterday,* 163.

43. "Lindbergh above the Clouds of Detraction," *Christian Advocate,* December 22, 1927, 1556.

44. Florence Emily Cain, "Idol Worship: 1927," *Christian Advocate,* January 12, 1928, 38.

45. *New York Times,* May 23, 1927, 3.

46. *Chicago Tribune*, May 23, 1927, 7.

47. *Kansas City Times*, May 23, 1927, 10.

48. Rev. E. Cameron, "Lindburgh [*sic*] in Prophecy," United Baptist Church, North Head, New Brunswick, May 22, 1927, CAL Papers, Box 19, MNHS.

49. *Kansas City Times*, May 23, 1927, 10.

50. CAL, autobiography draft, March 6, 1959, CAL Papers, Series V, Box 186, Yale.

51. Miles Jenks and Bryan Morey, "Lesser-Known Artists of the Lindbergh Collection," *History Happens Here: Digital Storytelling from the Missouri Historical Society*, March 18, 2020, https://mohistory.org/blog/lesser-known-artists-of-the-lindbergh-collection.

52. *New York Times*, June 20, 1927, 22.

53. ASB, *Lindbergh*, 218; "Stained-Glass Hagiology Claims Lindy," *Western Architect* 38 (August 1929): 144–45.

54. *New York Times*, May 30, 1927, 18; and June 13, 1927, 22.

55. F. Scott Fitzgerald, "Echoes of the Jazz Age" (1931), in *The Crack-Up, with Other Pieces and Stories* (New York: Penguin Books, 1965), 16–17.

56. On Sallman's *Head of Christ* and other white images of Jesus, see Edward J. Blum and Paul Harvey, *The Color of Christ: The Son of God and the Saga of Race in America* (Chapel Hill: University of North Carolina Press, 2012).

57. *Wisconsin State Journal*, May 22, 1927, 4.

58. Charles J. McGuirk, "The Tallness of the Great," *Liberty*, August 27, 1927, 7.

59. Quoted by John W. Ward, "The Meaning of Lindbergh's Flight," in *Studies in American Culture: Dominant Ideas and Images*, ed. Mary C. Turpie and Joseph J. Kwiat (Minneapolis: University of Minnesota Press, 1960), 33–34.

60. Mark Helbling, "The Response of African Americans to Lindbergh's Flight to Paris," *Prospects* 27 (October 2002): 384–85.

61. Kelly J. Baker, *Gospel according to the Klan: The KKK's Appeal to Protestant America, 1915–1930* (Lawrence: University Press of Kansas, 2011), 164.

62. Helbling, "The Response of African Americans," 376, 384.

63. William Weldon Johnson, "Three Achievements and Their Significance," in *The Selected Writings of William Weldon Johnson*, vol. 2, ed. Sondra Kathryn Wilson (New York: Oxford University Press, 1995), 91–92.

64. *Oakland Tribune*, May 30, 1927, 6.

65. *New York Times*, May 30, 1927, 18; and June 13, 1927, 22.

66. Quoted in FG, addendum to *"We,"* 311–12.

67. Allen, *Only Yesterday*, 183–84.

68. Quoted in "Angel like Lindbergh," *Time*, January 25, 1932, 40.

69. FG, addendum to *"We,"* 282.

70. GLN to CAL, December 11, 1942, and CAL to GLN, December 19, 1942, LFP, Box 2, MNHS. A photograph of the eugenics memorial and Dight's correspondence regarding Lindbergh can be found in the Charles Fremont Dight Papers, Box 5, MNHS.

71. See Gary Phelps, "The Eugenics Crusade of Charles Fremont Dight," *Minnesota History* 49 (Fall 1984): 99–108.

72. "Unjustified Sterilization," *America*, May 14, 1927, 102.

73. Christine Rosen, *Preaching Eugenics: Religious Leaders and the American Eugenics Movement* (New York: Oxford University Press, 2004), 4.

74. Quoted in Rosen, *Preaching Eugenics*, 3.

75. Quoted in Phelps, "The Eugenics Crusade," 105–6.

76. CAL, diary entry, November 14, 1938, CAL Papers, Series V, Box 214, Yale.

77. Joseph J. Corn, *The Winged Gospel: America's Romance with Aviation*, rev. ed. (Baltimore: Johns Hopkins University Press, 2001), 27.

78. CAL, *"We,"* 61.

79. Quoted by FG, addendum to *"We,"* 244.

80. Jim Brunton, "North Atlantic Skies—the Gateway to Europe," *NATS Blog*, June 26, 2014, https://nats.aero/blog/2014/06/north-atlantic-skies-gateway-europe.

81. Gill, *Lindbergh Alone*, 6.

82. CAL, *"We,"* 216–24.

83. John Lardner, "The Lindbergh Legends," in *The Aspirin Age, 1919–1941*, ed. Isabel Leighton (New York: Simon & Schuster, 1949), 200–201.

84. CAL, March 15, 1939, draft, *Spirit of St. Louis* Collection, Box 1, LOC.

85. CAL, *The Spirit of St. Louis*, 389–90.

86. CAL, *Autobiography of Values* (San Diego: Harcourt Brace Jovanovich, 1978), 12; CAL, August 4, 1969, remarks on Kenneth S. Davis, *The Hero: Charles A. Lindbergh and the American Dream* (New York: Doubleday, 1959), CAL Papers, Box 11, MNHS.

Chapter Five

1. AML, diary entry, undated [May 1928], in AML, *Bring Me a Unicorn: Diaries and Letters of Anne Morrow Lindbergh, 1922–1928* (New York: Harcourt Brace Jovanovich, 1971), 169.

2. AML to Dwight Morrow, January 9, 1926, in *Bring Me a Unicorn*, 28.

3. RL, *Under a Wing: A Memoir* (New York: Simon & Schuster, 1998), 207.

4. CAL, *Autobiography of Values* (San Diego: Harcourt Brace Jovanovich, 1978), 119.

5. AML, *War within and Without: Diaries and Letters of Anne Morrow Lindbergh, 1939–1944* (New York: Harcourt Brace Jovanovich, 1980), xiv. See also, AML, diary entry, July 8, 1956, in *Against Wind and Tide: Letters and Journals, 1947–1986*, ed. RL (New York: Pantheon Books, 2012), 153.

6. HN, *Dwight Morrow* (New York: Harcourt, Brace and Co., 1935), 12–14.

7. Julius Seelye Bixler, "Charles E. Garman—Amherst's Scholar-Teacher," *American Scholar* 1 (January 1932): 103.

8. Quoted in HN, *Dwight Morrow*, 30–31.

9. Quoted in HN, *Dwight Morrow*, 73–74.

10. CMM, *A Distant Moment* (Northampton, MA: Smith College, 1978), 12–13.

11. CMM, *A Distant Moment*, 143; "Elizabeth Cutter Morrow," *Smithipedia*, accessed September 23, 2020, https://sophia.smith.edu/blog/smithipedia/administration/elizabeth-cutter-morrow.

12. RL, *Under a Wing*, 134.

13. AML, *Bring Me a Unicorn*, xv–xvi.

14. Quoted in HN to Vita Sackville-West, November 25, 1934, in HN, *Diaries and Letters, 1930–1939*, ed. Nigel Nicolson (New York: Atheneum, 1966), 191.

15. AML, diary entry, September 17, 1922, in *Bring Me a Unicorn*, 5.

16. AML, *Bring Me a Unicorn*, xx.

17. AML, *Bring Me a Unicorn*, xiv, xv.

18. Quoted in HN, *Dwight Morrow*, 117. On his connections to Union and Yale, see 226 and 248, respectively.

19. HN, *Dwight Morrow*, 249–53.

20. AML to ECM, September 23, 1924, in *Bring Me a Unicorn*, 15.

21. AML to ECM, October 10, 1925, in *Bring Me a Unicorn*, 22.

22. AML to ECM, January 31, 1927, in *Bring Me a Unicorn*, 65.

23. AML, undated diary entry [late November/early December 1927], in *Bring Me a Unicorn*, 85–86.

24. AML, diary entry, December 20, 1927, in *Bring Me a Unicorn*, 87.

25. CAL, *Autobiography of Values*, 81–83.

26. See Charles F. Downs II, "Calvin Coolidge, Dwight Morrow, and the Air

Commerce Act of 1926," June 26, 2001, Calvin Coolidge Presidential Foundation, https://www.coolidgefoundation.org/resources/essays-papers-addresses-13.

27. See, for example, telegram, Jefferson Caffery to Frank Kellogg, February 7, 1929, in *Foreign Relations of the United States, 1929*, vol. 1 (Washington: Government Printing Office, 1943), https://history.state.gov/historical documents/frus1929v01/d333.

28. CAL, *Autobiography of Values*, 88–93.

29. Jenifer Van Vleck, *Empire of the Air: Aviation and the American Ascendancy* (Cambridge, MA: Harvard University Press, 2013), 60–61. Lindbergh's popularity in that part of the world has not entirely dissipated; thanks to Mark Healey for drawing my attention to the Brazilian politician Lindbergh Farias.

30. See L. Ethan Ellis, "Dwight Morrow and the Church-State Controversy in Mexico," *Hispanic-American Historical Review* 38 (November 1958): 482–505; HN, *Dwight Morrow*, 339–47.

31. CAL, *Autobiography of Values*, 85–88.

32. Quoted in HN, *Dwight Morrow*, 313.

33. CAL, *Autobiography of Values*, 122–23.

34. CAL, *Autobiography of Values*, 122–23; CAL, August 4, 1969, remarks on Kenneth S. Davis, *The Hero: Charles A. Lindbergh and the American Dream* (New York: Doubleday, 1959), CAL Papers, Box 11, MNHS; AML, diary entry, December 21, 1927, in *Bring Me a Unicorn*, 89–90.

35. AML, diary entries, December 21, 25, 28, 1927, in *Bring Me a Unicorn*, 89, 91, 95, 103, 109.

36. AML, diary entries, January–April 1928, in *Bring Me a Unicorn*, 113, 126–27, 129, 147.

37. AML, diary entries, April–July 1928, in *Bring Me a Unicorn*, 152, 182.

38. CAL, *Autobiography of Values*, 123.

39. AML, diary entries, October 1928, in *Bring Me a Unicorn*, 196, 202.

40. CAL, *Autobiography of Values*, 124.

41. AML to CMM, October 16, 1928, in *Bring Me a Unicorn*, 211, 215.

42. AML to EMM, late November 1928, in *Bring Me a Unicorn*, 239.

43. AML to ECM, May 27, 1929, in AML, *Hour of Gold, Hour of Lead: Anne Morrow Lindbergh, Diaries and Letters, 1929–1932* (New York: Harcourt Brace Jovanovich, 1973), 39.

44. AML, *Hour of Gold, Hour of Lead*, 2.

45. AML, *Hour of Gold, Hour of Lead*, 1.

46. CAL, *Autobiography of Values*, 129.

47. CAL, *Autobiography of Values*, 129–30; CAL to Joseph T. Durkin, May 20, 1966, CAL Papers, Series I, Box 41, Yale.

48. CAL, *Autobiography of Values*, 132. See also Paluel Flagg, "Lindberghs [*sic*] Introduction to Medicine," June 22, 1930, CAL Papers, Series I, Box 10, Yale.

49. CAL to George Corner, January 7, 1965, CAL Papers, Series I, Box 41, Yale; CAL to Corner, March 16, 1969, CAL Papers, Series I, Box 42, Yale.

50. See AC, *The Voyage to Lourdes*, trans. Virgilia Peterson (New York: Harper, 1950), and Joseph T. Durkin, *Hope for Our Time: Alexis Carrel on Man and Society* (New York: Harper & Row, 1965), 111–17.

51. CAL to Durkin, May 20, 1966.

52. For example, CAL, "A Method for Washing Corpuscles in Suspension," *Science*, n.s., 75 (April 15, 1932): 415–16, and AC and CAL, "The Culture of Whole Organs," *Science*, n.s., 81 (June 21, 1935): 621–23.

53. Flagg to CAL, June 22, 1935, CAL Papers, Series I, Box 10, Yale.

54. AC to W. M. Weishaar, September 22, 1931, CAL Papers, Series I, Box 7, Yale.

55. CAL, autobiography draft, April 27, 1963, CAL Papers, Series V, Box 190, Yale. John D. Rockefeller Jr. later called Lindbergh to ask if that church's "steel-girdered 'skyscraper' steeple . . . constituted such a menace to low-flying airplanes that a red light should be placed upon it"; CAL, autobiography drafts, January 5 and March 6, 1959, CAL Papers, Series V, Box 186, Yale.

56. C. A. Lindbergh, speech in the US House of Representatives, March 10, 1916, quoted in Charles [August] Lindbergh, *Why Is Your Country at War and What Happens to You after the War and Related Subjects* (Washington, DC: National Capital Press, 1917), 40n.

57. CAL, statement on AC centenary celebration, Georgetown University, Washington, DC, June 28, 1973, CAL Papers, Series V, Box 205, Yale.

58. CAL, *Autobiography of Values*, 139.

59. CAL, *Autobiography of Values*, 129.

60. AML, diary entry, December 25, 1927, in *Bring Me a Unicorn*, 104.

61. AML to CMM, December 2, 1928, in *Bring Me a Unicorn*, 245.

62. AML, *Hour of Gold, Hour of Lead*, 7–8.

63. AML to ECM, January 30, 1930, in *Hour of Gold, Hour of Lead*, 124.

64. AML, *Hour of Gold, Hour of Lead*, 2.

65. AML, *The Steep Ascent* (New York: Harcourt, Brace, 1944), 77.

66. CAL, *Autobiography of Values*, 203–6; ASB, *Lindbergh* (New York: Berkley Books, 1998), 209–10.

67. AML to EMM, September 23, 1929, in *Hour of Gold, Hour of Lead*, 86–87.

68. See, for example, Anne's description of the Reformation memorial in Geneva, Switzerland, diary entry, September 4, 1926, in *Bring Me a Unicorn*, 48.

69. AML to ECM, August 6 and 10, 1931, in *Hour of Gold, Hour of Lead*, 163–66, 169–70.

70. AML to ECM, August 17, 1931, in *Hour of Gold, Hour of Lead*, 174–75; AML, *North to the Orient* (New York: Harcourt, Brace, 1935), 105–8.

71. ASB, *Lindbergh*, 229.

Chapter Six

1. AML, *Hour of Gold, Hour of Lead: Anne Morrow Lindbergh, Diaries and Letters, 1929–1932* (New York: Harcourt Brace Jovanovich, 1973), 213.

2. AML to ELLL, November 12, 1931, in *Hour of Gold, Hour of Lead*, 202.

3. AML to CMM, October 1931, in *Hour of Gold, Hour of Lead*, 201.

4. AML, *Hour of Gold, Hour of Lead*, 210–11.

5. *Nashville Banner*, March 6, 1932, 1.

6. *Kansas City Times*, March 7, 1932, 1.

7. AML to ELLL, March 12, 1932, in *Hour of Gold, Hour of Lead*, 233.

8. ASB, *Lindbergh* (New York: Berkley Books, 1998), 254, 257, 264.

9. ASB, *Lindbergh*, 265–67.

10. AML, *Hour of Gold, Hour of Lead*, 211; AML, diary entry, May 11, 1932, in *Hour of Gold, Hour of Lead*, 246.

11. AML, diary entry, May 16, 1932, in *Hour of Gold, Hour of Lead*, 251.

12. ASB, *Lindbergh*, 277.

13. *Cincinnati Enquirer*, May 16, 1932, 18.

14. *Philadelphia Inquirer*, March 7, 1932, 11.

15. AML, "First Year after Death," undated manuscript [1974–1975], in *Against Wind and Tide: Letters and Journals, 1947–1986*, ed. RL (New York: Pantheon Books, 2012), 290.

16. AML, *Hour of Gold, Hour of Lead*, 214.

17. CAL, *Autobiography of Values* (San Diego: Harcourt Brace Jovanovich, 1978), 139–40.

18. Quoted in AML, diary entry, May 17, 1932, in *Hour of Gold, Hour of Lead*, 252.

19. AML, diary entry, August 16, 1932, in *Hour of Gold, Hour of Lead*, 300–301.

20. Quoted in AML, diary entry, August 18, 1932, in *Hour of Gold, Hour of Lead*, 302.

21. Quoted in AML, diary entry, February 6, 1933, in *Locked Rooms and Open Doors: Diaries and Letters of Anne Morrow Lindbergh, 1933–1935* (New York: Harcourt Brace Jovanovich, 1974), 13.

22. CAL, *Autobiography of Values*, 17; CAL, foreword to AML, *Listen! The Wind* (New York: Harcourt, Brace, 1938), v.

23. AML, *Locked Rooms and Open Doors*, xvii–xviii.

24. Quoted in Lauren D. Lyman, "The Lindbergh I Know," *Saturday Evening Post*, April 4, 1953, 85.

25. CAL, diary entry, July 10, 1933, CAL Papers, Series V, Box 214, Yale.

26. AML, *The Flower and the Nettle: Diaries and Letters of Anne Morrow Lindbergh, 1936–1939* (New York: Harcourt Brace Jovanovich, 1976), xiv.

27. AML, diary entry, July 21, 1933, in *Locked Rooms and Open Doors*, 59.

28. AML, diary entry, September 26, 1933, in *Locked Rooms and Open Doors*, 118.

29. AML to EMM, October 26, 1933, in *Locked Rooms and Open Doors*, 137.

30. ASB, *Lindbergh*, 290–96.

31. CAL, "Maine, 1934" draft, CAL Papers, Series V, Box 174, Yale.

32. AML to EMM, October 16, 1934, in *Locked Rooms and Open Doors*, 205.

33. AML, diary entry, December 30, 1934, in *Locked Rooms and Open Doors*, 232.

34. HN to Sackville-West, October 1, 1934, in HN, *Diaries and Letters, 1930–1939*, ed. Nigel Nicolson (New York: Atheneum, 1966), 182–83.

35. Not that one of America's most famous skeptics believed in *that* story. "For Mencken," his most recent biographer concludes, "the peaceful and joyous hereafter was another ideal that lacked proof, simply a tender-minded idea to get through the hard night of human misery"; D. G. Hart, *Damning Words: The Life and Religious Times of H. L. Mencken* (Grand Rapids: Eerdmans, 2016), 244.

36. Quoted in ASB, *Lindbergh*, 314–15.

37. *New York Times*, February 12, 1935, 12.

38. CAL, *Autobiography of Values*, 18, 142.

39. Brian Horrigan, "'My Own Mind and Pen': Charles Lindbergh, Autobiography, and Memory," *Minnesota History* 58 (Spring 2002): 12.

40. CAL, August 4, 1969, remarks on Kenneth S. Davis, *The Hero: Charles A.*

Lindbergh and the American Dream (New York: Doubleday, 1959), CAL Papers, Box 11, MNHS.

41. CAL, diary entry, June 15, 1941, CAL Papers, Series V, Box 214, Yale. This is one of many passages that Lindbergh edited before publishing his diaries from the time; compare with *The Wartime Journals of Charles A. Lindbergh* (New York: Harcourt Brace Jovanovich, 1970), 502–3.

42. AML, *Locked Rooms and Open Doors*, xxii–xxiii.

43. AML to Mrs. Goodkind, October 27, 1948, in *Against Wind and Tide*, 50.

44. AML, *Locked Rooms and Open Doors*, xxiii–xxiv.

45. RL, *Under a Wing: A Memoir* (New York: Simon & Schuster, 1998), 64–65.

46. RL, *No More Words: A Journal of My Mother, Anne Morrow Lindbergh* (New York: Simon & Schuster, 2001), 171; Rainer Maria Rilke, "The Swan," trans. Stephen Mitchell, accessed September 23, 2020, https://allpoetry .com/poem/8505631-The-Swan-by-Rainer-Maria-Rilke.

47. Susan Hertog, *Anne Morrow Lindbergh: Her Life* (New York: Anchor Books, 1999), 274.

48. AML, diary entry, June 17, 1935, in *Locked Rooms and Open Doors*, 277.

49. AML, diary entry, July 3, 1935, in *Locked Rooms and Open Doors*, 279.

50. AML, diary entry, July 16, 1935, in *Locked Rooms and Open Doors*, 285–86.

51. AML, diary entry, September 17, 1935, in *Locked Rooms and Open Doors*, 312.

52. AML, diary entry, December 7, 1935, in *Locked Rooms and Open Doors*, 331; CAL, *Autobiography of Values*, 18.

53. AML to ELLL, December 21, 1935, in *Locked Rooms and Open Doors*, 332.

54. *New York Times*, December 23, 1935, 1.

55. AML to ECM, January 10, 1936, in *The Flower and the Nettle*, 3.

56. ASB, *Lindbergh*, 346–47.

57. ASB, *Lindbergh*, 353.

58. AML, *The Flower and the Nettle*, xiv.

Chapter Seven

1. CAL, autobiography draft, undated [1946–1947], CAL Papers, Series V, Box 182, Yale. That early paragraph found its way into the posthumously published *Autobiography of Values* (San Diego: Harcourt Brace Jovanovich, 1978), 151.

2. AML, *The Flower and the Nettle: Diaries and Letters of Anne Morrow Lindbergh, 1936–1939* (New York: Harcourt Brace Jovanovich, 1976), xiv.

3. For example, CAL, diary entry, November 30, 1938, in *The Wartime Journals of Charles A. Lindbergh* (New York: Harcourt Brace Jovanovich, 1970), 122.

4. Breckinridge to CAL, May 22, 1936, CAL Papers, Series I, Box 6, Yale.

5. Quoted in Philip Boobbyer, *The Spiritual Vision of Frank Buchman* (University Park: Pennsylvania State University Press, 2013), 12.

6. Boobbyer, *Spiritual Vision of Frank Buchman*, 2.

7. CAL to Breckinridge, June 1, 1936, CAL Papers, Series I, Box 34, Yale.

8. *Revelation*, May 1936, 196.

9. CAL to Breckinridge, June 1, 1936, CAL Papers, Series I, Box 34, Yale.

10. "'Personal Work,'" *Time*, October 18, 1926, 28.

11. Daniel Sack, "Men Want Something Real: Frank Buchman and Anglo-American College Religion in the 1920s," *Journal of Religious History* 28 (October 2004): 273–74.

12. *Time*, April 20, 1936.

13. CAL to Carol Guggenheim, June 15, 1936.

14. Alexis Carrel, *Man, the Unknown* (New York: Harper & Row, 1935), 9, 29.

15. *New York Times Book Review*, September 29, 1935, 3.

16. AML, diary entry, May 25–26, 1936, in *The Flower and the Nettle*, 59.

17. AC, *Man, the Unknown*, 118–19, 123–26.

18. AML, diary entry, June 20, 1936, in *The Flower and the Nettle*, 70.

19. CAL, *Autobiography of Values*, 21.

20. AML, diary entry, September 1, 1936, in *The Flower and the Nettle*, 108–9; ASB, *Lindbergh* (New York: Berkley Books, 1998), 354–55.

21. CAL to AC, November 16, 1936, CAL Papers, Series I, Box 35, Yale.

22. CAL to Younghusband, December 19, 1936, and January 10, 1937, and CAL to AC, January 2, 1937, CAL Papers, Series I, Box 35, Yale.

23. CAL to AC, January 13, 1937, CAL Papers, Series I, Box 35, Yale.

24. CAL to Younghusband, undated [January 1937], CAL Papers, Series I, Box 35, Yale.

25. AML, diary entry, February 1, 1937, in *The Flower and the Nettle*, 135–36.

26. AML, diary entry, February 9, 1937, in *The Flower and the Nettle*, 143–45; CAL, *Autobiography of Values*, 149.

27. AML to ECM, February 21, 1937, in *The Flower and the Nettle*, 146.

28. *New York Times*, March 5, 1937, 23. Naidu was one of only two speakers

that AML praised for giving "inspiring talks"; AML to ECM, March 8, 1937, in *The Flower and the Nettle*, 151.

29. B. C. Chatterjee et al., preface to *The Religions of the World* (Calcutta: Ramakrishna Mission Institute of Culture, 1938), 1:v.

30. CAL to AC, March 7, 1937, CAL Papers, Series I, Box 35, Yale.

31. AML to ECM, March 8, 1937, in *The Flower and the Nettle*, 150–51.

32. AML to ECM, March 8, 1937, in *The Flower and the Nettle*, 151; CAL to AC, March 7, 1937.

33. CAL to HG, March 14, 1937, CAL Papers, Series I, Box 35, Yale.

34. CAL, diary entry, November 29, 1937, CAL Papers, Series V, Box 214, Yale.

35. AC to CAL, January 30, 1937, CAL Papers, Series I, Box 7, Yale; CAL to AC, April 17 and July 21, 1937, CAL Papers, Series I, Box 35, Yale.

36. CAL, August 1968 remarks on Walter S. Ross, *The Last Hero: Charles A. Lindbergh* (New York: Harper & Row, 1967), CAL Papers, Box 11, MNHS.

37. Publisher's preface to AC, *Man, the Unknown*, ix.

38. AC, *Man, the Unknown*, 18.

39. AC, *Man, the Unknown*, 140–41.

40. AC, *Man, the Unknown*, 20.

41. AC, *Man, the Unknown*, 42, 155 (emphasis added).

42. Gary Phelps, "The Eugenics Crusade of Charles Fremont Dight," *Minnesota History* 49 (Fall 1984): 108.

43. AC, *Man, the Unknown*, 318–19.

44. AC to CAL, December 27, 1936, January 15, 1937, and July 12, 1937, CAL Papers, Series I, Box 7, Yale.

45. CAL to AC, July 21, 1937, CAL Papers, Series I, Box 35, Yale.

46. Andrés H. Reggiani, "'Drilling Eugenics into People's Minds': Expertise, Public Opinion, and Alexis Carrel's *Man, the Unknown*," in *Popular Eugenics: National Efficiency and American Mass Culture in the 1930s*, ed. Susan Currell and Christina Cogdell (Athens: Ohio University Press, 2006), 85. Lindbergh also tried to help Carrel raise funds for the institute; see, for example, CAL, diary entry, January 26, 1938, CAL Papers, Series V, Box 214, Yale.

47. CAL, October 1, 1937, draft, CAL Papers, Series V, Box 174, Yale.

48. CAL, diary entry, January 3, 1938, CAL Papers, Series V, Box 214, Yale.

49. CAL, diary entry, January 6, 1938, CAL Papers, Series V, Box 214, Yale.

50. JN, *Uncommon Friends: Life with Thomas Edison, Henry Ford, Harvey Firestone, Alexis Carrel & Charles Lindbergh* (San Diego: Harcourt, 1987), 154–56.

51. JN figures prominently in Dick B., *Turning Point: A History of Early A. A.'s Spiritual Roots and Successes* (San Rafael, CA: Paradise Research Publications, 1997), 117–26.

52. JN, *Uncommon Friends*, 121–22, 128–29.

53. AC to CAL, August 31, 1937, CAL Papers, Series I, Box 7, Yale; CAL to AC, September 9, 1937, CAL Papers, Series I, Box 36, Yale.

54. JN, *Uncommon Friends*, 151–52.

55. JN, *Uncommon Friends*, 152–57.

56. CAL, diary entry, January 25, 1938, CAL Papers, Series V, Box 214, Yale.

57. AML, diary entries, January 17, February 1, and February 3, 1938, in *The Flower and the Nettle*, 199, 209, 210.

58. AML, diary entry, February 3, 1938, in *The Flower and the Nettle*, 210. The "Buddahood" quotation likely came from Allan Bennett, *The Wisdom of the Aryas* (London: Kegan Paul, 1923), 41.

59. CAL, diary entries, March 5 and April 30, 1941, in *Wartime Journals*, 455, 480.

60. CAL, August 4, 1969, remarks on Kenneth S. Davis, *The Hero: Charles A. Lindbergh and the American Dream* (New York: Doubleday, 1959), CAL Papers, Box 11, MNHS.

61. AML, diary entry, undated [December 24, 1936], in *The Flower and the Nettle*, 117.

62. AML, diary entry, March 8, 1938, in *The Flower and the Nettle*, 222. Here AML slightly misquotes Ps. 103:15–16.

63. AML, diary entry, March 12, 1938, in *The Flower and the Nettle*, 226.

64. AML, diary entry, December 11, 1938, in *The Flower and the Nettle*, 470.

65. CAL, diary entry, March 6, 1938, CAL Papers, Series V, Box 214, Yale.

66. CAL, *Autobiography of Values*, 21.

67. CAL to Anne Carrel, October 11, 1936, CAL Papers, Series I, Box 35, Yale.

68. AML, diary entries, August 24, 25, and 29, 1936, in *The Flower and the Nettle*, 105–7.

69. CAL to AC, April 9, 1938, CAL Papers, Series I, Box 36, Yale.

70. CAL, *Autobiography of Values*, 161–62; CAL, diary entry, February 25, 1938, CAL Papers, Series V, Box 214, Yale.

71. AC to CAL, August 24, 1937, CAL Papers, Series I, Box 7, Yale; JN, *Uncommon Friends*, 147–48.

72. AML, diary entry, September 13, 1938, in *The Flower and the Nettle*, 404–5.

73. Quoted in JN, *Uncommon Friends*, 162–63.

Chapter Eight

1. ASB, *Lindbergh* (New York: Berkley Books, 1998), 381–82.

2. CAL, September 17, 1938, draft, CAL Papers, Series V, Box 174, Yale.

3. David M. Friedman, *The Immortalists: Charles Lindbergh, Dr. Alexis Carrel, and Their Daring Quest to Live Forever* (New York: HarperCollins, 2007), 45–46.

4. Quoted in BLL, *Lindbergh of Minnesota: A Political Biography* (New York: Harcourt Brace Jovanovich, 1971), 36–37.

5. BLL, *Lindbergh of Minnesota*, 269–70.

6. See James Q. Whitman, *Hitler's American Model: The United States and the Making of Nazi Race Law* (Princeton: Princeton University Press, 2017). He discusses Herbert Kier's 1934 analysis of American racial laws on 121–23.

7. Anne Morrow Lindbergh, diary entry, October 8, 1944, in *War within and Without: Diaries and Letters of Anne Morrow Lindbergh, 1939–1944* (New York: Harcourt Brace Jovanovich, 1980), 443–44.

8. CAL, *Autobiography of Values* (San Diego: Harcourt Brace Jovanovich, 1978), 152.

9. CAL, September 17, 1938, draft, CAL Papers, Series V, Box 174, Yale.

10. CAL to Smith, June 5, 1936, CAL Papers, Series I, Box 34, Yale.

11. AML, diary entries, July 24 and 26, 1936, in *The Flower and the Nettle: Diaries and Letters of Anne Morrow Lindbergh, 1936–1939* (New York: Harcourt Brace Jovanovich, 1976), 89–90, 97.

12. AML to ECM, August 5, 1936, in *The Flower and the Nettle*, 100–101.

13. HG to CAL, August 1, 1936, CAL Papers, Series I, Box 13, Yale.

14. CAL to HG, September 15, 1936, CAL Papers, Series I, Box 34, Yale.

15. CAL to HG, September 15, 1936, CAL Papers, Series I, Box 34, Yale.

16. CAL to Harry Davison, October 28, 1937, CAL Papers, Series I, Box 36, Yale.

17. CAL, diary entry, March 16, 1938, in *The Wartime Journals of Charles A. Lindbergh* (New York: Harcourt Brace Jovanovich, 1970), 5.

18. CAL to Smith, May 9, 1938, CAL Papers, Series I, Box 36, Yale.

19. HN, diary entry, September 8, 1936, in HN, *Diaries and Letters, 1930–1939*, ed. Nigel Nicolson (New York: Atheneum, 1966), 272.

20. Breckinridge to CAL, October 6, 1936, CAL Papers, Series I, Box 6, Yale; CAL to Breckinridge, September 23, 1936, CAL Papers, Series I, Box 34, Yale.

21. CAL, diary entry, August 13, 1938, CAL Papers, Series V, Box 214, Yale.

22. AML, diary entry, August 18 and 19, 1938, in *The Flower and the Nettle*, 354, 361.

23. CAL to Raymond Lee, September 13, 1938, CAL Papers, Series I, Box 37, Yale; CAL, diary entry, August 27, 1938, in *Wartime Journals*, 61.

24. AML diary entries, August 18 and 28, 1938, in *The Flower and the Nettle*, 355–56, 389–90; CAL, diary entry, August 28, 1938, in *Wartime Journals*, 64.

25. AML, diary entry, August 19, 1938, in *The Flower and the Nettle*, 363.

26. HN, diary entry, May 22, 1938, in *Diaries and Letters*, 343; AML, *War within and Without: Diaries and Letters of Anne Morrow Lindbergh, 1939–1944* (New York: Harcourt Brace Jovanovich, 1980), xxiv.

27. CAL to Kennedy, September 22, 1938, CAL Papers, Series I, Box 37, Yale.

28. Telegram, Kennedy to Hull, September 22, 1938, in *Foreign Relations of the United States, 1938*, vol. 1 (Washington: Government Printing Office, 1955), https://history.state.gov/historicaldocuments/frus1938v01/d38.

29. CAL, diary entries, September 26–27, 1938, in *Wartime Journals*, 75–78.

30. CAL, November 1938 draft, CAL Papers, Series V, Box 174, Yale.

31. CAL to Göring, October 25, 1938, CAL Papers, Series I, Box 37, Yale; see also CAL, diary entry, October 18, 1938, in *Wartime Journals*, 101–3. Lindbergh discusses that encounter with Göring in *Autobiography of Values* (San Diego: Harcourt Brace Jovanovich, 1978), 180–82.

32. AML, diary entries, October 18 and 22, 1938, in *The Flower and the Nettle*, 437–38.

33. AML, diary entries, November 11–12, 1938, in *The Flower and the Nettle*, 449–50.

34. CAL, diary entry, November 13, 1938, in *Wartime Journals*, 115.

35. AC to CAL, November 18, 1938, CAL Papers, Series I, Box 7, Yale.

36. CAL, diary entry, November 19, 1938, CAL Papers, Series V, Box 214, Yale.

37. Frank Newport, "Historical Review: Americans' Views on Refugees Coming to U. S.," *Gallup* (blog), November 19, 2015, https://news.gallup .com/opinion/polling-matters/186716/historical-review-americans-views-ref ugees-coming.aspx.

38. AML to ECM, December 11, 1938, in *The Flower and the Nettle*, 470–71.

39. CAL, autobiography draft, December 1938, CAL Papers, Series V, Box 182, Yale.

40. CAL, diary entry, December 29, 1938, in *Wartime Journals*, 133–34.

41. CAL, autobiography draft, July 15, 1963, CAL Papers, Series V, Box 190, Yale.

42. AML, diary entries, January 8 and 30, February 6 and 8, and March 6, 1939, in *The Flower and the Nettle*, 486, 497, 512–14, 542–43. On Anne's enduring admiration for Teilhard, see the religious reflections she shared with one of

her granddaughters in AML to Kristina Lindbergh, January 21, 1973, in AML, *Against Wind and Tide: Letters and Journals, 1947–1986*, ed. RL (New York: Pantheon Books, 2012), 273–74.

43. AML, diary entry, January 30, 1939, in *The Flower and the Nettle*, 497.

44. CAL, diary entry, March 21, 1939, in *Wartime Journals*, 167.

45. The sculptor's own memoir makes only a glancing reference to Lindbergh; Jo Davidson, *Between Sittings: An Informal Autobiography* (New York: Dial, 1951), 317.

46. CAL, diary entry, February 22, 1939, CAL Papers, Series V, Box 214, Yale.

47. CAL, diary entry, December 13, 1938, CAL Papers, Series V, Box 214, Yale.

48. AML, diary entry, March 16, 1939, in *The Flower and the Nettle*, 554.

49. CAL, diary entry, March 20, 1939, CAL Papers, Series V, Box 215, Yale. Contrast the original text with the edited version published in *Wartime Journals*, 166.

50. CAL, diary entry, April 10, 1939, CAL Papers, Series V, Box 215, Yale. Here, too, contrast with *Wartime Journals*, 177.

51. WSC, *Charles A. Lindbergh and the Battle against American Intervention in World War II* (New York: Harcourt Brace Jovanovich, 1974), 125.

52. CAL, diary entry, April 20, 1939, in *Wartime Journals*, 186–87.

53. CAL, diary entry, June 3, 1938, CAL Papers, Series V, Box 214, Yale.

54. ASB, *Lindbergh*, 380.

55. John F. Woolverton and James D. Bratt, *A Christian and a Democrat: A Religious Biography of Franklin D. Roosevelt* (Grand Rapids: Eerdmans, 2019), 154.

56. FDR, Annual Message to Congress, January 4, 1939, in The American Presidency Project, https://www.presidency.ucsb.edu/documents/annual-message-congress.

57. R. J. Reinhart, "Gallup Vault: U. S. Opinion and the Start of World War II," *Gallup Vault*, August 29, 2019, https://news.gallup.com/vault/265865/gallup-vault-opinion-start-world-war.aspx.

58. CAL, diary entry, September 7, 1939, in *Wartime Journals*, 252.

Chapter Nine

1. Quoted in ASB, *Lindbergh* (New York: Berkley Books, 1998), 433.

2. AML, *The Flower and the Nettle: Diaries and Letters of Anne Morrow Lindbergh, 1936–1939* (New York: Harcourt Brace Jovanovich, 1976), xvi–xxviii.

3. AML, *The Flower and the Nettle*, xvi–xvii.

4. AML, *The Flower and the Nettle*, xxvii.

5. CAL, autobiography draft, December 1938, CAL Papers, Series V, Box 182, Yale.

6. CAL, diary entry, September 15, 1939, in *The Wartime Journals of Charles A. Lindbergh* (New York: Harcourt Brace Jovanovich, 1970), 257–58.

7. CAL, diary entry, September 22, 1939, in *Wartime Journals*, 261.

8. CAL, radio address, September 15, 1939, published in *World Affairs* 102 (September 1939): 164–66.

9. CAL to Wallace, September 12, 1939, CAL Papers, Series I, Box 37, Yale.

10. CAL, "Aviation, Geography, and Race," *Reader's Digest*, November 1939, 64.

11. Michael Adas, *Machines as the Measure of Men: Science, Technology, and Ideologies of Western Dominance* (Ithaca, NY: Cornell University Press, 1989).

12. CAL, "Aviation, Geography, and Race," 64–67.

13. AML, diary entry, September 11, 1939, in *War within and Without: Diaries and Letters of Anne Morrow Lindbergh, 1939–1944* (New York: Harcourt Brace Jovanovich, 1980), 52.

14. Harry Curran Wilbur to CAL, November 10, 1939, CAL Papers, Series V, Box 197, Yale.

15. Nellie Oakes to CAL, February 21, 1940, CAL Papers, Series V, Box 197, Yale.

16. Salter to CAL, October 25, 1939, CAL Papers, Series V, Box 197, Yale.

17. On the origins of "Christian nation" rhetoric in conservative opposition to the New Deal, see Kevin M. Kruse, *One Nation under God: How Corporate America Invented Christian America* (New York: Basic Books, 2015), chap. 1.

18. See also Katharine Hayden Salter, "The Gentile Problem," *Christian Century*, August 28, 1940, 1051–53.

19. Antoine de Saint-Exupéry, *Wind, Sand, and Stars*, trans. Lewis Galantière (New York: Reynal & Hitchcock, 1940), 293–94, 306, excerpted in *Reader's Digest*, November 1939, 141–43.

20. CAL, diary entry, August 5, 1939, in *Wartime Journals*, 237.

21. AML, diary entries, August 5–7, 1939, in *War within and Without*, 23–35.

22. Susan Hertog, *Anne Morrow Lindbergh: Her Life* (New York: Anchor Books, 1999), 359.

23. AML, diary entry, August 7, 1939, in *War within and Without*, 35–36.

24. *New York Herald Tribune*, September 20, 1939, 25.

25. AML, diary entry, June 7, 1940, in *War within and Without*, 102–3.

26. AML to ECM, June 5, 1940, in *War within and Without*, 101.

27. Hertog, *Anne Morrow Lindbergh*, 368–69.

28. Quoted in *New York Times*, June 5, 1940, 13.

29. AML to ECM, June 5, 1940, in *War within and Without*, 99–100.

30. AML, diary entries, September 2–3, 1939, in *War within and Without*, 46, 48.

31. AML, diary entries, September 26 and October 28, 1939, in *War within and Without*, 61–62, 64.

32. AML, "A Prayer for Peace," *Reader's Digest*, January 1940, 1–8.

33. AML, diary entry, June 19, 1940, in *War within and Without*, 113.

34. Hertog, *Anne Morrow Lindbergh*, 371, 378.

35. CAL, diary entry, June 21, 1940, in *Wartime Journals*, 360.

36. Gallup poll, July 7, 1940, accessed June 26, 2020, https://ibiblio.org/pha/Gallup/Gallup%201940.htm.

37. Philip Boobbyer, *The Spiritual Vision of Frank Buchman* (University Park: Pennsylvania State University Press, 2013), 138.

38. For example, see the program for the Moral Re-Armament rally at the Hollywood (CA) Bowl, July 19, 1939, CAL Papers, Series I, Box 22, Yale.

39. T. Willard Hunter, interview by Benedict K. Zobrist, August 9, 1988, Harry S. Truman Presidential Library, https://www.trumanlibrary.gov/library/oral-histories/huntertw.

40. CAL, diary entries, July 13 and September 23, 1939, in *Wartime Journals*, 232, 262.

41. CAL, diary entry, December 20, 1939, in *Wartime Journals*, 298.

42. CAL, diary entry, October 8, 1939, CAL Papers, Series V, Box 214, Yale.

43. CAL, diary entry, October 19, 1939, in *Wartime Journals*, 277.

44. CAL, diary entry, April 25, 1941, in *Wartime Journals*, 478.

45. CAL, diary entry, October 5, 1939, CAL Papers, Series V, Box 215, Yale.

46. CAL, diary entry, August 17, 1940, in *Wartime Journals*, 379. Sikorsky published his musings as *The Message of the Lord's Prayer* (New York: Scribner's Sons, 1942).

47. AML to ECM, September 4, 1940, in *War within and Without*, 145. See also CAL, diary entry, September 25, 1940, in *Wartime Journals*, 392.

48. CAL, diary entries, September 4, October 22, and October 30, 1940, in *Wartime Journals*, 382, 409, 411.

49. William R. Castle Jr. to CAL, August 9, 1940, CAL Papers, Series I, Box 7, Yale.

50. CAL, address at Yale University, October 30, 1940, CAL Papers, Series V, Box 202, Yale (emphasis added).

51. CAL, diary entry, November 5, 1940, CAL Papers, Series V, Box 216, Yale. Contrast to *Wartime Journals*, 413–14.

52. AML, diary entry, November 12, 1940, in *War within and Without*, 150.

53. CAL, diary entry, December 17, 1940, CAL Papers, Series V, Box 216, Yale.

54. Theodore Irwin, *Inside the "Christian Front"* (Washington, DC: American Council on Public Affairs, 1940), 3, 20.

55. CAL, diary entry, April 14, 1941, CAL Papers, Series V, Box 216, Yale. There is no mention of Kelly in the published *Wartime Journals*.

56. Philip Jenkins, *Hoods and Shirts: The Extreme Right in Pennsylvania, 1925–1950* (Chapel Hill: University of North Carolina Press, 1997), 202–3.

57. AML, diary entry, November 12, 1940, in *War within and Without*, 150.

58. CAL, diary entry, March 2, 1940, in *Wartime Journals*, 320.

59. CAL, diary entry, July 13, 1941, in *Wartime Journals*, 517; on Thomas's efforts, see Justus D. Doenecke, "Non-interventionism of the Left: The Keep America out of the War Congress, 1938–41," *Journal of Contemporary History* 12 (April 1977): 221–36.

60. "The Attack on Lindbergh," *Christian Century*, August 21, 1940, 1022–23. On religious responses to the intervention debate, see David Zietsma, "'Sin Has No History': Religion, National Identity, and U. S. Intervention, 1937–1941," *Diplomatic History* 37 (June 2007): 531–65.

61. CAL, address in Minneapolis, May 10, 1941, CAL Papers, Series V, Box 202, Yale.

62. CAL, address in New York City, May 23, 1941, CAL Papers, Series V, Box 202, Yale.

63. CAL, address in Des Moines, IA, September 11, 1941, CAL Papers, Series V, Box 204, Yale (emphasis added). See also AML's numerous comments and suggested revisions in the same file.

64. RL, *Under a Wing: A Memoir* (New York: Simon & Schuster, 1998), 214.

65. RL, *Under a Wing*, 201–2.

66. CAL, diary entry, June 9, 1941, CAL Papers, Series V, Box 216, Yale.

67. RL, *Under a Wing*, 202.

68. WSC, *Charles A. Lindbergh and the Battle against American Intervention in World War II* (New York: Harcourt Brace Jovanovich, 1974), 151, 174.

69. Lynne Olson, *Those Angry Days: Roosevelt, Lindbergh, and America's Fight over World War II, 1939–1941* (New York: Random House, 2013), 387.

70. "The Forbidden Theme," *Christian Century*, September 24, 1941, 1167–69.

71. Gregory Mason to Thomas Caldecot Chubb, September 18, 1941, CAL Papers, Series I, Box 2, Yale.

72. Olson, *Those Angry Days*, 381.

73. Frank Newport, "Historical Review: Americans' Views on Refugees Coming to U. S.," *Gallup* (blog), November 19, 2015, https://news.gallup.com /opinion/polling-matters/186716/historical-review-americans-views-refugees -coming.aspx.

74. CAL, radio address, September 15, 1939.

75. CAL, diary entries, June 30 and August 23, 1939, CAL Papers, Series V, Box 215, Yale. The former entry was published in *Wartime Journals*, 218, but the latter was abridged, 245.

76. CAL, diary entry, May 1, 1941, CAL Papers, Series V, Box 216, Yale.

77. Olson, *Those Angry Days*, 385.

78. CAL, diary entry, April 15, 1940, CAL Papers, Series V, Box 215, Yale.

79. CAL, diary entry, February 28, 1941, CAL Papers, Series V, Box 216, Yale.

80. CAL, diary entry, February 4, 1941, CAL Papers, Series V, Box 216, Yale.

81. AML, diary entry, September 11, 1941, in *War within and Without*, 221.

82. CAL, August 1968 remarks on Walter S. Ross, *The Last Hero: Charles A. Lindbergh* (New York: Harper & Row, 1967), CAL Papers, Box 11, MNHS.

83. Cowles to Stuart, August 11, 1941, CAL Papers, Series I, Box 2, Yale.

84. CAL, diary entry, May 29, 1941, CAL Papers, Series V, Box 216, Yale.

85. CAL, diary entries, September 15–18 and October 6, 1941, CAL Papers, Series V, Box 216, Yale.

86. Quoted in John F. Woolverton and James D. Bratt, *A Christian and a Democrat: A Religious Biography of Franklin D. Roosevelt* (Grand Rapids: Eerdmans, 2019), 165.

87. Quoted in Olson, *Those Angry Days*, 388.

88. Letter from Stuart, September 23, 1941, CAL Papers, Series I, Box 2, Yale.

89. CAL to Wood, September 1941, CAL Papers, Series I, Box 39, Yale.

90. CAL, address in Fort Wayne, IN, October 3, 1941, CAL Papers, Series V, Box 204, Yale.

91. CAL, diary entries, October 3 and 30, 1941, in *Wartime Journals*, 544, 551.

92. CAL, draft address ("What Do We Mean by Democracy and Freedom?"), December 1941, *Spirit of St. Louis* Collection, Box 34, LOC.

93. CAL, diary entry, December 8, 1941, in *Wartime Journals*, 561.

Chapter Ten

1. Lauren D. Lyman, "The Lindbergh I Know," *Saturday Evening Post*, April 4, 1953, 23.

2. CAL, diary entry, December 11, 1941, in *The Wartime Journals of Charles A. Lindbergh* (New York: Harcourt Brace Jovanovich, 1970), 565.

3. CAL, diary entry, December 12, 1941, in *Wartime Journals*, 566–67.

4. CAL to Wood, December 26, 1941, CAL Papers, Series I, Box 39, Yale.

5. WSC, *Charles A. Lindbergh and the Battle against American Intervention in World War II* (New York: Harcourt Brace Jovanovich, 1974), 222–23.

6. CAL, diary entries, January 12–13, 1942, in *Wartime Journals*, 578–84.

7. ASB, *Lindbergh* (New York: Berkley Books, 1998), 434–35.

8. AML, diary entry, February 2, 1942, in *War within and Without: Diaries and Letters of Anne Morrow Lindbergh, 1939–1944* (New York: Harcourt Brace Jovanovich, 1980), 247.

9. CAL to Henrik Shipstead, undated [April 20, 1942], CAL Papers, Series I, Box 39, Yale.

10. AML, interview by Russell Fridley, October 23, 1977, LFP, Box 1, MNHS.

11. CAL to JN, March 23, 1942, CAL Papers, Series I, Box 39, Yale.

12. Lynne Olson, *Those Angry Days: Roosevelt, Lindbergh, and America's Fight over World War II, 1939–1941* (New York: Random House, 2013), 237–38.

13. WSC, *Charles A. Lindbergh and the Battle*, 221.

14. "Lindbergh Gets a Job," *Time*, April 6, 1942, 15.

15. CAL, diary entry, April 1–2, 1942, in *Wartime Journals*, 613.

16. CAL, diary entry, April 1–2, 1942, in *Wartime Journals*, 613.

17. Tim Trainor, "How Ford's Willow Run Assembly Plant Helped Win World War II," *Assembly Magazine*, January 3, 2019, https://www.assemblymag.com/articles/94614-how-fords-willow-run-assembly-plant-helped-win-world-war-ii.

18. CAL, diary entry, July 26, 1942, in *Wartime Journals*, 681.

19. CAL, diary entry, March 30, 1942, CAL Papers, Series V, Box 216, Yale.

20. CAL to AML, April 28, 1942, in *War within and Without*, 262.

21. CAL, diary entry, July 9, 1942, in *Wartime Journals*, 674.

22. CAL, diary entry, August 13, 1942, in *Wartime Journals*, 695–96.

23. CAL, diary entry, March 30, 1942.

24. RL, *Under a Wing: A Memoir* (New York: Simon & Schuster, 1998), 181–82.

25. AML, *The Steep Ascent* (New York: Harcourt, Brace, 1944), 109–10.

26. AML to CAL, June 13, 1942, in *War within and Without*, 269–70.

27. AML, diary entry, November 6, 1941, in *War within and Without*, 236.

28. CAL, November 6, 1941, draft, *Spirit of St. Louis* Collection, Box 1, LOC.

29. AML, diary entry, March 12, 1942, in *War within and Without*, 252.

30. CAL, January 1, 1942, draft, *Spirit of St. Louis* Collection, Box 1, LOC.

31. CAL, December 1942, draft, *Spirit of St. Louis* Collection, Box 2, LOC.

32. AML, diary entry, November 14, 1942, in *War within and Without*, 304; CAL, diary entry, March 22, 1942, CAL Papers, Series V, Box 216, Yale.

33. CAL, undated drafts [1941?–1944], CAL Papers, Series V, Box 174, Yale.

34. CAL, diary entries, March 14 and 17, 1940, in *Wartime Journals*, 325–27; JN to CAL, April 7, 1942, CAL Papers, Series I, Box 22, Yale.

35. CAL, diary entry, August 30, 1942, CAL Papers, Series V, Box 217, Yale.

36. AML, "Relief in Europe" radio address, December 24, 1940, *Spirit of St. Louis* Collection, Box 34, LOC.

37. AML, diary entry, February 26, 1942, in *War within and Without*, 248.

38. On Lewis, see AML, diary entry, January 27, 1944, in *War within and Without*, 407. On Eliot, see AML, "Musical Chairs," February 23, 1981, speech, in *Against Wind and Tide: Letters and Journals, 1947–1986*, ed. RL (New York: Pantheon Books, 2012), 306, 313; and RL, *No More Words: A Journal of My Mother, Anne Morrow Lindbergh* (New York: Simon & Schuster, 2001), 19, 21.

39. AML, diary entry, February 26, 1942, in *War within and Without*, 249.

40. AML, diary entry, December 20, 1942, in *War within and Without*, 312.

41. AML, diary entry, November 28–December 10, 1943, in *War within and Without*, 397.

42. AML, *The Steep Ascent*, 58.

43. AML, diary entry, February 26, 1942, in *War within and Without*, 249.

44. AML, diary entry, April [6], 1942, in *War within and Without*, 254.

45. AML, diary entry, May 5, 1943, in *War within and Without*, 348–49.

46. AML, diary entries, December 27, 1942, and April 25, 1943, in *War within and Without*, 313, 343.

47. AML, diary entry, December 24, 1943, in *War within and Without*, 398–99.

48. CAL, diary entry, December 24, 1943, in *Wartime Journals*, 753.

49. CAL, diary entry, December 25, 1940, in *Wartime Journals*, 434.

50. Daniel Sack, *Moral Re-Armament: The Reinventions of an American Religious Movement* (New York: Palgrave Macmillan, 2009), 119–27.

51. CAL, diary entries, July 1 and 9, 1942, in *Wartime Journals*, 670, 674.

52. AML, diary entry, January 20, 1944, in *War within and Without*, 404, 406 (emphasis added).

53. CAL, diary entry, April 3, 1944, in *Wartime Journals*, 775.

54. John Glenn, with Nick Taylor, *John Glenn: A Memoir* (New York: Bantam Books, 1999), 78–79, 93–94.

55. CAL, diary entry, May 22, 1944, in *Wartime Journals*, 818.

56. Quoted in JN, *Uncommon Friends: Life with Thomas Edison, Henry Ford, Harvey Firestone, Alexis Carrel & Charles Lindbergh* (San Diego: Harcourt, 1987), 335.

57. CAL, diary entry, August 22, 1944, in *Wartime Journals*, 912.

58. CAL, diary entry, May 29, 1944, in *Wartime Journals*, 834.

59. CAL, diary entry, May 22, 1944, in *Wartime Journals*, 816–17.

60. CAL, diary entry, May 24, 1944, in *Wartime Journals*, 820–21.

61. CAL, diary entry, May 6, 1944, in *Wartime Journals*, 799.

62. CAL, diary entry, May 23, 1944, in *Wartime Journals*, 819.

63. CAL, diary entry, September 8, 1944, CAL Papers, Series V, Box 217, Yale.

64. CAL, diary entry, June 21, 1944, in *Wartime Journals*, 853–54.

65. CAL, diary entry, June 28, 1944, in *Wartime Journals*, 859.

66. CAL, diary entries, July 13 and 21, 1944, in *Wartime Journals*, 875, 879–80.

67. John W. Dower, *War without Mercy: Race and Power in the Pacific War* (New York: Pantheon Books, 1986).

68. AML, diary entry, October 8, 1944, in *War within and Without*, 447.

69. Anne Carrel, preface to Alexis Carrel, *Reflections on Life*, trans. Antonia White (New York: Hawthorn Books, 1952), 9.

70. CAL, diary entry, November 6, 1944, CAL Papers, Series V, Box 213, Yale.

71. CAL, preface to AC, *Voyage to Lourdes*, trans. Virgilia Peterson (New York: Harper, 1950).

72. ASB, *Lindbergh*, 462.

73. CAL, diary entry, April 12, 1945, CAL Papers, Series V, Box 213, Yale.

74. CAL, diary entry, April 15, 1945, CAL Papers, Series V, Box 213, Yale.

75. CAL, diary entry, May 17, 1945, in *Wartime Journals*, 943.

76. CAL, diary entries, June 6–7, 1945, in *Wartime Journals*, 979.

77. CAL, diary entry, May 18, 1945, in *Wartime Journals*, 949.

78. CAL, diary entry, June 11, 1945, in *Wartime Journals*, 993–96.

79. CAL, diary entry, June 11, 1945, in *Wartime Journals*, 996–98.

Chapter Eleven

1. CAL, address to the Aero Club of Washington, DC, December 17, 1945, *Spirit of St. Louis* Collection, Box 34, LOC.

2. Richard J. Overy, *Why the Allies Won* (New York: Norton, 1995), 225, 321–23.

3. Quoted in Joseph J. Corn, *The Winged Gospel: America's Romance with Aviation*, rev. ed. (Baltimore: Johns Hopkins University Press, 2001), 68.

4. Dan Hampton, *The Flight: Charles Lindbergh's Daring and Immortal 1927 Transatlantic Crossing* (New York: Morrow, 2016), xii.

5. AML, interview by Russell Fridley, October 23, 1977, LFP, Box 1, MNHS.

6. CAL, address at the Aero Club of Washington, DC.

7. CAL, *Of Flight and Life* (New York: Scribner's Sons, 1948), 19.

8. CAL, diary entry, August 6, 1945, CAL Papers, Series V, Box 213, Yale.

9. CAL, autobiography draft, July 3, 1954, CAL Papers, Series V, Box 184, Yale.

10. CAL, diary entry, September 14, 1945, CAL Papers, Series V, Box 213, Yale.

11. CAL, diary entry, September 14, 1945, CAL Papers, Series V, Box 213, Yale.

12. CAL, diary entry, September 19, 1945, CAL Papers, Series V, Box 213, Yale.

13. CAL, address at the Aero Club of Washington, DC.

14. CAL, *Of Flight and Life*, 25–26.

15. Vereide to CAL, July 8, 1946, CAL Papers, Series I, Box 17, Yale. Jeff Sharlet claims that Lindbergh led a "prayer circle" modeled on Vereide's, but I can find no evidence confirming this, nor any written response to Vereide's invitations; Sharlet, *The Family: The Secret Fundamentalism at the Heart of American Power* (New York: Harper Perennial, 2009), 123–24.

16. AML to Kitty Taquey, June 18, 1954, in *Against Wind and Tide: Letters and Journals, 1947–1986*, ed. RL (New York: Pantheon Books, 2012), 104–5.

17. ASB, *Lindbergh* (New York: Berkley Books, 1998), 475–77.

18. CAL, undated draft [1942–1945?], CAL Papers, Series V, Box 174, Yale.

19. CAL, *Of Flight and Life*, vi–vii. Hereafter, page references to this work will be placed in parentheses in the text.

20. CAL, address to the Institute of Aeronautical Sciences, New York, NY, January 25, 1954, *Spirit of St. Louis* Collection, Box 32, LOC.

21. *New York Herald Tribune Weekly Book Review*, October 24, 1948, 6.

22. *Catholic World*, December 1948, 255–56.

23. *Time*, September 6, 1948, 72.

24. Flagg to CAL, September 10, 1948, CAL Papers, Series I, Box 10, Yale.

25. Gluhareff to CAL, August 16, 1948, CAL Papers, Series V, Box 176, Yale. This letter (like those in the following two notes) comes from a folder of reader mail marked "special" by Lindbergh.

26. Fred Cloud to CAL, August 17, 1948, and F. E. Davison to CAL, August 26, 1948, CAL Papers, Series V, Box 176, Yale.

27. Charles W. Leader to CAL, October 4, 1948, CAL Papers, Series V, Box 177, Yale.

28. Atchley to CAL, September 19, 1948, CAL Papers, Series I, Box 4, Yale.

29. *The Westminster Shorter Catechism*, question 1, Presbyterian Church (U.S.A.), accessed August 28, 2020, https://www.presbyterianmission.org/wp-content/uploads/wsc-english1.pdf.

30. Bartky to CAL, undated [1948–1949], CAL Papers, Series V, Box 176, Yale.

31. AML, undated comments on *Of Flight and Life* [1947?], CAL Papers, Series V, Box 182, Yale.

32. AML, diary entry, May 21, 1948, in *Against Wind and Tide*, 45.

33. CAL, *Of Flight and Life*, 35 (emphasis added).

34. CAL, *Of Flight and Life*, 34–36; JN to CAL, April 29, 1948, CAL Papers, Series I, Box 22, Yale; *New Yorker*, August 28, 1948, 71.

35. RMH to CAL, January 8, 1949, CAL Papers, Series V, Box 176, Yale.

36. RMH, commencement address at University of Chicago, June 14, 1946; enclosed in RMH to CAL, October 24, 1946, CAL Papers, Series I, Box 17, Yale.

37. CAL to RMH, November 25, 1946, CAL Papers, Series I, Box 39, Yale.

38. CAL to RMH, July 31, 1952, CAL Papers, Series I, Box 40, Yale.

39. CAL to Keith, August 4, 1952, CAL Papers, Series I, Box 40, Yale.

40. CAL to Harry Shapiro, December 29, 1952, CAL Papers, Series I, Box 40, Yale.

41. Memo by Helen G. Hammons, undated [December 1955], CAL Papers, Series I, Box 3, Yale.

42. AML, diary entry, January 5, 1947, in *Against Wind and Tide*, 17–22.

43. AML, *Gift from the Sea*, fiftieth anniversary ed. (New York: Pantheon Books, 2005), 39.

44. RL, *Under a Wing: A Memoir* (New York: Simon & Schuster, 1998), 69–70.

45. RL, *No More Words: A Journal of My Mother, Anne Morrow Lindbergh* (New York: Simon & Schuster, 2001), 36.

46. AML to Barbara and Jon Lindbergh, January 2, 1955, in *Against Wind and Tide*, 115.

47. RL, *No More Words*, 145.

48. Thanks to Reeve Lindbergh for sharing some of these memories of her religious upbringing, email to author, June 16, 2020.

49. AML to Barbara and Jon Lindbergh, January 20 and February 15, 1955, in *Against Wind and Tide*, 116–18.

50. AML, diary entry, September 18, 1954, in *Against Wind and Tide*, 107.

51. RL, *Under a Wing*, 118.

52. RL, *Under a Wing*, 97.

53. RL, introduction to *Against Wind and Tide*, 6; RL, *No More Words*, 154.

54. AML to CAL, December 18, 1947, in *Against Wind and Tide*, 32–33.

55. AML, undated diary entry [May 1949], in *Against Wind and Tide*, 54–56.

56. Susan Hertog, *Anne Morrow Lindbergh: Her Life* (New York: Anchor Books, 1999), 444.

57. RL, introduction to *Against Wind and Tide*, 11.

58. RL, introduction to *Against Wind and Tide*, 7. See also RL, *Under a Wing*, 209.

59. AML, *Gift from the Sea*, 17.

60. AML, *Gift from the Sea*, 48.

61. AML, *Gift from the Sea*, 37–38.

62. AML, diary entry, July 27, 1953, in *Against Wind and Tide*, 85.

63. Brian Horrigan, "'My Own Mind and Pen': Charles Lindbergh, Autobiography, and Memory," *Minnesota History* 58 (Spring 2002): 10, 12.

64. *Christian Science Monitor*, September 17, 1953, 11.

65. RL, *Under a Wing*, 210.

66. CAL, *The Spirit of St. Louis* (New York: Scribner's Sons, 1953), 340–41.

67. CAL, *The Spirit of St. Louis*, 389–90.

68. CAL, autobiography draft, July 19, 1953, CAL Papers, Series V, Box 184, Yale.

69. CAL, *The Spirit of St. Louis*, xi, 288–89.

70. CAL, *The Spirit of St. Louis*, 321–22.

71. Lauren D. Lyman, "The Lindbergh I Know," *Saturday Evening Post*, April 4, 1953, 88.

72. James G. Keller, "What about the Hundred Million?" *American Ecclesiastical Review* 112 (May 5, 1945): 321.

73. CAL, "Thoughts of a Combat Pilot," *Saturday Evening Post*, October 2, 1954, 78–79.

74. Robert N. Lohr to CAL, October 4, 1954, and Linda S. Locke to CAL, December 13, 1954, CAL Papers, Series V, Box 198, Yale.

75. CAL, *Of Flight and Life*, 52.

76. CAL, "Thoughts of a Combat Pilot," 79.

77. Synopsis of *The Spirit of St. Louis* script, undated [1954–1955?], Billy Wilder Papers, Folder 91, Margaret Herrick Library, Beverly Hills, CA.

78. Jimmy Stewart and Bartlett Robinson, "Airplane in the Making," *The Spirit of St. Louis*, directed by Billy Wilder (1957; Burbank, CA: Warner Brothers, 2006), DVD.

79. CAL to Wilder, May 20, 1954, CAL Papers, Series I, Box 40, Yale.

80. CAL to Leland Hayward, April 1, 1955, CAL Papers, Series I, Box 40, Yale.

81. Jimmy Stewart and Marc Connelly, "Father Hussman [sic]," *The Spirit of St. Louis*.

82. Synopsis of *The Spirit of St. Louis* script.

83. Jimmy Stewart, "Landing Prayer," *The Spirit of St. Louis*.

84. Keller to Wilder, May 1, 1957, Wilder Papers, Folder 83, Herrick Library. On the work of that organization, see Keller, "You Can Be a Christopher," *Catholic World* 162 (January 1946): 316–25.

85. Wilder to Keller, May 16, 1957, Wilder Papers, Folder 83.

86. CAL to Wilder, April 9, 1957, CAL Papers, Series I, Box 40, Yale.

87. CAL to Harold Bixby, April 10, 1957, CAL Papers, Series I, Box 40, Yale.

Chapter Twelve

1. CAL, autobiography draft, December 29, 1966, CAL Papers, Series V, Box 192, Yale.

2. "Germans Claim Charles Lindbergh Is Their Father," *Deutsche Welle*, Au-

gust 19, 2003, https://www.dw.com/en/germans-claim-charles-lindbergh-is
-their-father/a-951603; Rudolf Schröck, with Dyrk Hesshaimer, Astrid Bouteuil, and David Hesshaimer, *Das Doppelleben des Charles A. Lindbergh: Der
berühmteste Flugpionier aller Zeiten-seine wahre Geschichte* (Munich: Wilhelm
Heyne, 2005).

3. RL, *Forward from Here: Leaving Middle Age—and Other Unexpected Adventures* (New York: Simon & Schuster, 2008), 201.

4. RL, introduction to AML, *Against Wind and Tide: Letters and Journals,
1947–1986*, ed. RL (New York: Pantheon Books, 2012), 7.

5. RL, *Forward from Here*, 203.

6. Jabeen Bhatti, "Lindbergh's Double Life," *Deutsche Welle*, June 20, 2005,
https://www.dw.com/en/lindberghs-double-life/a-1620936-0.

7. RL, *Forward from Here*, 218.

8. CAL, autobiography draft, August 18, 1957, CAL Papers, Series V, Box
185, Yale.

9. EAL, "Martin Luther and the Reformation," undated lecture [1859], CAL
Papers, Series VI, Box 274, Yale.

10. CAL, autobiography draft, May 9, 1959, CAL Papers, Series V, Box 186, Yale.

11. CAL to HG, April 24, 1968, CAL Papers, Series I, Box 42, Yale.

12. CAL to HG, March 16, 1960, CAL Papers, Series I, Box 41, Yale.

13. CAL, autobiography outline, May 22, 1961, CAL Papers, Series V, Box
188, Yale.

14. CAL, autobiography drafts, December 24 and 29, 1966, CAL Papers,
Series V, Box 192, Yale.

15. AML to CMM, March 1950, in *Against Wind and Tide*, 62.

16. CAL to Ellie Newton, May 22, 1957, CAL Papers, Series I, Box 40, Yale.

17. CAL to JN, April 14, 1961, CAL Papers, Series I, Box 41, Yale; the letter is
reprinted in JN, *Uncommon Friends: Life with Thomas Edison, Henry Ford, Harvey
Firestone, Alexis Carrel & Charles Lindbergh* (San Diego: Harcourt, 1987), 314–15.

18. JN, *Uncommon Friends*, 313.

19. CAL, *Autobiography of Values* (San Diego: Harcourt Brace Jovanovich,
1978), 281–82.

20. RL, *Forward from Here*, 212–13.

21. CAL to JN, July 24, 1961, CAL Papers, Series I, Box 41, Yale; reprinted in
JN, *Uncommon Friends*, 315–16.

22. CAL, June 5 and 14, 1961, notes, CAL Papers, Series V, Box 188, Yale.

23. *Christianity Today*, August 28, 1961, 45.

24. CAL, June 16, 1961, notes, CAL Papers, Series V, Box 188, Yale.

25. CAL, autobiography draft, December 1962–January 1963, CAL Papers, Series V, Box 189, Yale.

26. CAL, "Is Civilization Progress?" *Reader's Digest*, July 1964, 69.

27. Stanley Diamond, *In Search of the Primitive: A Critique of Civilization* (New Brunswick, NJ: Transaction Publishers, 1974), 207.

28. CAL, autobiography drafts, August 29 and September 1, 1965, CAL Papers, Series V, Box 191, Yale.

29. CAL, autobiography drafts, September 1952–July 1953, CAL Papers, Series V, Box 184, Yale.

30. CAL, autobiography draft, August 22, 1965, CAL Papers, Series V, Box 191, Yale. See also CAL, June 1964 notes, CAL Papers, Series V, Box 190, Yale.

31. CAL, diary entry, May 23, 1944, in *The Wartime Journals of Charles A. Lindbergh* (New York: Harcourt Brace Jovanovich, 1970), 819.

32. CAL, autobiography draft, 1957, CAL Papers, Series V, Box 185, Yale.

33. CAL, autobiography draft, August 22, 1965, CAL Papers, Series V, Box 191, Yale.

34. CAL, July 17 and 26, 1970, notes, CAL Papers, Series V, Box 194, Yale.

35. CAL, "Lessons from the Primitive," *Reader's Digest*, November 1972, 148–50.

36. Neal Thompson, *Light This Candle: The Life and Times of Alan Shepard* (New York: Three Rivers Press, 2004), 17–18.

37. Susan Faludi, *Stiffed: The Betrayal of the American Man* (New York: HarperCollins, 1999), 454.

38. Quoted in James R. Hansen, *First Man: The Life of Neil A. Armstrong* (New York: Simon & Schuster, 2005), 371.

39. AML, "The Heron and the Astronaut," *Life*, February 28, 1969, 20.

40. CAL, "A Letter from Lindbergh," *Life*, July 4, 1969, 60B.

41. Thompson, *Light This Candle*, 394.

42. Kendrick Oliver, *To Touch the Face of God: The Sacred, the Profane, and the American Space Program, 1957–1975* (Baltimore: Johns Hopkins University Press, 2013), 17, 43.

43. AML, "The Heron and the Astronaut," 26.

44. CAL, "A Letter from Lindbergh," 61.

45. CAL, autobiography draft, June 12–13, 1959, CAL Papers, Series V, Box 186, Yale.

46. CAL, foreword to Michael Collins, *Carrying the Fire: An Astronaut's Journeys* (New York: Farrar, Straus & Giroux, 1974), x–xiii.

47. Quoted in Hansen, *First Man*, 621.

48. CAL, address to the Society of Experimental Test Pilots, Los Angeles, California, September 27, 1969, CAL Papers, Series V, Box 205, Yale. Reprinted in *Cockpit*, November 1969, 26–28.

49. CAL, letter for World Wildlife Fund, November 16, 1966, CAL Papers, Series V, Box 192, Yale.

50. Glen Jeansonne and David Luhrssen, "Between Heaven and Earth—Lindbergh: Technology and Environmentalism," *History Today* 58 (January 2008): 58.

51. See, for example, CAL to Rep. Sidney R. Yates, CAL Papers, Series I, Box 43, Yale.

52. RL, *Under a Wing: A Memoir* (New York: Simon & Schuster, 1998), 204.

53. CAL, "Some Remarks at Dedication of Lindbergh State Park Interpretive Center," *Minnesota History* 43 (Fall 1973): 275–76.

54. CAL, diary entry, April 1, 1938, in *Wartime Journals*, 10.

55. CAL, "Aviation, Geography, and Race," *Reader's Digest*, November 1939, 64.

56. CAL, address to the Aero Club, Washington, DC, December 17, 1949, *Spirit of St. Louis* Collection, Box 34, LOC.

57. CAL, autobiography drafts, September 1952–July 1953.

58. CAL, "Feel the Earth," *Reader's Digest*, July 1972, 65.

59. CAL, address to International Union for the Conservation of Nature, Tananarive, Madagascar, October 9, 1970, CAL Papers, Series V, Box 205, Yale.

60. CAL, address at Georgetown University, Washington, DC, June 28, 1973, CAL Papers, Series V, Box 205, Yale.

61. CAL to Sister Hildegard, June 24, 1971, CAL Papers, Series I, Box 43, Yale.

62. "Our History," Abbey of Regina Laudis, accessed September 29, 2020, https://abbeyofreginalaudis.org/community-history.html.

63. CAL to Sister Hildegard, July 30, 1971, CAL Papers, Series I, Box 43, Yale.

64. CAL to Mother Benedict, May 7, 1973, CAL Papers, Series I, Box 43, Yale.

65. CAL, "The Way of Wildness," *Reader's Digest*, November 1971, 90–91.

66. CAL to Rep. Emilio Daddario, July 1, 1970, CAL Papers, Series I, Box 43, Yale.

67. CAL to Jovanovich, August 12, 1971, Series I, Box 43, Yale.

68. CAL, *Autobiography of Values*, 379–80, 385.

69. CAL, *Autobiography of Values*, 385–87.

Chapter Thirteen

1. CAL, November 6, 1941, draft, *Spirit of St. Louis* Collection, Box 1, LOC.

2. CAL, July 1943 draft, *Spirit of St. Louis* Collection, Box 2, LOC.

3. AML to Scott Lindbergh, April 5, 1968, in AML, *Against Wind and Tide: Letters and Journals, 1947–1986*, ed. RL (New York: Pantheon Books, 2012), 241.

4. AML to Dana Atchley, February 1, 1969, in *Against Wind and Tide*, 246.

5. AML to Margot Wilkie, March 6, 1973, in *Against Wind and Tide*, 276.

6. CAL to Mother Benedict, May 6, 1973, CAL Papers, Series I, Box 43, Yale.

7. CAL, *Autobiography of Values* (San Diego: Harcourt Brace Jovanovich, 1978), 390.

8. CAL, *Autobiography of Values*, 27.

9. CAL, *Autobiography of Values*, 391.

10. AML to Stephen Mitchell, May 31, 1973, in *Against Wind and Tide*, 277.

11. AML to Margot Wilkie, July 7, 1973, in *Against Wind and Tide*, 283.

12. Quoted in ASB, *Lindbergh* (New York: Berkley Books, 1998), 552.

13. RL, *Under a Wing: A Memoir* (New York: Simon & Schuster, 1998), 185–87.

14. Milton Howell, interview by TWH, December 4, 1984, TWH Files, CLHM.

15. Henry Kahula, interview by TWH, January 3, 1981, TWH Files, CLHM.

16. ASB, *Lindbergh*, 549–50; "A Brief History of Palapala Ho'omau Church," accessed September 29, 2020, https://www.palapalahoomau.org/history.

17. AML, "First Year after Death," undated manuscript [1974–1975], in *Against Wind and Tide*, 297.

18. RL, *Under a Wing*, 190.

19. Henry Kahula interview.

20. Robert Lowry, "Angel's Welcome (Ka Lani Ku'u Home)," *Na Himeni Haipule Hawaii* (Honolulu: Hawaii Conference United Church of Christ, 1972), no. 175.

21. ASB, *Lindbergh*, 558; Roselle Howell, interview by TWH, January 2, 1981, TWH Files, CLHM.

22. Milton Howell interview.

23. Roselle Howell interview.

24. AML, "First Year after Death," 290.

25. AML, diary entry, July 21, 1983, in *Against Wind and Tide*, 327; RL, *Under a Wing*, 191.

26. Quoted by TWH, *The Spirit of Charles Lindbergh: Another Dimension* (Lanham, MD: Madison Books, 1993), 136.

27. RL, *Under a Wing*, 193.

28. Quoted in AML, diary entry, August 18, 1932, in *Hour of Gold, Hour of Lead: Anne Morrow Lindbergh, Diaries and Letters, 1929–1932* (New York: Harcourt Brace Jovanovich, 1973), 302.

29. AML, "First Year after Death," 300.

30. AML, diary entry, July 27, 1985, in *Against Wind and Tide*, 338.

31. CAL, December 4, 1973, comments on galley proofs of WSC, *Charles A. Lindbergh and the Battle against American Intervention in World War II* (New York: Harcourt Brace Jovanovich, 1974); and CAL to WSC, December 23, 1973, CAL Papers, Series I, Box 43, Yale.

32. WSC to William Goodman, December 14, 1973; WSC to CAL, December 26, 1973, and January 1, 1974, CAL Papers, Series I, Box 8, Yale.

33. Rudolf Schröck, with Dyrk Hesshaimer, Astrid Bouteuil, and David Hesshaimer, *Das Doppelleben des Charles A. Lindbergh: Der berühmteste Flugpionier aller Zeiten-seine wahre Geschichte* (Munich: Wilhelm Heyne, 2005), 310.

34. AML, address to the Minnesota Historical Society, Minneapolis, MN, October 27, 1979; published as "The Changing Concept of Heroes," *Minnesota History* 46 (Winter 1979): 309.

35. RL, *No More Words: A Journal of My Mother, Anne Morrow Lindbergh* (New York: Simon & Schuster, 2001), 69.

36. TWH, *The Spirit of Charles Lindbergh*, xi.

37. Transcript of "Faith of the Lone Eagle" service, Wananalua Church, Hana, HI, December 14, 1980, TWH Files, CLHM.

38. CAL to Leland Hayward, April 1, 1955, CAL Papers, Series I, Box 40, Yale.

39. TWH, *The Spirit of Charles Lindbergh*, xiii.

40. RL, interview by Russell Fridley, October 23, 1977, LFP, Box 1, MNHS.

41. RL, "The Lindbergh Heritage: What Do We Do with It Now?" (address at Westminster Presbyterian Church, Minneapolis, MN, May 23, 1985), http://www.westminsterforum.org/forum/the-lindbergh-heritage-what-do-we-do-with-it-now.

42. RL, ed., *In Every Tiny Grain of Sand: A Child's Book of Prayers and Praise* (Cambridge, MA: Candlewick, 2000).

43. RL, *On Morning Wings* (Cambridge, MA: Candlewick, 2002).

Afterword

1. CAL, diary entry, April 15, 1945, CAL Papers, Series V, Box 213, Yale.

2. CAL, *Autobiography of Values* (San Diego: Harcourt Brace Jovanovich, 1978), 152.

3. Robert P. Jones, *White Too Long: The Legacy of White Supremacy in American Christianity* (New York: Simon & Schuster, 2020), 6, 170.

4. On Christianity and systemic racism, I highly recommend Jemar Tisby, *The Color of Compromise: The Truth about the American Church's Complicity in Racism* (Grand Rapids: Zondervan, 2019) and—older, but still sadly relevant—Michael O. Emerson and Christian Smith, *Divided by Faith: Evangelical Religion and the Problem of Race in America* (New York: Oxford University Press, 2000).

Selected Bibliography

Unpublished Sources

Sterling Memorial Library, Yale University—New Haven, Connecticut
Charles Augustus Lindbergh Papers
Manuscript Division, Library of Congress—Washington, DC
Charles A. Lindbergh *Spirit of St. Louis* Collection
Gale Family Library, Minnesota Historical Society—St. Paul, Minnesota
Charles Augustus Lindbergh Papers
Charles August Lindbergh Papers
Lindbergh Family Papers
Charles Lindbergh House and Museum—Little Falls, Minnesota
T. Willard Hunter Files
Books owned by Charles August Lindbergh and Evangeline Lodge
Land Lindbergh
Morrison County Historical Society—Little Falls, Minnesota
WPA Histories
Margaret Herrick Library—Beverly Hills, California
Billy Wilder Papers

Books and Articles

B., Dick. *Turning Point: A History of Early A.A.'s Spiritual Roots and Successes.*
San Rafael, CA: Paradise Research Publications, 1997.
Boobbyer, Philip. *The Spiritual Vision of Frank Buchman.* University Park: Pennsylvania State University Press, 2013.
Bruno, Harry A., and William S. Dutton. "Lindbergh, the Famous Unknown."
Saturday Evening Post, October 21, 1933, 23–40.

Bryson, Bill. *One Summer: America, 1927.* New York: Anchor Books, 2013.

Carrel, Alexis. *Man, the Unknown.* New York: Harper & Row, 1935.

——. *Reflections on Life.* Translated by Antonia White. New York: Hawthorn Books, 1953.

——. *Voyage to Lourdes.* Translated by Virgilia Peterson. Foreword by Charles A. Lindbergh. New York: Harper, 1950.

Cole, Wayne S. *Charles A. Lindbergh and the Battle against American Intervention in World War II.* New York: Harcourt Brace Jovanovich, 1974.

Collins, Michael. *Carrying the Fire: An Astronaut's Journeys.* Foreword by Charles A. Lindbergh. New York: Farrar, Straus & Giroux, 1974.

Corn, Joseph J. *The Winged Gospel: America's Romance with Aviation.* Rev. ed. Baltimore: Johns Hopkins University Press, 2001.

Davis, Kenneth S. *The Hero: Charles A. Lindbergh and the American Dream.* New York: Doubleday, 1959.

Durkin, Joseph T. *Hope for Our Time: Alexis Carrel on Man and Society.* New York: Harper & Row, 1965.

Eksteins, Modris. *Rites of Spring: The Great War and the Birth of the Modern Age.* New York: Anchor Books, 1989.

Fisher, Harold L. *The Land Called Morrison.* Rev. ed. St. Cloud, MN: Volkmuth Publishing, 1976.

Fitzgerald, F. Scott. *The Crack-Up, with Other Pieces and Stories.* New York: Penguin Books, 1965.

Friedman, David M. *The Immortalists: Charles Lindbergh, Dr. Alexis Carrel, and Their Daring Quest to Live Forever.* New York: HarperCollins, 2007.

Gill, Brendan. "The Doom of Heroes." *New Yorker,* September 19, 1953, 110–13.

——. *Lindbergh Alone: May 21, 1927.* New York: Harcourt Brace Jovanovich, 1977.

Glenn, John, with Nick Taylor. *John Glenn: A Memoir.* New York: Bantam Books, 1999.

Gray, Susan M. *Charles A. Lindbergh and the American Dilemma: The Conflict of Technology and Human Values.* Bowling Green, OH: Bowling Green State University Popular Press, 1988.

Hampton, Dan. *The Flight: Charles Lindbergh's Daring and Immortal 1927 Transatlantic Crossing.* New York: Morrow, 2017.

Hansen, James R. *First Man: The Life of Neil A. Armstrong.* New York: Simon & Schuster, 2005.

Hart, Bradley W. *Hitler's American Friends: The Third Reich's Supporters in the United States.* New York: St. Martin's, 2018.

Helbling, Mark. "The Response of African Americans to Lindbergh's Flight to Paris." *Prospects* 27 (October 2002): 375–98.

Hertog, Susan. *Anne Morrow Lindbergh: Her Life.* New York: Anchor Books, 1999.

Hixson, Walter L. *Charles A. Lindbergh, Lone Eagle.* New York: HarperCollins, 1996.

Horrigan, Brian. "'My Own Mind and Pen': Charles Lindbergh, Autobiography, and Memory." *Minnesota History* 58 (Spring 2002): 2–15.

Hunter, T. Willard. *The Spirit of Charles Lindbergh: Another Dimension.* Lanham, MD: Madison Books, 1993.

Jeansonne, Glen, and David Luhrssen. "Between Heaven and Earth—Lindbergh: Technology and Environmentalism." *History Today* 58 (January 2008): 54–59.

Jenson, Carol. "Loyalty as a Political Weapon: The 1918 Campaign in Minnesota." *Minnesota History* 43 (Summer 1972): 42–57.

Kessner, Thomas. *The Flight of the Century: Charles Lindbergh and the Rise of American Aviation.* New York: Oxford University Press, 2010.

Lardner, John. "The Lindbergh Legends." In *The Aspirin Age, 1919–1941,* edited by Isabel Leighton, 190–213. New York: Simon & Schuster, 1949.

Larson, Bruce L. "Barnstorming with Lindbergh." *Minnesota History* 52 (Summer 1991): 230–38.

———. "Charles A. Lindbergh: The Swedish Connection." *Scandinavian Review* 90 (Summer 2002): 6–15.

———. *Lindbergh of Minnesota: A Political Biography.* New York: Harcourt Brace Jovanovich, 1971.

———. "Lindbergh's Return to Minnesota, 1927." *Minnesota History* 42 (Winter 1970): 141–52.

———. "Little Falls Lawyer, 1884–1906: Charles A. Lindbergh, Sr." *Minnesota History* 43 (Spring 1973): 158–74.

Lindbergh, Anne Morrow. *Against Wind and Tide: Letters and Journals, 1947–1986.* Edited by Reeve Lindbergh. New York: Pantheon Books, 2012.

———. *Bring Me a Unicorn: Diaries and Letters of Anne Morrow Lindbergh, 1922–1928.* New York: Harcourt Brace Jovanovich, 1971.

———. "The Changing Concept of Heroes." *Minnesota History* 46 (Winter 1979): 306–11.

———. *Dearly Beloved*. New York: Harcourt, Brace, 1962.

———. *Earth Shine*. New York: Harcourt, Brace, 1969.

———. *The Flower and the Nettle: Diaries and Letters of Anne Morrow Lindbergh, 1936–1939*. New York: Harcourt Brace Jovanovich, 1976.

———. *Gift from the Sea*. Fiftieth anniversary edition. Introduction by Reeve Lindbergh. New York: Random House, 2005.

———. "The Heron and the Astronaut." *Life*, February 28, 1969, 14–26.

———. *Hour of Gold, Hour of Lead: Anne Morrow Lindbergh, Diaries and Letters, 1929–1932*. New York: Harcourt Brace Jovanovich, 1973.

———. *Listen! The Wind*. New York: Harcourt, Brace. 1938.

———. *Locked Rooms and Open Doors: Diaries and Letters of Anne Morrow Lindbergh, 1933–1935*. New York: Harcourt Brace Jovanovich, 1974.

———. *North to the Orient*. New York: Harcourt, Brace, 1935.

———. "Prayer for Peace." *Reader's Digest*, January 1940, 1–8.

———. *The Steep Ascent*. New York: Harcourt, Brace, 1944.

———. *War within and Without: Diaries and Letters of Anne Morrow Lindbergh, 1939–1944*. New York: Harcourt Brace Jovanovich, 1980.

———. *The Wave of the Future: A Confession of Faith*. New York: Harcourt, Brace, 1940.

Lindbergh, Charles August. *Why Is Your Country at War and What Happens to You after the War and Related Subjects*. Washington, DC: National Capital Press, 1917.

Lindbergh, Charles Augustus. *Autobiography of Values*. San Diego: Harcourt Brace Jovanovich, 1978.

———. "Aviation, Geography, and Race." *Reader's Digest*, November 1939, 64–67.

———. *Boyhood on the Upper Mississippi: A Reminiscent Letter*. St. Paul: Minnesota Historical Society Press, 1972. Republished as *Lindbergh Looks Back: A Boyhood Reminiscence*. Foreword by Reeve Lindbergh. St. Paul: Minnesota Historical Society Press, 2002.

———. "Feel the Earth." *Reader's Digest*, July 1972, 62–65.

———. "Is Civilization Progress?" *Reader's Digest*, July 1964, 67–74.

———. "Lessons from the Primitive." *Reader's Digest*, November 1972, 147–50.

———. "A Letter from Lindbergh." *Life*, July 4, 1969, 60–61.

———. "A Letter to Americans." *Collier's*, March 29, 1941, 14–15, 75–77.

———. *Of Flight and Life*. New York: Scribner's Sons, 1948.

———. "Some Remarks at Dedication of Lindbergh State Park Interpretive Center." *Minnesota History* 43 (Fall 1973): 275–76.

———. *The Spirit of St. Louis.* New York: Scribner's Sons, 1953.

———. "Thoughts of a Combat Pilot." *Saturday Evening Post,* October 2, 1954, 20–21, 78–79.

———. *The Wartime Journals of Charles A. Lindbergh.* New York: Harcourt Brace Jovanovich, 1970.

———. "The Way of Wildness." *Reader's Digest,* November 1971, 90–93.

———. *"We": The Famous Flier's Own Story of His Life and His Transatlantic Flight, Together with His Views on the Future of Aviation.* New York: Grosset & Dunlap, 1927.

Lindbergh, Reeve, ed. *In Every Tiny Grain of Sand: A Child's Book of Prayers and Praise.* Cambridge, MA: Candlewick, 2000.

———. *Forward from Here: Leaving Middle Age—and Other Unexpected Adventures.* New York: Simon & Schuster, 2008.

———. *No More Words: A Journal of My Mother, Anne Morrow Lindbergh.* New York: Simon & Schuster, 2001.

———. *On Morning Wings.* Cambridge, MA: Candlewick, 2002.

———. *Under a Wing: A Memoir.* New York: Simon & Schuster, 1998.

Lyman, Lauren D. "The Lindbergh I Know." *Saturday Evening Post,* April 4, 1953, 22–23, 84–88.

McCullough, David. *The Wright Brothers.* New York: Simon & Schuster, 2015.

Milton, Joyce. *Loss of Eden: A Biography of Charles and Anne Morrow Lindbergh.* New York: HarperCollins, 1993.

Morgan, Constance Morrow. *A Distant Moment.* Northampton, MA: Smith College, 1978.

Morlan, Robert. "The Nonpartisan League and the Minnesota Campaign of 1918." *Minnesota History* 34 (Summer 1955): 221–32.

Mosley, Leonard. *Lindbergh: A Biography.* Garden City, NY: Doubleday, 1976.

Newton, James. *Uncommon Friends: Life with Thomas Edison, Henry Ford, Harvey Firestone, Alexis Carrel & Charles Lindbergh.* Foreword by Anne Morrow Lindbergh. San Diego: Harcourt, 1987.

Nicolson, Harold. *Diaries and Letters, 1930–1939.* Edited by Nigel Nicolson. New York: Atheneum, 1966.

———. *Dwight Morrow.* New York: Harcourt, Brace and Co., 1935.

Nute, Grace Lee. "The Lindbergh Colony." *Minnesota History* 20 (September 1939): 243–58.

Oliver, Kendrick. *To Touch the Face of God: The Sacred, the Profane, and the American Space Program, 1957–1975*. Baltimore: Johns Hopkins University Press, 2013.

Olson, Lynne. *Those Angry Days: Roosevelt, Lindbergh, and America's Fight over World War II, 1939–1941*. New York: Random House, 2013.

Reggiani, Andrés H. "'Drilling Eugenics into People's Minds': Expertise, Public Opinion, and Biopolitics in Alexis Carrel's *Man, the Unknown*." In *Popular Eugenics: National Efficiency and American Mass Culture in the 1930s*, edited by Susan Currell and Christina Cogdell, 70–90. Athens: Ohio University Press, 2006.

Reich, Leonard S. "From the 'Spirit of St. Louis' to the SST: Charles Lindbergh, Technology, and Environment." *Technology & Culture* 36 (April 1995): 351–93.

Ross, Walter S. *The Last Hero: Charles A. Lindbergh*. New York: Harper & Row, 1967.

Roth, Philip. *The Plot against America: A Novel*. New York: Vintage International, 2004.

Sack, Daniel. "Men Want Something Real: Frank Buchman and Anglo-American College Religion in the 1920s." *Journal of Religious History* 28 (October 2004): 260–75.

———. *Moral Re-Armament: The Reinventions of an American Religious Movement*. New York: Palgrave Macmillan, 2009.

Schröck, Rudolf, with Dyrk Hesshaimer, Astrid Bouteuil, and David Hesshaimer. *Das Doppelleben des Charles A. Lindbergh: Der berühmteste Flugpionier aller Zeiten-seine wahre Geschichte*. Munich: Wilhelm Heyne, 2005.

Thompson, Neal. *Light This Candle: The Life and Times of Alan Shepard*. New York: Three Rivers Press, 2004.

Van Every, Dale, and Morris DeHaven Tracy. *Charles Lindbergh: His Life*. New York: D. Appleton, 1927.

Van Vleck, Jenifer. *Empire of the Air: Aviation and the American Ascendancy*. Cambridge, MA: Harvard University Press, 2013.

Wallace, Max. *The American Axis: Henry Ford, Charles Lindbergh, and the Rise of the Third Reich*. New York: St. Martin's, 2003.

Index

Titles published in the

LIBRARY OF RELIGIOUS BIOGRAPHY SERIES